Research and Practice in Applied Linguistics

General Editors: **Christopher N. Candlin and David R. Hall**, Linguistics Department, Macquarie University, Australia.

All books in this series are written by leading researchers and teachers in Applied Linguistics, with broad international experience. They are designed for the MA or PhD student in Applied Linguistics, TESOL or similar subject areas and for the language professional keen to extend their research experience.

Titles include:

Forthcoming titles:

Marilyn Martin-Jones
BILINGUALISM

Martha Pennington
PRONUNCIATION

Annamaria Pinter
TEACHING ENGLISH TO YOUNG LEARNERS

Norbert Schmitt
VOCABULARY

Helen Spencer-Oatey and Peter Franklin
INTERCULTURAL INTERACTION

Devon Woods and Emese Bukor
INSTRUCTIONAL STRATEGIES AND PROCESSES IN LANGUAGE EDUCATION

Research and Practice in Applied Linguistics
Series Standing Order ISBN 978–1–4039–1184–1 hardcover
Series Standing Order ISBN 978–1–4039–1185–8 paperback
(*outside North America only*)

You can receive future titles in this series as they are published by placing a standing order. Please contact your bookseller or, in case of difficulty, write to us at the address below with your name and address, the title of the series and the ISBN quoted above.

Customer Services Department, Macmillan Distribution Ltd, Houndmills, Basingstoke, Hampshire RG21 6XS, England

Researching Communication Disorders

Alison Ferguson

and

Elizabeth Armstrong

palgrave
macmillan

First published 2009 by
PALGRAVE MACMILLAN

Palgrave Macmillan in the UK is an imprint of Macmillan Publishers Limited, registered in England, company number 785998, of Houndmills, Basingstoke, Hampshire RG21 6XS.

Palgrave Macmillan in the US is a division of St Martin's Press LLC, 175 Fifth Avenue, New York, NY 10010.

Palgrave Macmillan is the global academic imprint of the above companies and has companies and representatives throughout the world.

Palgrave® and Macmillan® are registered trademarks in the United States, the United Kingdom, Europe and other countries.

ISBN-13: 978–0–230–00450–4 hardback
ISBN-10: 0–230–00450–4 hardback
ISBN-13: 978–0–230–00451–1 paperback
ISBN-10: 0–230–00451–2 paperback

This book is printed on paper suitable for recycling and made from fully managed and sustained forest sources. Logging, pulping and manufacturing processes are expected to conform to the environmental regulations of the country of origin.

A catalogue record for this book is available from the British Library.

A catalog record for this book is available from the Library of Congress.

10 9 8 7 6 5 4 3 2 1
18 17 16 15 14 13 12 11 10 09

Printed and bound in Great Britain by
CPI Antony Rowe, Chippenham and Eastbourne

6/30/10

Contents

Series Editor's Preface

Research and Practice in Applied Linguistics is an international book series from Palgrave Macmillan which brings together leading researchers and teachers in Applied Linguistics to provide readers with the knowledge and tools they need to undertake their own practice-related research. Books in the series are designed for students and researchers in Applied Linguistics, TESOL, Language Education and related subject areas, and for language professionals keen to extend their research experience.

Every book in this innovative series is designed to be user-friendly, with clear illustrations and accessible style. The quotations and definitions of key concepts that punctuate the main text are intended to ensure that many, often competing, voices are heard. Each book presents a concise historical and conceptual overview of its chosen field, identifying many lines of enquiry and findings, but also gaps and disagreements. It provides readers with an overall framework for further examination of how research and practice inform each other, and how practitioners can develop their own problem-based research.

The focus throughout is on exploring the relationship between research and practice in Applied Linguistics. How far can research provide answers to the questions and issues that arise in practice? Can research questions that arise and are examined in very specific circumstances be informed by, and inform, the global body of research and practice? What different kinds of information can be obtained from different research methodologies? How should we make a selection between the options available, and how far are different methods compatible with each other? How can the results of research be turned into practical action?

The books in this series identify some of the key researchable areas in the field and provide workable examples of research projects, backed up by details of appropriate research tools and resources. Case studies and exemplars of research and practice are drawn on throughout the books. References to key institutions, individual research lists, journals and professional organizations provide starting points for gathering information and embarking on research. The books also include annotated lists of key works in the field for further study.

The overall objective of the series is to illustrate the message that in Applied Linguistics there can be no good professional practice that isn't based on good research, and there can be no good research that isn't informed by practice.

CHRISTOPHER N. CANDLIN and DAVID R. HALL
Macquarie University, Sydney

Illustrations

Figures

Tables

Abbreviations

AAC	Alternative and Augmentative Communication
ASD	Autism Spectrum Disorders
BPVS	British Picture Vocabulary Scales
BAAL	British Association for Applied Linguistics
EBP	Evidence-based Practice
LSVT	Lee Silverman Voice Technique
MLD	Moderate Learning Difficulty
PET	Positron Emission Tomography
SLI	Specific Language Impairment
SPAA	Speech Pathology Association of Australia
TBI	Traumatic Brain Injury
TTP	Time to Peak
ToM	Theory of Mind
TROG	Test of Reception of Grammar
WHO	World Health Organisation

Acknowledgements

The majority of the work for this book was undertaken while Professor Armstrong was Program Convenor of the Master of Speech & Language Pathology program at Macquarie University, Sydney.

We gratefully acknowledge the many speech pathologists and linguists who have guided the development of our own understanding of researching communication disorders. We hope that we have been able to pass on some of this understanding in this book. In particular, we would like to thank Ruqaiya Hasan and Christopher Candlin for their theoretical guidance over many years, and Christopher Candlin and David Hall for their editorial assistance in the preparation of this book. For helping our understanding of living with communication disorders, we thank our clients who have guided us in distinguishing reality from abstraction, and in assisting us in setting our priorities for research. We both owe many thanks also to our partners, Malcolm and Ian, families and friends for their support for our research and in the process of completing this book.

Note on Authors

Associate Professor Alison Ferguson has over twenty years experience in the field of speech-language pathology, and established the speech-language pathology programme at the University of Newcastle in 1994. Her internationally recognized research explores the application of sociolinguistic theory to the analysis of interactions involving people with aphasia, students and speech-language pathologists. Alison received the University of Newcastle's inaugural 'Supervisor of the Year' Award in 2007 in recognition of her contribution to the supervision of master's and doctoral level students, and in 2008 her book *Expert Practice: A Critical Discourse* was published (Plural Publishing).

Professor Elizabeth Armstrong is Foundation Chair in Speech Pathology at Edith Cowan University in Perth, with over 20 years experience in the field of speech-language pathology. She has pioneered the application of Systemic Functional Linguistics to the field of speech-language pathology, with her published work appearing in both book chapters and international peer-reviewed publications. Professor Armstrong was the Founding Editor of the *International Journal of Speech Language Pathology* (formerly *Advances in Speech Language Pathology*), first published in 1999.

Glossary

Acquired: Describes a condition which came about after a period of typical development, and hence is most usually seen when referring to adults, for example, the slurred speech associated with dysarthria following a stroke. However, note that an adult can have a 'developmental' disorder, for example, intellectual impairment since birth, and a child can have an 'acquired' disorder, for example, a typically developing five-year-old might acquire a language impairment following brain injury from a motor vehicle accident.

Action research: Research framework which aims to bring about positive changes in the situation being researched. Described as 'participatory action research' when it involves participants in all stages of the research.

Alternative and Augmentative Communication (AAC): Describes the use of methods and modalities other than verbal communication, for example, the use of gestures, signs, symbols and drawing. With the developments in information technology, AAC is increasingly 'high tech'. The term 'assistive technology' is becoming more frequently used to describe this kind of AAC.

Anonymity: Refers to conditions under which information regarding the identity of the participants is never collected or able to be retrieved from any data collected during the course of the research, for example, a survey conducted in a supermarket. (See also, Confidentiality)

Aphasia: Occurs after neurological damage (e.g.) stroke to specific parts of the brain responsible for semantic and syntactic aspects of language (usually the left cerebral hemisphere).

Aphonia: see Voice disorders.

Apraxia of Speech (AOS): Occurs after damage to the parts of the brain controlling motor speech, but often co-occurs with aphasia (see above). Involves difficulty with the planning of movements for speech, which is not attributable to changes to the peripheral muscles for speech. Speech is typically produced with groping movements of the articulators to achieve articulatory postures, with frequent substitution and distortion of sounds.

Approach: A term used with very general meaning to describe the paradigms, theories, models and frameworks which inform the researcher's work.

Childhood Apraxia of Speech (CAS): Describes problems with coordinated and accurate production of speech sounds and patterns of sounds. This is a controversial classification, and presents a diagnostic challenge.

Clinical education: Term for the professional practice experience which students undertake under the supervision of qualified speech-language pathologists during their professional preparation. Other terms such as 'field education', or 'professional education or experience' or 'practicum' are essentially synonymous. Note that the use of the term 'clinical' does not presuppose that the experience is within a formal clinic or conducted within a medical model of service delivery. For example, the term may be used equally to describe experience within a school setting with services provided in a collaborative model.

Cognitive-communication disorder: Occurs after damage to diffuse areas of the brain and/or to the right cerebral hemisphere (e.g. after TBI, dementia, right cerebral hemisphere damage). Communication symptoms reflect the damage to the cortical functions required for cognition, for example, problems with inhibition may result in verbosity or paucity of content.

Congenital: Describes a condition present at the time of birth. For example, cleft palate and cerebral palsy can both be described as 'congenital', even though the cleft palate manifested in the early stages of embryonic development, and cerebral palsy may not necessarily be identified until a later stage in the child's development.

Confidentiality: Refers to conditions under which the information about the identity of the participants is collected, but maintained securely so that only the researchers have access that that information, for example, a study involving audio or video recording of interaction. (see also, Anonymity)

Cross-sectional: Describes a research design in which data are taken from a number of subjects at one particular point in time, for example, in studies of typical speech development, separate groups of children in different age groups are tested, and the groups compared.

Decontextualized: Describes the elicitation of speech or language performance in conditions in which there is an attempt to control all factors which might affect performance other than the particular factor under study. So, for example, if the researcher is attempting to research the recognition of spoken words, then a decontextualized task would be to ask the person to point to single words written down on separate cards from a choice of four other words ('distractors') which differ from the target word semantically and/or phonologically. Control of contextual factors is seen as increasing the validity of research from a psycholinguistic perspective, but is seen as contaminating the validity of data from a sociolinguistic perspective.

Delay: Speech or language which is typical of a younger child.

Delayed language: Describes the language of a child who is slow to develop language skills, in the context of typical development of motor and other cognitive skills.

Developmental: Describes a condition which not only manifests itself during the developmental period (i.e. early through to late childhood), but also involves the compromised attainment of typically expected developmental milestones, for example, physically, cognitively, socially, emotionally.

Developmental articulation disorder: Describes difficulty with particular sounds (rather than with particular patterns of sounds), which may relate to structural differences (e.g. cleft palate), or learned movements (e.g. lisp).

Differential diagnosis: Describes the process by which symptoms and other relevant information are weighed against each other, through processes of both deductive and inferential reasoning.

Disorder: Speech or language is qualitatively different from either same age or same language-age peers.

Dissertation: Written thesis.

Disfluency: see also Dysfluency. Moments of disruption to the flow of speech which are considered 'normal', and not to be part of stuttering or stammering behaviour.

Double dissociation: Describes a diagnostic process in which there is a requirement for both particular functions and dysfunctions to be observed in order to strengthen the diagnosis.

Dysarthria: Occurs after damage to the parts of the brain controlling motor speech. Usually involves pathological changes to muscle tone, and results in slurred speech (imprecise consonant production) and reduced intelligibility.

Dysphonia: see Voice disorders.

Dysfluency: Moments of disruption to the flow of speech considered to be part of stuttering or stammering behaviour.

Effectiveness: Research which investigates effectiveness seeks to establish whether one treatment works better than the other, for example, in a shorter time, or at less cost, or with more carry-over into everyday life. Research into effectiveness typically compares two treatments with previously established efficacy.

Efficacy: Efficacy research seeks to establish whether a particular treatment brings about a change.

Etiology: (sometimes spelled 'aetiology') – cause of a condition, usually implies a medical cause.

Fluency: see Stuttering.

Framework: A broad encapsulation of the key issues to be considered in an area of knowledge. Frameworks allow for the systematic study of issues, without pre-empting any conceptions of explanatory or predictive relationships.

Impact factor: The impact factor of a journal refers to a measure of citations of articles contained in that journal to other science and social science journals over a three-year period.

Incidence: Generally considered to be the number of new cases which appear in a given population in a given period.

Intra-rater reliability: Comparison of measures by one rater on the same data on two occasions.

Inter-rater reliability: Comparison of measures of more than one rater on the same data.

Longitudinal: Describes a research design in which data are taken from the same subjects at repeated points over time, for example, instead of the more commonly used cross-sectional design, typical speech development could be investigated using a longitudinal research design, by testing a group of children as they develop at particular ages.

Model: An explanation of the structural or causal relationships within a set of knowledge or process.

Monograph: Publication in book form.

Normal: see Typical.

Operational definition: Working definition for the purposes of a particular investigation.

Paradigm: Fundamental way of conceptualizing a field of knowledge or a methodology.

Participatory action research: see Action research.

Peer-reviewed: Articles, or journals in which all articles go through a process of selection involving critique from an independent expert in the field. The process may be 'blind' to varying extents, for example, usually the researcher will not know the identity of the reviewer, and in many cases the identity of the researcher will not be made explicitly known to the reviewer. (Synonymous with 'refereed')

Perspective: This term is often used when the research or conceptualization of knowledge are not sufficiently wide-ranging to warrant the term 'paradigm', and so are focused primarily on descriptive rather than explanatory or predictive aims.

Phonological disorder: Describes difficulty with the phonological rules which govern the patterns of speech production.

Placebo: A 'placebo' treatment broadly speaking is one which is expected to achieve little or no change, but which has a number of features which are similar enough to the intervention to control for general features such as, for example, improvement associated with receiving attention and social contact. It should be noted that placebo treatments are often very efficacious. These effects are themselves subject to research, as they raise important possibilities of 'mind over matter' treatment effects, as well as possible changes associated with monitoring.

Praxis: Broadly this term equates to 'practice', but embodies the embedded philosophies, knowledges, and expertise which combine in the carrying out of complex work.

Prevalence: Number of cases which exist in the population at any particular time.

Psychometric: Refers to the properties of test instruments with regard to validity and reliability, and these psychometric properties need to have been established through empirical research.

Refereed: see Peer-reviewed.

Rigour: Refers to the aspects of qualitative research methodology which will allow researchers to validly draw conclusions from their data. The key aspects of rigour are that sampling should be valid (e.g. sampling should be from data that is as natural as possible, and as uncontaminated by the researcher's presence or observation activities as possible), data analysis methods such as thematic coding should be systematic and comprehensive, interpretations of analysis should be checked against participants' perspectives, and that both data analysis and interpretation should be sufficiently transparent to allow for others to consider the validity of the conclusions drawn by the researcher.

Scaffolding: Describes the assistance or support provided by a teacher or therapist to facilitate the performance or learning of a child or adult. For example, the provision of prompts or cues.

Serial: Publication in journal form.

Specific Language Impairment (SLI): Describes the language of a child who is developing these skills in a different pattern, but who is developing typically in terms of motor and other cognitive skills.

Symptom: Observed or reported physical, cognitive, emotional, or behavioural manifestation of the individual.

Syndrome: Set of symptoms which are commonly observed to co-occur in some meaningful relationship, for example, which suggests a particular underlying etiology, or which requires a particular approach to management.

Stammering: see Stuttering.

Standardized: Describes assessment tools or tests which prescribe the content and method of administration in order to minimize variation. Most standardized tools have a background of prior research which has demonstrated the test's validity and reliability, and which report on the performance of a set of normal subjects on the test.

Stuttering: Fluency disorders involve disruption to the smooth flow of speech and usually manifest as stuttering or stammering.

Taxonomy: A systematic categorization system that allows the description of members of the same type of thing in relation to each other, and also in relation to sub-types, and in relation to broader groupings.

Test-retest reliability: Comparison of measures for an elicitation task (e.g. test or sampling method) on the same individual on two occasions.

Theory: Specifically articulated formulation of knowledge in a particular component or aspect of knowledge within a field of study. Theories generally have the capacity to not only describe current observations but also to provide an explanation, and predict future possibilities.

Typical: In recent years, children with speech and language disorders are increasingly referred to with reference to 'typically developing' children. Much of the earlier research literature in the field of communication disorders uses the term 'normal' to describe control groups, and this term is arguably still appropriate for comparison groups to those with medical conditions, or for large-scale comparison groups for whom substantial 'normative' data are available. However, the use of the term 'normal' evokes the antonym 'abnormal' which carries a highly negative value load, and is questionable particularly in situations where conditions or difficulties may represent simply a different point on a continuum of proficiency rather than an 'abnormality'.

For these reasons, the alternative terms 'typical' in contrast to 'atypical' are often preferred.

Voice disorders: Involve disruption to normal voice quality, that is, the voice can become *dysphonic* (harsh, strained or husky), and when extreme, the person can lose their voice completely (*aphonia*).

Part I

Key Concepts And Research Issues

1
Paradigms and Research Practice

1.1 Introduction

The study of language and communication has been an interdisciplinary endeavour since the 1970s, with linguistic, anthropological, psychological and sociological theories being developed and applied since the late 1800s. The study of communication disorders is a relatively newer undertaking, although observations of individuals with various kinds of communication difficulties have been made throughout history, for example the nineteenth century work of Broca and Wernicke (see Broca, 1861; Tesak & Code, 2008; Wernicke, 1893) on the disorder of aphasia occurring after a stroke or head injury. The study of communication disorders is an inherently multidisciplinary one, given the different perspectives on language available in the theoretical domain, as well as the inherent and logical links to questions on mind and brain, and the clinical challenges to provide services and treatment for individuals identified as having a communication disorder. Disciplines involved to date include psychology, linguistics, speech pathology, audiology, education and medicine, each using slightly different paradigms and methodologies.

This volume aims to provide an overview of the field of communication disorders for researchers interested in exploring this area, providing both theoretical and practical perspectives on this endeavour. The very multidisciplinary nature of the area can be daunting to those embarking on projects which constitute a small part of an overall field. For applied linguists, for example, the area of communication disorder is often seen as a highly medicalized speciality area, into which applied linguists and linguists enter with some trepidation. There are a number of perceived theoretical barriers (e.g. biological/neuroscientific knowledge required in order to deal with populations whose

3

communication disorder is associated with specific brain damage), as well as practical ones (e.g. the need for ethics approval from multiple medical institutions, and gaining access to people with speech and language disorders). For speech-language pathologists, for example, the diverse theories and methodologies which may inform an understanding of a particular clinical population can be daunting to master. For all disciplines, research in the area of communication disorders has utilized numerous theoretical approaches and methodologies that need to be put into perspective in order to contextualize any new project being undertaken. Such contextualization is important so that the project is informed by previous relevant work, and so that the researcher is clear as to the potential contribution of the work to ongoing questions and issues in the field.

Bearing in mind the diversity of approaches to the study of communication disorders, this chapter aims to provide the reader with a window into the various paradigms used in the field, their relationship to each other and a discussion on potential complementarity.

1.2   What is a 'communication disorder'?

For the purposes of the current discussion, it is also important to establish at the outset the areas that are usually addressed under the heading of 'communication disorders'. The term 'communication' is usually used to describe all aspects which make up any exchange of meaning, including speech, language, voice, fluency and non-verbal and pragmatic communication behaviours. A generally accepted taxonomy used in the study of communication disorders separates speech from language disorders, with speech disorders including sub-types of articulation, voice and fluency disorders (see Concept 1.1). These could be caused by physical phenomena such as hearing impairment, cleft palate, cerebral palsy, stroke or on the other hand, may have no known cause. Language disorders include disruptions to phonology, syntax, semantic and pragmatic aspects of communication, again related to either physical causes such as stroke, brain injury or are developmental in nature with no known aetiology.

There are different ways of looking at issues that will illuminate different aspects of communication disorders. Different terms, for example, 'paradigm', 'theory', 'model', 'framework', 'approach' and 'perspective', reflect such differences. Definitions and examples of the same are provided in Table 1.1. Two paradigms that currently inform the study of communication disorders can be described as

Concept 1.1   Taxonomy of communication disorders

In the study of communication disorders, a generally accepted taxonomy involves separating speech from language disorders, with speech disorders including sub-types of articulation, voice and fluency disorders.

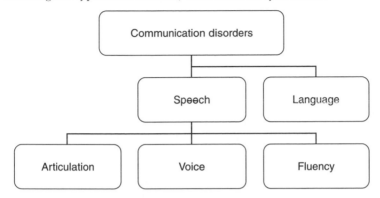

Such a simple taxonomy of communication disorders provides only a basic descriptive framework. For example, stuttering may be described as a motor speech problem, but at the same time it is clear that language issues are an important consideration, for example, the variation noted in stuttering with the propositionality of the language use.

'quantitative' and 'qualitative'. Approaching the issue of defining or identifying when communication can be considered 'disordered' from a quantitative perspective, communication 'performance' can be viewed from a statistical standpoint in terms of what falls in the 'normal range' of behaviours for a particular population, and what could be classified as 'disordered', that is, outside the normal range, for example, two standard deviations from 'the mean' on a particular language test. This paradigm is most often engendered in standardized testing regimes in which individuals receive scores for accurate responses on a range of language tasks that involve the four modalities of speaking, writing, reading and auditory comprehension. Tasks include oral naming, oral formulation of sentences given a cue word, spelling to dictation, reading words and sentences aloud, comprehension of short written stories and comprehension of stories read to the person. As part of the overall construction of such tests, large populations across different age groups are tested for the purpose of establishing normative data against which individuals suspected of

Table 1.1   Paradigms

Term	Definition	Communication disorders example
Paradigm	A fundamental way of conceptualizing a field of knowledge or a methodology.	Quantitative and qualitative descriptions of typical communication (Damico & Simmons-Mackie, 2003)
Theory	Specifically articulated formulation of knowledge in a particular component or aspect of knowledge within a field of study.	Vygotsky's theory of proximal development – therapeutic intervention will be more effective when targeted at skills which can be performed with scaffolding (Avent & Austermann, 2003)
Model	Explanation of the structural or causal relationships within a set of knowledge or process.	Models of phonology applied to intervention for speech disorders in children (Nelson & Ball, 2003)
Framework	Broad encapsulation of the key issues to be considered in an area of knowledge.	Description of the therapeutic process (Horton, 2006)
Approach	General term to describe the integration of paradigms, theories, models and frameworks informing the research.	'Life Participation Approach' for intervention for people with aphasia (Chapey *et al.*, 2001) 'Cognitive neuropsychological approaches' (Nickels, 2002)
Perspective	Conceptualization of knowledge or process which is descriptive rather than explanatory or predictive.	Application of Systemic Functional Linguistic (SFL) perspective (Armstrong *et al.*, 2007)

having difficulties can be compared. One outcome of using such data in testing children, is that a child can either be confirmed as being on a par with his/her peers, or can be identified as being delayed in some way, for example, the Clinical Evaluation of Language Fundamental – Fourth Edition (CELF-IV) (Semel *et al.*, 2003, 2006) is often used in the education system for determining which children require extra assistance.

When examining the abilities of adults with communication disorders, more potentially influential sociolinguistic variables affecting performance such as level of education and socioeconomic status of participants have been acknowledged. However, the notion of a 'norm' is still inherent in tests such as the Boston Diagnostic Aphasia Exam (Goodglass *et al.*, 2001), Western Aphasia Battery (Kertesz, 2006) and the Psycholinguistic Assessment of Language Processing in Aphasia (Kay *et al.*, 1992) – often used tests for adult aphasia.

Approaching the issue of disorder from a more descriptive or qualitative perspective, one might look at an individual's communicative functioning differently. Instead of trying to determine if the person acts/communicates like others of similar age, gender and educational background, the question of labelling or suggesting 'disorder' involves the investigation of the person's functioning from social, vocational and educational perspectives. Armstrong suggests that language use, for example, is identified as disordered when 'the language user regularly fails or is regularly compromised in some way in the negotiation of meaning in either social, academic or workplace environments. That is, s/he is perhaps unable to communicate ideas or needs in everyday talk, is unable to explain complex arguments, or is unable to sustain organized discourse' (Armstrong, 2005, p. 138). Such an approach investigates different abilities from that examined in a more quantitative framework. While it can also be quantitative in nature, as it is possible to operationalize and quantify linguistic behaviours or phenomena, this approach is less concerned with comparing 'disordered' vs 'normal' language, and more concerned with detailed description of pragmatic communicative behaviour.

1.3 Theoretical perspectives

The two perspectives referred to above in terms of defining a communication disorder relate largely to two theoretical perspectives on communication disorder that predominate in the field of speech and language disorders. These are the psycholinguistic/cognitive and sociolinguistic/social-semiotic perspectives. The psycholinguistic perspective sees language as a cognitive function that is formulated in a modular format according to a set of internal rules, then 'used' for social purposes. This framework suggests that components of language such as syntax and semantics are relatively separate parts of the language system and operate either sequentially or in parallel to produce a final expressive output, or to decode incoming information. A sociolinguistic/social-semiotic approach, on the other hand, views language as inseparable from the context in which it is used. In this approach, syntax is not seen separately from semantics – syntax contributes to meaning in the same way that individual lexical items do. Hence, it is not possible to

Table 1.2   Contributions of psycholinguistic and sociolinguistic perspectives

Aspect of contribution	Psycholinguistic perspective	Sociolinguistic perspective
Role of context	Context is controlled, e.g., standardized instruction	Natural context for elicitation
Nature of language elicited and examined	Decontextualized words, sentences – goal is to identify replicable performance	Discourse – goal is to identify range of variation in performance
Description of observed language performance	Described with reference to accuracy (error analysis), in relation to language theory (e.g. generative grammar) or model (e.g. Quirk grammar – Greenbaum & Quirk, 1990)	Described with reference to appropriateness or adequacy for social purposes, in relation to potential linguistic resources
Paradigm influence	Quantitative, e.g., statistical examination of averaged performance	Qualitative, e.g., 'rich' or 'thick' description of individual performance
Examples of models, theories, approaches and perspectives used	(Garrett, 1988) (Levelt, 1989)	(Gumperz, 1982) (Halliday & Matthiessen, 2004)
Communication disorders example	(Dell *et al.*, 1993)	(Bates *et al.*, 1991)

divide language into areas that operate independently from each other; see Table 1.2.

It is important at this point to highlight the potential dichotomy between quantitative and qualitative paradigms as alluded to above. Finding a definition for either of these two terms is problematic, and in fact, as noted by Damico and Simmons-Mackie, contrasting the two actually creates 'a false dichotomy between research paradigms' (Damico & Simmons-Mackie, 2003, p. 131). For example, qualitative research, while focusing more on description of social phenomena, can also involve numerical indices that are useful in correlating with that description. Damico and Simmons-Mackie suggest an operational definition of qualitative research that encompasses this notion: 'Qualitative research refers to a variety of analytic procedures described to systematically collect and describe authentic contextualized social phenomena with the goal of interpretive adequacy' (Damico and Simmons-Mackie, 2003 p. 132). However, it is equally important to acknowledge that in the more quantitative paradigms, more emphasis is placed on numerical indices and statistical significance, and that the type of data utilized by the different approaches does vary.

There is another distinction that can be made in terms of analytical approaches which also drives methodologies and that is the top-down/ bottom-up distinction. Top-down approaches to analysis operate with predetermined categories, in which the theoretical model determines the behaviours/characteristics to be investigated. Those behaviours emanate from the theoretical model employed. For example, SFL analyses involve detailed examination of certain characteristics such as cohesive devices (Halliday & Hasan, 1976), particular process types (mental, material, verbal – see Halliday, 1994a; Halliday & Matthiessen, 2004) and instances of appraisal sub-types (Martin, 2000). Similarly, formal grammatical analyses (Crystal *et al.*, 1976) and pragmatic analyses (e.g. Prutting & Kirchner, 1987) would be considered top-down in nature. On the other hand, bottom-up approaches use the data itself to form categories from which conclusions can be drawn about the nature of the data. Conversation Analysis (CA) (Sacks *et al.*, 1974) is an example of a bottom-up framework. Using this analysis, detailed observations can be made of interactions and their nature. For example, researchers have described how speakers handle breakdown of conversation in both normal and aphasic discourse (Ferguson, 1994; Laakso & Klippi, 1999; Lesser, 2003; Lindsay & Wilkinson, 1999). Use of co-text by the non-aphasic conversation partner to guess what the aphasic partner is attempting to say has been explored, as well as a variety of patterns of responses that can either facilitate or hinder the flow of conversation after the breakdown.

Thematic analysis of interview data also constitutes a bottom-up approach to analysis, where there are no preconceived categories prior to the examination of the data, and the responses of interviewees are analysed for content and recurrent themes (Liamputtong & Ezzy, 2005a). As in other areas of applied linguistics, for example, discourse analysis, many researchers in the field of communication disorders employ both top-down and bottom-up approaches, in what is increasingly being referred to as a 'mixed methodology' (Creswell, 2003).

1.4   What kind of research questions arise in the field?

As an illustration of the ways in which theoretical models can be applied to the area of communication disorders, it is useful to introduce the kinds of questions that are asked in the area. Questions can fall into a number of different domains, which might be grouped broadly here into two main areas (see Chapter 3 for further discussion of these broad areas of research): understanding the nature of communication disorders (e.g. theoretical issues about speech/language and brain function, processing of linguistic information from a cognitive perspective, behavioural manifestations of disorders, psychosocial consequences – see also Section 3.2), and treatment efficacy (see also Section 3.3).

1.4.1   Understanding the nature of communication disorders

Possibly the longest history of research into communication disorders is that associated with language/brain relationships. The 1800s produced seminal works by neurologists such as Paul Broca and Carl Wernicke who detailed their observations of patients with brain lesions exhibiting particular disturbances in speech function. While many case studies were reported over the ensuing years, the 1900s saw both further case studies and large group studies undertaken to investigate the localization of particular linguistic functions in the brain (Penfield & Roberts, 1959). While localizationist theory has moved on considerably in terms of notions of language function, new technology has renewed interest in the area of speech/language and neurological correlates. The functional Magnetic Resonance Imaging (fMRI) technology in particular has enabled studies of language function to be undertaken involving such questions as: Are areas of the brain known to be implicated in attention and memory function less active in children with Specific Language Impairment (SLI) than typically developing children? (Weismer *et al.*, 2005). Are areas of the right hemisphere more activated after left hemisphere damage? (Voets *et al.*, 2006). Can rehabilitation of specific skills such as word-finding affect cortical activation? (Peck *et al.*, 2004).

Another perspective on speech/language functioning addresses language as a cognitive function as described above in Section 1.3. As noted, cognitive models suggest that particular linguistic skills can be broken down into sub-components and that each of these sub-components can be impaired by brain damage. These models are not specifically concerned with neurological correlates but postulate hypothetical processes associated with language decoding and encoding. To date, they are primarily single word based (see Nickels 2002 for overview), although both syntactic (Garrett 1988) and discourse models

(Fredericksen, 1986; Kintsch & Van Dijk, 1978) have also been posited. Questions asked within this realm include:

- What are the sub-components of particular linguistic skills such as naming?
- What skills/processes underlie a syntactically correct clause?
- In terms of pathological phenomena observed in such disorders as aphasia, for example, word-finding difficulty, paraphasia and neologism, what are the underlying bases of the phenomena?
- Are different parts of speech more vulnerable to disorder than others? (e.g. are nouns more vulnerable to breakdown in aphasia than verbs?).
- What is the underlying nature of agrammatism?
- Questions can also relate to more socio-behavioural issues. Consider the following:

  ○ How do communication disorders manifest themselves in everyday conversational contexts at the level of discourse?
  ○ How do aspects such as cohesion/coherence break down in the discourse of an individual with a communication disorder?
  ○ How do communication partners interact with individuals with communication disorders, for example, do they change their own communication style in order to accommodate their partner?
  ○ How do dyads manage conversational breakdown? That is, how is repair managed when one of the speakers has a communication disorder?

Questions of contextual factors affecting communication behaviour are also asked, investigating issues such as:

- Do people with aphasia vary their language according to normal contextual variables such as genre?
- Does topic affect discourse parameters?
- Does familiarity of communication partner affect language patterns used by children with SLI (e.g. degree of explicitness in situations of shared/unshared knowledge)?

As communication disorders make a significant impact on an individual's life, research questions also extend to the nature of this impact in terms of psychosocial functioning:

- Do communication disorders induce anxiety and/or depression in the person having the disorder?

- How do communication disorders affect the person's social participation within his/her community?
- How does the communication disorder affect significant others in the person's life?
- Another perspective is the exploration of the experience of having a communication problem, and indeed undergoing treatment for the problem.

1.4.2   Treatment efficacy

Other important questions relate to treatment of the disorder – both restitutive in nature dealing with improving the skills of the person with the identified disorder (e.g. can naming therapy improve the naming skills of a person with aphasia?), and compensatory (e.g. can training the person in the use of gesture or an alternative communication device improve their abilities to get their message across in social situations?). Treatments can involve very individual or group treatment regimes, as well as classroom-based interventions. Both clinical practice and research in the area of treatment efficacy is currently strongly influenced by the paradigm of 'Evidence-Based Practice' (Reilly *et al.*, 2004). The evidence-based practice (EBP) paradigm began in the field of medicine and emerged largely in response to the issue of how the explosion of research in the field could be effectively translated into the everyday practice of clinicians. One of the key ways to facilitate this integration of research findings into practice was seen as being able to identify the findings upon which the greatest reliance could be placed (i.e. the 'best' research), and to use these in the development of guidelines for practice. The prevailing scientific paradigm within the field of medicine meant that the notion of 'best' rested upon features of research from within the quantitative research methodologies such as controlled experimental design (see Section 3.3.2 for more detail). More recently, however, there has been an emerging recognition of the usefulness of mixed methodologies in intervention research, in order to increase relevance to the 'clinical bottom-line' as well as to increase the validity and rigour of the research.

1.5   Different methodologies

As could be expected, different methodologies will be used for each of the above groups of questions, and within these groups as well. Numerous questions can be addressed from a number of theoretical and methodological perspectives, while others are more akin to some in particular. Let us examine further the particular types of questions noted above in terms of possible methodological frameworks (see Chapter 8 for further development of these issues).

When addressing language/brain issues, research may incorporate both large group studies, aimed at drawing conclusions about particular brain function and localization, and single case studies that might challenge a previously accepted tenet by presenting an individual who does not fit the findings of previous research. An example of the latter would be a case of crossed aphasia. Most individuals who become aphasic after brain damage have suffered damage to their left hemisphere, known to be dominant for primary language skills. However, single case studies have appeared in the literature documenting individuals who are aphasic after right hemisphere damage, thus expanding our knowledge of hemispheric dominance for language. While both decontextualized language tasks, and discourse tasks can be utilized in such investigations, to date the former have provided the primary language data for fMRI studies. This is largely because specific tasks requiring single word or sentence stimuli and responses are easier to control for in terms of contextual variables, than the more complex language behaviours involved in discourse.

Studies using a cognitive neuropsychologial model tend to use the single-case-study design as their gold standard, since it is through testing the model in detail within one system, that is, one individual, that patterns of intact and impaired functioning can be identified (Ellis & Young, 1988).

When addressing what might be called communication behavioural issues, behaviours must be sampled appropriately so that the researchers can be confident that what they are seeing is representative, to some degree, of the individual's overall skills. These behaviours might involve the individual's ability to retrieve names in either a metalinguistic task such as naming pictures, or in an everyday conversation. The use of standardized language tests vs spontaneous speech sampling as methods to investigate an individual's language skill/behaviours will obviously relate to the theoretical issues discussed above. Where a modular approach to language will encourage testing different language skills separately and on particular metalinguistic tasks, a more social approach to language will suggest obtaining samples of the individual's communication across a variety of social situations/genres in order to examine language functioning. If one goes down the latter path, however, the optimal amount of data to be gathered will become problematic and will be dependent on a number of issues. First, if simple clause level phenomena such as length of utterance, number of paraphasias (word substitutions e.g. 'chair' is used instead of 'table' are tabulated e.g. I ate lunch at the chair), tense errors are to be analysed and counted, then relatively short monologic texts may be seen as representative. For example, a quantitative psycholinguistic approach looking to identify disorders of discourse might suggest that a 300-word narrative is a sufficiently representative speech sample in order to be able to draw conclusions about the speaker's abilities in terms of such parameters as length of utterance, vocabulary level and use of cohesive devices (Brookshire & Nicholas, 1994). A more qualitative sociolinguistic approach to the same problem will be interested in contextual influences on these parameters and recommend a longer sample, preferably across different contexts. Hence, while both approaches may be interested in questions related to discourse, theoretical notions about discourse will influence both length and types of samples required. If a researcher is interested in interactional behaviours, then obviously conversational samples, rather than monologue, will be required. Selection of conversational partners may be significant to the type of sample gained, for example, familiar vs unfamiliar partners.

Ethnographic studies also constitute an option for the researcher interested in totally naturalistic data – using a bottom-up approach as described in Section 1.3. Such studies are undertaken in everyday social situations such as the classroom, nursing home and individual's home – recording communicative interactions in these settings. In these situations, the researcher does not pre-define or structure the research context, but observes and records communication as it occurs in everyday contexts.

Issues related to social consequences of communication disorder can be approached in a variety of ways as well. As well as exploring specific language/communication patterns of behaviour, an ethnographic framework can also enable the researcher to explore social issues such as the nature of interactions in therapy sessions (Simmons-Mackie *et al.*, 1999) and the social implications of diagnostic labels (Damico & Augustine, 1995). Other qualitative methods for investigating such issues involve in-depth interviews in which individuals are asked to discuss their experiences/attitudes to a variety of communication-related issues. For example, Parr and colleagues explored the experiences of people with aphasia from the initial stages in hospital up to later experiences post onset of the disorder (Parr *et al.*, 1997). Thematic analysis of the interview data produced a series of issues that highlighted the relative importance of different consequences of aphasia, including attitudes to speech therapy. Other studies have used qualitative methods to investigate child speech and language disorders, for example, researching the attitudes of parents attending speech therapy for their children and addressing such issues as involvement, expectations and satisfaction (Glogowska & Campbell, 2000).

From a quantitative perspective, numerous scales and questionnaires exist which tap such issues as depression and quality of life (Code & Muller, 1992; Hilari *et al.*, 2001). In the area of adult communication disorders, activities of daily living can also be assessed and quantified in terms of either how the person performs tasks under testing conditions that simulate everyday situations – see (e.g. CADL-2, Holland *et al.*, 1999) or the reported frequency and success with which they engage in everyday activities, for example, the Communicative Effectiveness Index (Lomas *et al.*, 1989).

Example 1.1 Examples of quantitative communication instruments

Communicative Effectiveness Index (Lomas et al., 1989)
10 cm Likert scale. Partner to rate the person's ability at (see below) on scale between 'not at all able' to 'as able as before stroke'.

Getting someone's attention
Giving 'yes' and 'no' answers appropriately
Communicating his/her emotions
Starting a conversation with people who are not close family

Code-Muller Protocol (Code & Muller, 1992)
Five-point scale probing the following (possible responses: get much worse, get a little worse, stay the same, improve a little, improve a lot)
For example, Do you think the ability to speak to strangers will....

If one is attempting to show that a particular sort of therapy improves communication, then comparing a treated to a non-treated group might be a viable option. On the other hand, if one believes that individual differences might mask important changes achieved by some participants, then single case studies might be more illuminating. Simple testing of an individual before and after a treatment regime (pre- and post-testing) is the most basic test of efficacy. However, two primary issues related to efficacy involve (a) confidence that the behaviour being treated was stable prior to treatment and was not already improving (establishing a baseline) and (b) teasing out the effect of the actual treatment regime implemented, as opposed to other treatments, interventions, and social experiences the participant in the research may be having outside but concurrent to the research project treatment. Simple solutions to these issues involve testing/sampling a participant repeatedly before commencing treatment to establish a baseline of behaviour, and employing a multiple baseline involving both the behaviour under focus, as well as other behaviours. The principle involved in multiple baselines is that one can see whether other behaviours change along with the treated behaviour, even when they are not being treated. This issue is particularly important in studies where improvement of behaviours could be attributed to maturation (e.g. in young children) or 'spontaneous recovery' (e.g. in adults after stroke, where the brain is expected to undergo some spontaneous recovery even without rehabilitation). More detailed methodological discussion regarding multiple baseline design can be found in Barlow & Hersen (1984), Kazdin (1982, 2003) and McReynolds & Kearns (1983).

Longitudinal studies can also answer particular questions such as 'How does language recover after a stroke?', 'Does one language recover differently from the other in a bilingual person with aphasia?' They can also track the development of speech and language skills, highlighting the ways in which children acquire language. Again, group vs single case studies are both options in this area.

1.6   Applying theory to practice

Theories (models, approaches and perspectives) play a major role in guiding both research and practice. One recent example is in the cognitive neuropsychological approach. In this approach, the theoretical underpinnings of the model rest with generative grammar based on the work of Chomsky (Cook, 1996), and theories of modular language processing (Fodor, 1983). The model of how language is processed has been built up through successive research findings with both brain-damaged and non-brain-damaged individuals. Instead of then describing individual's language performance with reference to normative performance on tests based on the model, each individual's language performance is considered directly with reference to the model, for example, considering which modules of language processing may be differentially impaired (Whitworth *et al.*, 2005). Thus, theory and practice remain inextricably linked on a case-by-case basis.

However, when considering the issues discussed above, it is important to note that research into communication disorders, as in any applied linguistic endeavour, is not simply about applying theory to practice – see Quote 1.1. It is also about informing theories *through* practice. Due to the complex nature of behaviours occurring in real life contexts, translation of theory is never straightforward. It is not sufficient for the applied field to simply describe a practice based on a particular theoretical framework. The practice itself generates its own theoretical principles, hence producing a basis for ongoing and systematic investigation of questions relevant to the area at hand, and recursively feeding back into the original theory.

Quote 1.1   Theory and practice

Hasan and Perrett discussing the shortcomings of theories in providing clear directions for applications (Hasan & Perrett, 1994):

> it seems that the fundamental issues of applied linguistics have remained problematic because linguistic revolutions have not delivered what they promised. (p. 179)
> The conception of language that has emerged from these revolutions and which applied linguistics has typically chosen to work with calls for revision because it fails to do justice to the complex issues that have to be addressed in doing applied linguistics. (pp. 179–80)

Candlin and Sarangi (2004) discussing the notion of theoretical development in Applied Linguistics:

> [Applied Linguistics] ... has constantly to work to develop generalizable principles of theoretical and analytic insights which will enable it to say not only what it does, but why what it does is grounded in coherent and sustainable argument. (Candlin & Sarangi, 2004, p. 3)

The study of behaviours of individuals with brain damage is a good example of how applied research can inform theoretical issues. Traditionally, theories of cognitive and linguistic function have been based on data from 'normal' speakers, listeners, readers and writers. However, knowledge derived from the study of 'non-typical' or 'non-normal' data has also informed theory. This has been more frequently the case in cognitive psychology than in linguistics. In fact, Ellis and Young (1988) pointed out that one of the main aims of cognitive neuropsychology is 'to draw conclusions about normal, intact cognitive processes from the patterns of impaired and intact capabilities seen in brain-injured patients' (Ellis & Young, 1988, p. 4). Ellis and Young go on to say that 'the cognitive psychologist wishes to be in a position to assert that observed patterns of symptoms could not occur if the normal, intact cognitive system were not organized in a certain way. (Ellis & Young, 1988, p. 4). For example, if two aspects of language functions such as X and Y can be found to be differentially impaired in brain damaged individuals (a dissociation), then it can be inferred that these are indeed separate functions/entities, requiring separate processing.

When applying linguistic theory to practice, numerous non-standard language and speech behaviours are encountered that do not fall within the traditional realms of analysis and the analysis must be immediately modified to accommodate them. For example, the substitution of one word for another (as in *I ate the book* instead of *I ate the apple*) may happen occasionally by error in a non-brain damaged person's speech, but is a regular feature of aphasic discourse. Such substitutions are known as paraphasias, their presence reflecting either semantic or phonemic disruption to the linguistic system. Interpretation of analyses must also be modified as phenomena are encountered that have not been considered during a theory's construction. For example, pathological repetition of words, phrases, ideas is often a feature of the discourse of individuals with brain damage. A cohesion analysis of discourse containing such features may reveal numerous cohesive ties, and yet the effect of these ties is not to contribute to cohesion and ultimately overall coherence, in fact sometimes quite the opposite. Problematic usage, such as when clauses remain incomplete, becomes difficult to interpret as to whether ellipsis has occurred or whether words have been inadvertently omitted. Some applied analyses (e.g. Language Assessment, Remediation and Screening Procedure (LARSP) Crystal *et al.*, 1976) originally classified such phenomena as 'other', which obviously does not shed much light on the nature or effect of such clauses. On the other hand, description of the surrounding context of the clause, while not definitively supplying the meaning of the incomplete one, may provide some clues as to the meaning being attempted and possible difficulties being encountered by the speaker.

Considering the above issues, it is important for the researcher to come to the field of communication disorders with an expectation of the need for flexibility in terms of theoretical models or analyses. Theoretical models may not automatically resonate with the populations encountered and the data obtained. Such difficulties provide the impetus for continued theory-building, and so provide an important challenge to researchers from a range of disciplines.

There are also expectations for research in the area that emanate from the scientific model which has been the traditional research model used in research into communication disorders. These relate to the psychometric constructs of validity and reliability (see Chapter 3 for more details). As in the area of second language testing, these two constructs have received much attention in the development of suitable and objective assessment materials (Weir, 2005). Face validity is of particular importance in this area, referring to the notion in this context, that our measures/analyses are truly reflecting the disorder as would be perceived by the general population. Reliability refers to the consistency of results obtained from a particular analysis both across analysts and within the one analyst (if s/he were to repeat the same analysis). While such constructs are not necessarily as central to more formal linguistic traditions, it is important to keep them in mind if one is advocating that particular procedures emanating from research undertaken may have use in clinical practice. Reliability in particular is one way to attempt to ensure consensus amongst clinicians who may be making decisions regarding particular diagnoses, educational options for clients, based on analyses undertaken.

1.7 Interdisciplinary collaboration

As mentioned at the outset, the study of communication has been approached from numerous perspectives and by numerous different disciplines. Interest in communication *disorders* has also come from numerous disciplines, although to a much more limited extent. Its investigative origins stem largely from medically related disciplines that were concerned with 'pathologies' in communication, evident after brain trauma, and also developmental delay. Issues of neurological functioning (e.g. localization of brain function), and later, treatment of such disorders were the primary focus of research in the area. However, as this area of study increased, interest grew in what breakdowns in communication could tell us about normal language processing. Psychologists, seeing language as but one part of a larger cognitive system, became interested in modelling language in similar ways to that of other cognitive systems such as memory and visual processing. Linguistic processing could serve to assist in completing the picture of cognitive processing in the brain. Linguists have also made significant contributions to describing the disorders in more detail and postulating possible linguistic processes occurring (Ball & Duckworth, 1996; Grodzinsky, 1990, 2006; Ulatowska *et al.*, 1990, 2004). Education is another discipline involved in the investigation of communication disorders, with a particular interest in the development of language in children, and its consequences for literacy and learning in general (Christie *et al.*, 2003). And most recently sociologists and anthropologists have contributed to issues such as identity after stroke (e.g. Hagstrom, 2004; Shadden & Agan, 2004).

From a treatment perspective, the primary allied health professional involved – the speech-language pathologist – is either employed within an educational setting, or children are referred to community health centres or hospitals for assessment and treatment. One of the exceptions to this scenario involves autism, which has had both medical and educational research histories dating back many years, and treatment of which is very multidisciplinary in nature and often occurs within an educational setting only. In some ways, the lack of clear aetiology of this spectrum of disorders has challenged many disciplines to search for answers, for example, neurologists, psychologists, educationalists, speech-language pathologists, psychiatrists and linguists. It has become clear that none of these knowledge bases individually explains the spectrum. However, the contribution of each in combination with each other, has slowly added to our knowledge of the disorder(s) involved.

In more recent times, a teamwork/collaborative approach has developed in many educational/clinical situations which fosters interdisciplinary research (Magill-Evans *et al.*, 2002). As individuals with communication disorders are increasingly being approached more holistically in terms of services provided to them, research is also following this path. The richness of collaborative research obviously lies in the different perspectives and knowledge bases that the collaborators bring to the project. Each brings different experiences, knowledge and access to the situation, hence should provide a broader and more in-depth approach to the problem at hand.

1.8   Communication disorders in a global community

Bilingualism and multilingualism in culturally and linguistically diverse communities also raise numerous issues in the area of communication disorders (see Isaac, 2002 for an overview). Questions related to what constitutes 'mastery' of a particular language and conversely, what is considered 'disordered language' are particularly relevant (see Chapter 5 for further discussion). If a child grows up in a bilingual environment but develops the two languages at different rates and with different levels of fluency, at what point can it be said that the child is having difficulty with one or other of his/her languages? Must a child be having difficulty learning both languages before it could be postulated that s/he has a language problem? In the case of multilingual adults after brain injury, differential loss of languages can inform us in terms of how languages are stored in the brain (Fabbro, 2001; Paradis, 1995). But in what way can treatment best be provided – in the strongest language? The language learned last? The language required the most for everyday usage?

The use of interpreters in such clinical endeavours is also an area for investigation, given that therapists may not speak the primary language of the client (Friedland & Penn, 2003; Isaac, 2002; Kambanaros & van Steenbrugge, 2004). The shared interest of many practitioners and researchers across the disciplines of linguistics, psychology, education and speech pathology are well served by interdisciplinary approaches to the study of bilingual and interpreted language use.

1.9   Concluding comments

This chapter has introduced a myriad of theoretical and methodological issues encountered in the field of communication disorders. While it has highlighted differences in approaches, it has hopefully also suggested complementarity of approaches and indeed different types of research. The book aims to provide an overview of research issues pertaining to the area, and to provide a pathway into this field of research for those individuals who are interested. As we explore these and other issues further in the quest to familiarize the reader with relevant questions, concerns and problems posed in the field, it is hoped that researchers will be encouraged to embark on projects that will shed their own particular light on some of these issues.

Further reading

Armstrong, E. (2005). Language disorder: A functional linguistic perspective. *Clinical Linguistics and Phonetics, 19*(3), 137–53.
This article discusses the nature and definition of 'disorder' as it relates to communication skills. While it provides a functional perspective, it addresses issues involved in different ways of approaching the notion of 'disorder'.
Ellis, A. W., & Young, A. W. (1988). *Human cognitive neuropsychology.* London: Lawrence Erlbaum.

This text provides an overview of approaches that examine acquired neurogenic communication disorders from a cognitive neuropsychological perspective. It outlines a framework that is an extension of the psycholinguistic approach to language that has been utilized traditionally in aphasia research.

2
The Research/Practice Context

Broadly speaking, the context for research in the field of communication disorders encompasses the theoretical and empirical work of other researchers in the field (both past and present), as well as the clinical and real-world manifestations, consequences and environments of the individuals who have communication disorders and those of their families, friends and the professionals with whom they may be involved. This chapter will at first focus on the practice context before moving on to examine the research context.

Researchers in the field of communication disorders work with people who have any one or more of the disorders which have been traditionally categorized into the areas of speech, language, voice and fluency (Owens, 2007). As discussed in Chapter 1, such disorders can be developmental in nature, that is, present from childhood, or they can be acquired subsequent to some neurological or other disease-related events such as stroke, trauma or laryngectomy. However, within this broad taxonomy are numerous subgroups that reflect a wide variety of disorders. One of the purposes of this chapter is to introduce the different types of disorders to potential researchers in order to clarify the different terminologies used within the field. This will be discussed in Section 2.1.

When embarking on research in this field, however, becoming familiar with the disorders is only the beginning of the endeavour. The contexts in which individuals with communication disorders find themselves is another important aspect to be considered, since this varies according to the kind of disorder they have, or indeed the cause of the disorder, as well as society's view of that disorder. For example, a child with a specific language disability with no obvious medical cause may be in a special class at school catering for children with language problems, or be seeing a special education teacher and/or speech-language pathologist for extra assistance. In many ways, the difficulty or disorder may be seen as an educational one, even in situations where medical factors are involved. For example, the child with cerebral palsy will often be at a special school, obtaining a variety of allied health and medical assistance, as well as educational input. Regular liaison with a medical practitioner may also be involved, as the physical cause and obvious manifestation places cerebral palsy more within the medical domain. Adults with acquired communication disorders from neurological events such as stroke, traumatic brain injury (TBI) or dementia may be in hospital, attending therapy at a variety of rehabilitation centres, or in a nursing home. If discharged from hospital, and living at home, they may be most likely accessing assistance through the healthcare system in some way.

In order to both gain access to research participants with communication disorders, and to understand some of the issues that confront them in their everyday lives, researchers need to have an overview of the circumstances which such individuals find themselves in. This can relate to educational and vocational issues, and residential settings and institutions, as well as the kinds of professionals involved in care and service delivery. The context in which the person functions also has ramifications for the kinds of issues that are relevant to research, and for ethical questions that are raised regarding the nature of the research proposed. A researcher in this area needs to be aware of the challenges that face the individual, both external and internal. This is discussed in Section 2.2.

The nature of the problems faced by the person with a communication disorder and the environmental settings in which they find themselves in mean that different types of professionals from varied disciplinary backgrounds may be involved. Researchers in the field of communication disorders need to have an appreciation of the contribution of other disciplines and their potential involvement within any research in this field. These issues are discussed in Section 2.3.

For all researchers in the field, it is important to contextualize the focus of research within the research that has been or is currently being conducted by others in the field and in related fields. Researchers need to have well-developed search skills to locate relevant research literature, as well as the ability to make discerning choices as to the relative contribution of other research to the research at-hand. This chapter concludes with a discussion on some of the aspects of these research skills that assist in researching the field of communication disorders (Section 2.4).

2.1 People with communication disorders

2.1.1 Descriptions with reference to diagnostic categorization

When working in any field, taxonomies (see Chapter 1, Concept 1.1) are useful to convey a common sense of what is being discussed. Certainly, a number of communication disorders have been identified over the years, with a specific referential term taking on the nature of 'diagnosis' when used in a medical setting. Within the medical paradigm, many communication disorders are part of symptom-complexes that can be described in detailed taxonomic systems such as the DSM-IV (APA, 1994; First & Tasman, 2004).

For example, *aphasia, dysarthria and apraxia* are used as diagnostic terms. Such terms are useful as they provide a general description of a set of behaviours or communication patterns that constitute a phenomenon generally agreed upon as existing as a separate entity. Individuals fitting such patterns can be classified as belonging to a particular group, the disorder is increasingly defined, and treatments established to deal with this particular disorder. However, in recent times, there has been much discussion on such terms, some of which, such as *specific language disorder, semantic/pragmatic disorder* remain very controversial (see Special Issue of *Advances in Speech and Language Pathology*, 7(2), 2005, for detailed discussion on terminology and its uses in the description of communication disorders). They are controversial because it would appear that a number of different 'symptoms' or descriptions of behaviours are classified as belonging to one diagnosis, when in fact there may be a variety of disorders involved. The autism spectrum is a classic case where a spectrum of disorders was acknowledged to exist in the 1990s, rather than individuals on the continuum all being labelled simply 'autistic' – a state of affairs which did not acknowledge difference and in many ways stifled research by continuing to assert that this was in fact one disorder. In more recent times, the term *aphasia,* traditionally accepted as language disorder occurring after neurological damage, has attracted controversy (Caramazza & Badecker, 1991; McNeil & Pratt, 2001; Rao, 1994). As a further example, scholars argue whether or not 'language' includes pragmatic skills, that is, language 'in use' and if so, why the term aphasia should be restricted to individuals with left hemisphere damage, and not be applied to those with right hemisphere damage whose communication abilities are affected in the social-pragmatic domain, but not primarily in the syntactic and semantic domains (Joanette & Ansoldo, 1999). Similarly, traditional subcategories of 'aphasia' have

Table 2.1 Overview of types of developmental speech and language communication disorders

Aspect of communication	Types of communication disorders
Language	*Delayed language*: Describes the language of a child who is slow to develop language skills, in the context of typical development of motor and other cognitive skills.
	Specific Language Impairment: Describes the language of child who is developing these skills in a different pattern, but typically in terms of motor and other cognitive skills.
Speech articulation	*Phonological disorder*: Describes difficulty with the phonological rules which govern the patterns of speech production.
	Developmental articulation disorder: Describes difficulty with particular sounds (rather than with particular patterns of sounds), which may relate to structural differences (e.g. cleft palate), or learned movements (e.g. lisp).
	Childhood Apraxia of Speech (CAS): Describes problems with coordinated and accurate production of speech sounds and patterns of sounds. This is a controversial classification, and presents a diagnostic challenge.

been accepted as clinical diagnoses, for example, Broca's aphasia, transcortical-sensory aphasia. While researchers have documented thousands of cases over the years, the use of these categories has also become controversial (for an overview of the issues involved, see Poeppel & Hickok, 2004).

Having prepared the reader for some inherent difficulties in the use of terminology in this field, it is important that the researcher also becomes familiar with traditionally accepted categories of communication disorders, and these are overviewed in Tables 2.1, 2.2 and 2.3. Communication disorders can exist in isolation. However, it is also possible that some may co-occur within the one individual. For example, when a general developmental disability exists, for example, intellectual impairment, a child may have delayed speech and language development. In addition, there may be some structural abnormalities, for example, dental/oral anomalies that cause articulation problems. Likewise, cerebral palsy, causing speech problems, may sometimes be accompanied by intellectual deficit, in which case the child may have language delay as well.

Table 2.2 Overview of the types of acquired speech and language communication disorders

Aspect of communication	Types of communication disorders
Language	*Aphasia*: Occurs after neurological damage (e.g. stroke) to specific parts of the brain responsible for semantic and syntactic aspects of language (usually the left cerebral hemisphere). Symptoms can include word-finding difficulty, paraphasias (e.g. substitution of one word for another) and syntactic disruption (e.g. telegrammatic style involving a relative lack of verbs and functors).
	Cognitive-communication disorder: Occurs after damage to diffuse areas of the brain and/or to the right cerebral hemisphere (e.g. after TBI, dementia, right cerebral hemisphere damage). Communication symptoms reflect damage to the cortical functions required for cognition, e.g. problems with inhibition may result in verbosity or paucity of content, problems with attention or self-monitoring may result in tangentiality, problems with executive function and judgement may result in inappropriate turn-taking or inappropriate management of the level of politeness required for particular situations.
Speech articulation	*Dysarthria*: Occurs after damage to the parts of the brain controlling motor speech. Usually involves pathological changes to muscle tone, and is typically characterized by slurred articulation due to effects on lip and tongue muscles, abnormal voice symptoms (e.g. harsh, hoarse, breathy or strained quality) due to laryngeal involvement, varying degrees of excessive or insufficient nasality due to effects on the movement of the soft palate, and lack of breath control during speech due to respiratory muscle involvement.
	Apraxia of Speech: Occurs after damage to the parts of the brain controlling motor speech, but often co-occurs with aphasia (see above). Involves difficulty with the planning of movements for speech, which is not attributable to changes to the peripheral muscles for speech. Speech is typically produced with groping movements of the articulators to achieve articulatory postures, with frequent substitution and distortion of sounds.

Table 2.3   Overview of the types of voice and fluency disorders

Aspect of communication	Types of communication disorders
Speech – Voice	*Voice disorders*: This involves disruption to normal voice quality, that is, the voice can become *dysphonic* (harsh, strained or husky), and when extreme, the person can lose his/her voice completely (*aphonia*). These disorders can be functional and/or structural in aetiology. Physical obstruction to the vocal tract such as vocal nodules or malignant tumours can result in such symptoms. On the other hand, vocal abuse (shouting too much, singing using a poor technique) and psychological factors such as stress may also be responsible.
Speech – Fluency	*Stuttering*: Fluency disorders involve disruption to the smooth flow of speech and usually manifest as stuttering or stammering. They are often developmental in nature – typical onset is between 3 to 5 years. Some stuttering behaviours resolve with age, while others persist into adulthood. Fluency disorders can also result from neurological damage, but these are different in nature from developmental disorders.

2.1.2   A different perspective on classification

Another approach to communication disorders resides within a framework developed in recent years by the World Health Organisation (Threats, 2006; WHO, 2001). WHO has proposed a framework by which to classify various aspects of functioning and disability (see website http://www.who.int/classifications/icf/en/ for more details). The International Classification of Functioning, Disability and Health (also known as International Classification of Functioning, or ICF) represents an attempt to go beyond the traditional medical diagnostic classification systems for diseases and conditions such as those described above (WHO, 2000, 2001, 2002). It classifies body structures and functions, but describes more than the actual impairment, encompassing how that disorder affects the individual's daily activities and their participation in social life, as well as the external factors in the environment that affect these experiences (see Figure 2.1).

As an example, a person who has aphasia has an impairment at the level of the brain that affects his/her semantic and/or syntactic systems and makes expression of words and sentences difficult. The impairment would be classified and rated as a particular severity. This translates in their everyday life into difficulties with such activities as talking with their partner, answering the telephone, shopping and so on. The person's

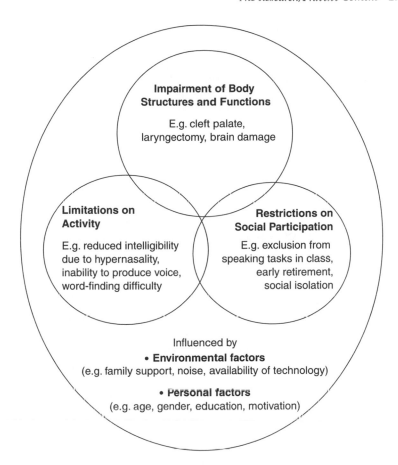

Figure 2.1 The International Classification of Functioning (ICF) and communication disorders

performance of these activities would be rated in terms of the degree to which it affects in his/her everyday life. However, the person's *capacity* to perform such activities is also examined and rated, that is, a person may have the capacity to perform, but for some reason, may not be able to in all situations. Conversely, a person may not have the capacity to perform a particular task unaided, and yet when given assistance, can actually accomplish the task. At a social participation level, they severely restrict themselves, often isolating themselves from friends and contacts such as those made at local social clubs and sporting events. In addition, friends, family and the general community find it difficult to communicate with them, and are often unprepared for communication with someone who has aphasia. Telephone bill-paying systems, for example, do not accommodate people with aphasia due to the rapid rate of responses required, and the relatively high level of comprehension for instructions needed. At the environment level, such factors are rated as being either facilitators or barriers and are rated again on a scale of impact.

The usefulness of this classification system continues to be debated (see Special Issue of *Advances in Speech Language Pathology*, 6(1), 2004, (now the International Journal of Speech-Language Pathology). However, its existence is an attempt to examine the social impact of communication disorders, in line with the social model of disability (Oliver, 1983) – a model that looks beyond the individual and their disorder, to the surrounding society and the ways in which that society either assists or hinders the individual from participating at a number of different levels.

2.2   Environmental contexts

The environment in which individuals with communication disorders live, study, work and socialize vary greatly depending on the country and their cultural affiliation. The following description of settings is based on a Western cultural model, although there are many variations from country to country and across and within cultures. Individual researchers need be alert to the variations which exist which will influence their own research endeavours.

2.2.1   The hospital/healthcare setting

Depending on the cause of the problem, individuals with communication disorders (both children and adults) are often referred to the health system for assistance. Children may be screened for speech and hearing problems from an early age by healthcare workers. If detected with potential problems, they may then be referred on to medical specialists (e.g. paediatricians; ear, nose and throat specialists), speech-language pathologists, audiologists, as well as professionals in the health and/ or educational systems. Most people will be dealt with as outpatients either on a one-off assessment basis, review basis for monitoring purposes or regularly for ongoing therapy.

However, when sudden incidents that involve the onset of a communication problem occur, or those from which a communication problem ensues, individuals are most likely to become hospital inpatients, although this is not always the case. This can happen in children or adults, although occurs much more often in adults in the case of communication disorders. Traumatic head injuries resulting from a variety of accidents can cause significant communication problems in both children and adults and often require long-term rehabilitation (in terms of months and sometimes years) for the person involved. Strokes and other neurological disease, for example, Parkinson's disease, Motor Neurone Disease can also cause communication disorders and again require long-term intervention. Individuals are often transferred from the acute hospital setting to a rehabilitation hospital if requiring longer term inpatient care. This may last from a few weeks to several months.

Other groups of people receiving treatment in a hospital setting may include those with voice disorders (e.g. vocal nodules) or individuals who stutter. The former group may or may not have a physical pathology, but require an assessment by an Ear, Nose and Throat physician in order to either detect or rule out this possibility so that treatment can be planned accordingly. The latter group, however, has no medical pathology, and usually attend only speech therapy. Many groups require multidisciplinary intervention because of concomitant disorders such as those related to stroke (e.g. body weakness requiring physiotherapy), hence will be seen in a multidisciplinary setting such as a rehabilitation centre.

As well as hospital settings, community centres often also provide services to individuals with communication disorders. Such centres provide a variety of services, including speech pathology, psychological counselling and support, social work assistance, nursing and medical services, dietary advice and so on. Some provide services to children only, while others cater for both children and adults.

Mental health services are offered in both hospital and community settings. Individuals with communication disorders may also be seen by a mental health team. They may have difficulties related to developmental disability, or their communication may be impaired either temporarily or permanently as a result of their mental health or as an adverse consequence of medication for their problem.

Hospital settings pose numerous challenges to individuals with communication disorders. Even for those without communication disorders, negotiating the medical system can be extremely problematic. Understanding the kinds of care and procedures provided, as well as actively participating in decision-making regarding the direction of care, can be challenging at the best of times. However, when handicapped by difficulty in speaking and/or understanding, the individual is placed in an extremely vulnerable position. Together with the fact that significant trauma usually surrounds the event which brings the

person to hospital in the first place, the realization of the ramifications of the event as time progresses can significantly immobilize a
person, even in the absence of any physical impairment. Individuals
with communication disorders are known to have particular difficulties when in hospital (Balandin *et al.*, 2001). For example, making simple needs known can be difficult, issues of consent for treatment are
problematic, and individuals often become isolated because they are
unable to participate in any social chat during routine interactions
with staff, other patients or family. In hospital, interactions range from
discussion with a nurse on alleviation of pain through medications or
change of physical position, to discussion with a doctor on prognosis for the future following stroke, or details on imminent surgery, to
attempting to make meal choices from a menu, with the assistance of
a dietician or dietary aide. Discussions with family regarding home
and financial situations as well as future residential status can be even
more significant. Individuals with communication disorders are often
excluded from many discussions and life decisions whilst in hospital.
When considering research in the hospital setting, potential researchers need to be aware of the demands already placed on the person who
is the inpatient as well as their families. Issues of informed consent can
also be problematic and must be carefully explored (see Chapter 6 for
further discussion).

2.2.2 The residential setting

Individuals with severe communication impairments are often found
to be living in situations outside the immediate family environment. In
the case of stroke, for example, they may have accompanying physical
disabilities that prevent them from living independently at home, or do
not have sufficient support to maintain themselves at home. In such
cases, the person may reside in a hostel or nursing home environment
depending on the level of care required. Depending on the person's
social situation, and the organization of the residence itself, they may
be socially active in that environment or may become extremely isolated. It is worth noting that nursing home accommodation is mostly
geared towards the elderly population. While some younger people may
also need nursing home care, there are few institutions that provide
other than a geriatric service, with most residents being elderly, several
suffering from dementia.

Similar to the hospital context, individuals with communication
disorders in nursing homes can experience considerable isolation. It
is estimated that up to 95% of residents in any nursing home suffer

from some degree of communication and/or swallowing impairment, whether it be a frank speech problem or a hearing-related condition (Worrall & Hickson, 2003).

In the case of people with developmental disorders, for example, intellectual impairment, group homes have become increasingly common over the last decade in particular. Such homes usually include between 2 and 6 residents with varying levels of disability and support needs. In this environment, independence is encouraged. Residents may or may not have family support.

In order to access individuals for research purposes within a nursing home, hostel, or group home, researchers will need to contact either the Director of the facility in the case of the nursing home/hostel, and/or the state department/company/institution operating the group home. To ensure protection of residents, ethics clearances must always be obtained, and clear explanations given to residents, residents' families where appropriate, and staff about the nature of the research being undertaken. It is also important to remember that the residential setting is the research participant's home and the same respect must be afforded both the person and the residence as if it was a private residence (see Chapter 6 for further discussion).

2.2.3 Support groups

As well as relying on institutional support, many individuals are involved in local, state, or national support groups that are initiated by individuals with communication disorders and their families. These support groups serve several functions. They provide emotional support for both the person with the communication disorder and their families in that they have the opportunity to meet other people with similar difficulties and in similar situations. Social outings, fund-raising, adult education seminars are sometimes organized that facilitate sometimes otherwise isolated families/individuals to re-engage in their community. They can also provide practical support – sometimes by providing information on respite care opportunities, government allowances and by providing temporary respite for a carer during the day when the support group meets and his/her relative can attend. Support groups are often disease/condition specific (see Chapter 10 for examples). Such groups function to support individuals with communication disorders and their families in the long term by providing information, social and psychological support, and sometimes therapy. They often have newsletters, and researchers can recruit by advertising in these newsletters – see Part IV, Section 10.5 for examples of support groups.

2.3.4   The educational setting

Children with communication problems attend mainstream and special schools and preschools, depending on the nature and severity of their difficulties, as well as on the prevailing educational service paradigm. In mainstream schools, they are sometimes integrated within a classroom of typically developing children, while others are placed in a class for children with special needs. While some such classes are 'disorder-specific' (e.g. for children with language difficulties), many include children with a variety of special needs including behaviour management, visual and auditory challenges, mobility limitations, learning difficulties, specific literacy problems, as well as communication disorders. Some may receive individual assistance, while others will be assisted in the group setting only.

Special schools also vary considerably in nature. Some special schools are devoted to children with specific disabilities, for example, visual and hearing impairments, autism, cerebral palsy, while others cater for children with multiple physical and cognitive impairments.

Schools may be public or private in terms of funding and administration, and hence different administrative frameworks will be encountered in terms of gaining access to students for research purposes. Government schools may have area or state boards that have to be approached, while private schools and preschools may be associated with religious or other charitable institutions and will have their own administrative structures that need to be negotiated.

2.2.5   Implications of diverse settings

As noted above, a variety of locational contexts exist, each having their own culture and history. It is important to be aware of how the research project fits in to the clinical/educational situation in which the person is already engaged:

- Does the project propose to replace a particular therapy or intervention?
- Does it complement it?
- Is the teacher/speech-language pathologist required to change his/her practice to accommodate the research project (see Example 2.1)?
- Is the family involved, and if so, are they to be considered research participants as well as the person with the communication disorder?

Example 2.1

A researcher wanted to investigate the efficacy of phonemic awareness therapy for children with reading difficulties in a group setting within a classroom. This involved negotiating with the school and classroom teacher on the best way to implement such a study. Phonemic awareness training was not a routine classroom activity for this class. Consent had to be obtained from the children's parents for their children to be involved in this training. Hence, justification had to be supplied as to why such training would be of benefit and what the children would be missing out on during this period of training when they would otherwise have been doing another activity.

When dealing with communication disorders within a healthcare situation, the researcher must be aware that clients may be in a variety of conditions with regard to their state of health. In the acute hospital setting, the person may have just had a stroke and may still be in a medically and psychologically unstable condition. The hospital may or may not approve of research being undertaken under these conditions. Hence, it is important for the researcher to be aware of the situation and to anticipate potential problems that might arise in undertaking the research (see Example 2.2).

Example 2.2

TD was admitted to hospital after suffering from a stroke. He had a hemiplegia and a severe aphasia, leaving him with impaired communication skills. He was frustrated and depressed and tired very easily at this stage post onset of the stroke. The researcher was investigating recovery patterns in the conversational skills of people with aphasia. As part of the ethics application to the hospital, the researcher had to specify how consent would be obtained from TD for his participation in the project. A speech pathologist experienced in communicating with people with aphasia explained the project to TD and his family using both written and verbal means – one supplementing the other. The language was simplified so that TD could understand and the speech pathologist constantly checked that TD understood what was being said by asking him a variety of questions. TD's family was present. One of the other conditions in the ethics application also specified that the data collection would stop if TD became tired or distressed. In the early stages after stroke, fatigue and poor concentration can be major difficulties for the person involved. Hence, while the researcher taped short conversations between the person with aphasia and his spouse, the researcher was alert to these factors and discontinued the taping sessions on more than one occasion at the person with aphasia's request.

In a therapy setting, the researcher should be aware of the frustration sometimes encountered by an adult or child with a communication problem, particularly if required to undergo testing of skills that are impaired, or even being asked to participate in a conversation when this is a difficult undertaking. Participating in a research project may require a lot of extra effort on the part of the individual and their family if the procedure is not part of the normal therapy process. Provisions should be made to avoid extra stress where possible. For example, the researcher may offer to see the individual in their home if more convenient. While this brings in other ethical issues (e.g. the need to have a third person present during interactions), it may assist the person/family greatly in participating. Such ethical issues are discussed further in Chapter 6.

2.3   Disciplinary context

As mentioned earlier in Chapter 1, research on communication disorders emanates from a variety of disciplines. For the researcher in the field, this has ramifications for the range of research literature that must be reviewed in order to absorb the nature of relevant research issues, (see below – Section 2.4). The medical, educational, speech pathology and psychology fields are the primary disciplines involved.

In both the paediatric and adult areas, various kinds of research questions can be asked that necessarily involve more than one discipline. For example, in the case of disordered development of articulation skills in children, complex phonological theories underpin many analyses of speech. While speech-language pathologists plan interventions, linguists specializing in phonetics and phonology can contribute to the development of these from a theoretical perspective (Ball & Muller, 2002).

One outstanding example of research which was underpinned by the interdisciplinary collaboration between researchers in linguistics and speech pathology can be seen in the work on the development of a number of assessment methodologies for children and adults with language impairments which were guided by the work of David Crystal – for example, the PRISM (Profile in Semantics), and the PROPH (Profile in Phonology) (Crystal, 1992), and the Language Assessment, Remediation and Screening Procedure (LARSP) (Crystal *et al.*, 1976) – see Example 2.3 for example of collaboration on a small-scale project.

Example 2.3 Example of interdisciplinary research (Ferguson & Peterson, 2002)

This single case study was carried out by one of the authors (Ferguson, a speech pathologist) with the assistance of a linguistic researcher (Peterson). The research looked at the role of intonation in interaction involving a person with aphasia. The question arose from the observation during an interview involving the person with aphasia (a man in his seventies), his wife (also in her seventies), and their neighbour (a woman in her fifties), that the neighbour's intonation pattern appeared to become noticeably different when talking with the man with aphasia – more 'sing-song'.

Interdisciplinary research context: Intonation has been observed to change when speakers differ in terms of power and age, for example, the way nursing staff sometimes talk with elderly institutionalized nursing home residents has been described as 'elderspeak' (Kemper et al., 1998). Linguists working from a sociolinguistic perspective have been able to describe the perceptual features of such intonational patterns in a way that provides an explanatory description of the social relationships between interactants (Brazil, 1981). Social psychologists describe such shifts in intonation with reference to 'Communication Accommodation Theory' (Giles *et al.*, 1973). Gallois and others (1995) continue to explore this model with reference to accommodation for disability.

Research question: Is there a difference in the intonation pattern used by the neighbour when addressing the person with aphasia, as compared to that used when addressing his wife? If so, what is the nature of this difference?

This man had a moderate-severe fluent aphasia, resulting from a left cerebrovascular accident (stroke) some years before. He had limitations on his ability to understand rapid or complex conversational language, and experienced frequent word-finding difficulty. He also had a mild hearing loss, for which he used hearing aids. He reported that he found socializing to be an effort, but he enjoyed attending a social group for people who had experienced disability following a stroke.

Environmental context: As this man lived at home, data were collected in his home, with conversational language use being recorded (video and audio) as all participants and the researcher (Ferguson) sat around the dining table having a cup of tea.

Collaborative contributions: Ferguson contributed her speech pathology expertise to the diagnostic assessment, data collection, and preliminary transcription and analysis. Peterson contributed his linguistic experience to the detailed perceptual notation and subsequent analysis. Interpretation of findings was conducted in collaboration.

Similarly, researchers from the discipline of psychology have worked collaboratively with both linguistics and speech pathology over many years. For example, the contribution of the psychologist Roger Ingham to the measurement of stuttering behaviours over the last 30 years continues to provide productive outcomes for the assessment and intervention for stuttering (e.g. Ingham & Cordes, 1997; Ingham *et al.*, 1989).

2.4   Research context

As indicated at the beginning of both Chapters 1 and this chapter, no researcher is working in a vacuum. While ideas for research often spring to mind in the context of clinical practice or from observations in everyday life, it is important to thoroughly test and develop the research plan or question in light of what is already known about the issues of relevance. Examples of designing projects are given in Part 3, Chapter 10.

Exploring the research context involves conducting a search on previous research studies which have been published in the field. For researchers entering an area which is relatively unfamiliar, it can be useful to look first through recent reference books which provide overviews of key paradigms, theories, frameworks, approaches and per-spectives in the area of interest. This first stage provides the researcher with an idea as to the names of key researchers in the field, and of key words that may prove useful in later searches of literature databases, as well as a 'big picture' understanding of the area. A useful question to consider at this stage is the significance of the question or direction for research, for example, what would be the outcome of knowing the answer to this question, or of knowing more about the problem? This is very much a practical question, as from this point on, considerable time and effort will need to be expended, much of it prior to being able to obtain resources to support the research.

In the field of communication disorders, most of the research con-ducted is to be found in the form of journal articles, published in what are described as peer-reviewed (or 'refereed') journals (see Chapter 7). These journals may be accessed in hard copy, and/or are increas-ingly available electronically. Large electronic databases are available through library or work-related services, as well as some are available to the general public (for example, through Google Scholar™ -http:// scholar.google.com.au/) – see Part IV, Section 10.6 for some examples of journals in the field of communication disorders.

Generally, the first trawl through previous research results in one of two outcomes. The first outcome is that not many articles are located, and in this situation it helps to review key words used in the search. Sometimes it can be useful to start reading in detail a couple of poten-tially relevant articles, and start following up the references cited by these papers. From this preliminary reading, it often becomes more apparent what search terms might be useful. The second possibility is that too many articles get located, and it begins to become difficult to know which articles constitute the 'best' research, and which to peruse. It can be helpful at this stage to start using category systems along similar lines to those developed within the paradigm of EBP (see Chapter 3) to sort the previous research, for example, categorizing articles in terms of randomized controlled experimental studies (such studies usually self-identify as these), controlled cohort comparisons (e.g. comparing two groups, or the same group under more than one condition), group descriptions (e.g. just one group in one condition), single case studies (noting whether including controlled experimental comparisons, or whether descriptive), and expert opinion (e.g. scholarly or clinical guidelines or discussion). Within each of these categories it is likely that some articles stand out as more relevant to the topic of interest and/or more rigorously conducted, and so it will be helpful to make a note of this.

Through this reading, it sometimes becomes clear that a particular researcher, or group of researchers, or perhaps a particular centre for research, have an ongoing research programme which is relevant to the topic of interest. If appropriate, it may be useful to find out more about the nature of their ongoing research (e.g. via internet, email), for example, they may have presented conference papers on work in progress, which are yet to be published, or it may be possible to attend a conference at which they will be discussing their work.

After some reading and continued critical evaluation of the significance of the research direction, it is usually a good idea to discuss some of the issues and quandaries with people who might become collaborative researchers, whether from the same or other disciplines – new ideas will emerge from such discussions, and time will be saved through the generation of alternative options. Intellectual property is sometimes of concern to researchers, particularly researchers in the initial stage of research who may feel relatively disempowered – these issues are discussed in Chapter 7 with reference to dissemination of research, but it is also worth noting the simple practices such as the sending of brief notes (e.g. through email) of discussions to check on understandings formed regarding matters discussed and plans made can provide a basis for an open working relationship.

2.5 Global community of researchers

As noted above, a large research community exists in this field of communication disorders, encompassing numerous disciplines from all over the world. International conferences and the internet provide valuable opportunities for the twenty-first century researcher to remain in constant contact with developments from across the globe. While cultural/linguistic boundaries still sometimes restrict the flow of ideas within and across disciplines, such boundaries are becoming increasingly irrelevant. Researchers in this area need to be aware of the depth and breadth of research being undertaken in different contexts and with different foci depending on that context. As countries become increasingly multicultural and multilingual, the study of communication disorders will have to become increasingly broad, encompassing cross-cultural values and issues of multilingualism not previously addressed due to political, economic or educational constraints.

2.6   Concluding comments

This chapter has set the stage upon which research on communication disorders can be conducted, through consideration of the people and places involved. In this chapter a number of points have been raised which suggest the importance of preparation in the research process, for example, through consideration of the feasibility and significance of the planned research. In the Chapter 3 we move to consider some of the key problems in the field in general terms, highlighting key methodological considerations in the process.

Further readings

Owens, R. E. (2007). *Introduction to communication disorders: A lifespan perspective* (3rd edn). Boston: Pearson/Allyn&Bacon.
    This book provides an overview of the different types of communication disorders experienced across the lifespan. It also describes general assessment and treatment approaches taken to these disorders by speech pathologists.
Threats, T. T. (2006). Towards an international framework for communication disorders: Use of the ICF. *Journal of Communication Disorders, 39*(4), 251–65.
    This article provides an introduction to the ICF framework and its applicability to communication disorders. It covers studies already using the framework in this field and the ways in which it may form the basis of collaborative and international research in the future.

Part II

Practical Applications of Research

3
What are the Key Problems in the Field?

This chapter identifies areas research has been focused on historically within the field, as well as looks at some of the current 'hot topics'. Extending on the coverage provided in Chapter 1, the present chapter looks more closely at research which seeks to understand the nature of communication disorders (Section 3.1), which is discussed under the general term 'epidemiology'. The term 'epidemiology' in its purest form is the study of disease and disorders in *populations*, as opposed to *individuals*, so for example, exploring questions such as the incidence and prevalence of particular communication disorders (for definition see Concept 3.1). However, epidemiology also encompasses research that attempts to increase the understanding of the nature of particular disorders, since ascertaining the nature of disorders is fundamental to broader epidemiological studies. In Section 3.2, this chapter also looks further at research that explores aspects of 'efficacy', that is, research that investigates whether and how particular approaches to remediation may contribute to improvement for children and adults with communication disorders. This section provides an opportunity to examine more closely the paradigms of EBP, and the types of research designs which are involved in such research. In the final section (Section 3.3), this chapter explores research that looks at issues 'around' the person with the communication disorder, for example, at the impact on families and carers, at interventions designed to educate those living and working with individuals with communication disorders, and at issues relevant to the education of professionals working with these individuals. This section includes coverage of examples of research into professional communication, including intra- and inter-professional communication. As we introduce each of these aspects of research, we will identify some of the main methodological issues for studies in the field of communication disorders (for further details, see Irwin *et al.*, 2008; Pring, 2005).

Concept 3.1 Incidence and prevalence

Incidence is generally considered to be the number of new cases which appear in a given population in a given period, e.g. number of people with a long-term disability caused through road accidents during 2007.

Prevalence is generally considered to be the number of cases which exist in the population at any particular time, e.g. number of people with long-term disability from road accidents. In this example, prevalence is likely to exceed incidence, since there are likely to be more survivors with disability than new cases. The reverse is true for the case of stuttering, as while many new cases arise during early childhood, it is estimated that between 60% and 80% of children will recover.

An important issue to be kept in mind throughout this chapter is the need to recognize that not all important questions or issues are 'researchable'. Often a particular theory is built on key assumptions that are fundamental to frameworks derived within that theoretical perspective, but not all key assumptions may be open to empirical testing. An example of this is in the area of formal linguistics where in the 1960s some theorists have argued for a universal language acquisition device which was essentially hard-wired into the human brain, requiring only minimal environmental input to trigger its activation. Those arguing against this view considered that there was no specific language acquisition device, but rather that the brain developed in response to environmental stimuli. Such stimuli inevitably involved communication, and development proceeded for communication in the same way as for any of the aspects of human development. Both these theoretical positions were essentially unable to be tested through research, since even case studies of severely neglected and environmentally deprived children were confounded by the impact of the deprivation on overall cognitive development. As a corollary to the first point that not all theoretical positions are researchable, it is also important to recognize that potentially there are many aspects of communication that could provide data, but not all data yield findings that are important to a particular research question. An example of this is in the area of what is sometimes described as 'body language', which can be recognized as an important source of communication in many situations, but which would clearly be irrelevant to a study of telephone conversations. Unfortunately, the situation is rarely as black and white as the telephone example. A researcher may need to make decisions about what data to include or exclude and these decisions are crucial since exclusion of data runs the risk of missing pivotal information. For example, in most studies of aphasic language in which the research focus is on underlying cognitive-linguistic processing, hesitations and revisions will be excluded from transcription and hence from later analysis (Saffran *et al.*, 1989). The 'cleaned-up' data are highly informative for research in which cognitive-linguistic processing is seen from within a static 'functional architecture' perspective. However, the data are significantly impoverished for research in which hesitation phenomena are seen as indicators of linguistic formulation difficulty, for example, in research on the dynamic aspects of cognitive-linguistic processing, or in research on the role of such phenomena in assisting with turn-taking.

3.1 Epidemiology

Epidemiological research is concerned with establishing the nature of disorder in the population, and is important in ascertaining how important particular disorders are for particular communities.

Concept 3.2 Epidemiological research

An example of the power of epidemiological research comes from the story of how cholera was curbed in London in the 1800s. Up until this time, doctors had been dealing with a deluge of individual cases of this devastating disease as best they could. One particular doctor took upon himself to map each case of cholera as it occurred against a map of London. After a while a pattern emerged indicating that the majority of cases were concentrated about a particular line of the water supply. At that time, people obtained their drinking water from public pumps, and so this doctor argued successfully for the need to shut off the pumps supplied by this particular water line. Miraculously, the plague of cholera ceased. Only later was the connection between faecally contaminated water as the bacterial basis for cholera definitively established, but in the meantime, an epidemiological study had been responsible for saving many lives (Vinten-Johansen *et al.*, 2003).

Epidemiological research into communication disorders is unlikely to yield quite such dramatic results as seen in Concept 3.2, but the global and societal perspective offered through epidemiological research is worth consideration. Government support and charitable funding for particular diseases and disorders within the community are only possible when arguments can be submitted based on established need for services. When disorders remain unrecognized in the community and when it is not possible to say how many people are affected and in what ways, support for individuals remains inadequate. For example, Parkinson's disease is well recognized in the community, with most people being aware of high-profile individuals with the disorder (e.g. actor Michael J. Fox), and with a known prevalence of around 50 people per 100,000 over the age of 50 (Duffy, 2005, p. 190), and with particular programmes of support directed to the services for people with this disorder. For people with dysarthria from Parkinson's disease, public awareness has assisted in the development of particular therapy programmes aimed specifically at the types of communication difficulty associated with the disease. For example, the Lee Silverman Voice Technique (LSVT) is a therapy approach which results in more audible and more intelligible speech, and is currently the most well-researched treatment for any type of dysarthria, with the strongest levels of evidence for its efficacy (see the case example of this approach in Section 3.2 below). The development of the treatment methods and the research that has established its efficacy has only been possible through the clear identification of the population in need. As a counter example, aphasia is a poorly recognized communication problem which is associated with brain damage from stroke and head injury. In a survey of 978 people in the street conducted in Australia, United States and United Kingdom, researchers found that only 5.4% of people knew what this disorder was, and how it might affect communication (Simmons-Mackie *et al.*, 2002). Nor are there any reliable or comprehensive data available in any country in the world as to the incidence and prevalence of this problem. However, it is known from minor research studies that aphasia is typically present in about one-third of cases of stroke, and there is incidence and prevalence information about stroke. On the basis of this kind of inferential data, it is estimated that aphasia is at least as prevalent as Parkinson's disease. Currently, there is an established need for an improved evidence base for aphasia treatments, but support for such research is hampered by basic data establishing the community need.

3.1.1   Describing communication problems

Describing communication problems requires an appreciation of complex taxonomies, as discussed in Chapter 1 (Section 1.2), and a recognition of what makes for a valid description or measure. If a communication problem with high recognition in society such as stuttering is considered, it might be thought that this problem would be relatively straightforward to describe and measure. In studies which have attempted to establish how many people stutter, the researchers typically have not defined stuttering, but instead they have relied on an assumed societal consensus as to what is stuttering. For example, such studies have simply surveyed teachers in schools, asking them how many children in their class stutter. However, the results from such studies show variation in reported prevalence, for example, 0.3 per cent to 3.9 per cent (Blum-Harasty & Rosenthal, 1992, p. 67). One of the reasons for this variation in reports probably centres on differences in the identification of stuttering as well as sampling differences. The communication behaviour of hesitation and repetition occurs normally across most individuals, and is commonly observed to occur more often in children who are still in the stage of developing their communication skills. Many people who observe such disfluency[1] in young children will simply consider this as normal, and hence the label 'stuttering' will not be applied. So depending on the age of children reported upon in a survey, it is possible to get very different identification of the numbers of children who stutter. Even in the adult population it is unclear as to the amount and type of dysfluency that might prompt a listener or the person themselves to identify 'stuttering'. For example, a large number of relatively effortlessly produced simple initial syllable repetitions are unlikely to be noticed by an observer (or the speaker themselves), while a small number of lengthy and effortful prolonged vowels are likely to alert an observer (or speaker) to identify stuttering.

One response to this kind of issue for identification of communication disorder has been to closely define a set of particular observable behavioural features, making use of an 'operational definition' (see Concept 3.3). Stuttering again provides an example of this. Stuttering is often behaviourally defined as including repetitions, prolongations and blocks, or alternatively defined as per Onslow's 'data language' as involving interruptions of speech by repeated movements or fixed postures (Teesson *et al.*, 2003) . Reliability studies (see Concept 3.4) have shown that even experienced judges (e.g. experienced speech-language pathologists working with a stuttering caseload) can identify the same or similar numbers of stutters from the same speech sample on more than one occasion only with considerable training (Brundage *et al.*, 2006). Such experienced judges can, with repeated training, obtain what is considered to be acceptable inter-judge agreement, in that two such judges can identify similar numbers of stutters from the same speech sample. However, acceptable reliability is generally accepted as agreement on a minimum of 80 per cent of the total count, and in most studies of stuttering the inter-judge reliability is between 80 per cent and 90 per cent, leaving a considerable amount of disagreement about the identification of stuttering. The other issue with identification is that such studies are based on a comparison of total counts of identified stutters rather than on establishing agreement on each moment of stuttering. Exact identification of moments of stuttering have proved to be almost impossible to obtain adequate agreement in identification. Raters need to set up extensive sets of criteria in identifying what will count as one stutter. For example, if the syllable is taken as the basic unit of measurement for stuttering (Wingate, 1988) then is 're- re- re- re- repeat' to be considered one stutter or four? (Speech-language pathologists using syllable counts to measure stuttering would identify this as one stutter.) Many moments of stuttering consist of complex sets of dysfluency, for example repetition and prolongation, for example, 'reeee- re- reeeepeat, re- repeat'. Is this one moment of stuttering on the word 'repeat' (1 stutter), or two attempts at the word 'repeat' each of which is stuttered (2 stutters), or 4 stutters if each prolongation or partial or whole word production are considered?

Concept 3.3   Operational definition

When researchers 'operationally define' a particular behaviour or a set of behaviours which are being observed, they are attempting to develop a working definition for the purposes of a particular investigation. The aim of an operational definition is to increase the agreement between observers when identifying, counting or measuring the behaviour or set of behaviours.

The features of an operational definition are as follows:

- Specifies observable behaviours
- Specifies any relevant frequency or quality indices that are necessary to the identification
- Specifies the context(s) in which the behaviours need to occur

An example of a POOR operational definition of word-finding difficulty (anomia) would be,

- Moments when the person is struggling to find the word they want to say.

A BETTER operational definition would be,

- Moments where word-finding difficulty is indicated by any one of the following:
  - Delay between initiation and production of the word sought of a minimum of 3 seconds

- ○ Metalinguistic comment by the person regarding the struggle (e.g. 'I know the word, but just can't seem to find it', 'It's on the tip of my tongue')
- ○ Reformulation of the utterance to use an alternative word or phrasing to the word initially sought.

Operational definitions often need continued revision towards greater specificity, and the reliability process (discussed later) contributes to the development of the working definitions to be used in any particular research project.

Concept 3.4 Reliability of measurement

The reliability of measurement is an important issue in the field of communication disorders, both in order to ensure that objective measurement through instrumentation is obtaining consistent results, and in order that subjective perceptual judgements/ratings are validly reflecting the behaviour under study (consensus) and/or are being applied consistently.

Reliability may be established for one rater on the same data on two occasions (intra-rater reliability), or for more than one rater on the same data (inter-rater reliability) or for the elicitation task (e.g. test or sampling method) on the same individual on two occasions (test–retest reliability).

A good summary is available in the work of Stemler who notes that reliability may involve considerations of consensus (agreement), consistency and measurement estimates (Stemler, 2004).

Even when reliable identification of a feature of communication can be demonstrated, this does not guarantee the validity of the identification. There are many aspects of validity (see Concept 3.5), but probably the primary aspect for consideration is face validity (as previously discussed in Chapter 1). Considerations of face validity ask whether the descriptions or measures appear to be capturing the commonsense view, in the way that just about anyone in this particular society would see it. To take an extreme example, often height and weight are related so that the taller the person, the more they might weigh, and so the question would be which measure has the greater face validity in a study on the height of adolescents – a tape measurement in centimetres, or weight in kilograms? In this example, the option of measuring height would be a more obviously valid measure, and would be a readily obtainable one. However, it is not uncommon for researchers to have to rely on less obvious measures, since other measures may not be obtainable, and so the extent to which particular descriptions and measures hold face validity starts to matter. To continue with stuttering as an example from research into communication disorders, even reliable count data about moments of stuttering can be challenged as holding little face validity. For example, research by Ingham and Cordes has questioned whether moments of observed stuttering validly reflect the experience of the person who stutters (Ingham & Cordes, 1997). Their research has shown differences in how stuttering is experienced by the person who stutters and the listener's observations of moments of stuttering. For some research purposes, this discrepancy might not be of concern, for example, if the research was focused on the impact of stuttering on the listener. However, for other research purposes, this discrepancy would matter, for example, if the research was focused on the effect of an intervention. Possibly, for some individuals, a reduction in observable stuttering might not reflect a reduction in the trouble experienced by the person who stutters.

Concept 3.5   Key aspects of validity

The following aspects are important to be considered in the field of communication disorders:

Face validity: Does this research or measure appear to capture or describe the most important feature of the problem that is the focus of this research?

Construct validity: Is the test or method used to examine the feature of interest constructed in a way that is consistent with the theoretical underpinnings of the research? How does each part of the test or method relate to each other part, and what is the contribution of the parts to the end achievement of describing the focus of this research?

Concurrent validity: Does this test or method provide similar or different findings in comparison to other tests or methods which have been previously validated?

Ecological validity: Does this research use methods that allow for sampling of behaviour as it occurs in its natural context?

3.1.2   Aspects of communication

As previously introduced in Chapter 2 (Section 2.1.2), WHO has been concerned over many years to provide a way to describe both the functioning of individuals in terms that are not discriminatory, and which allows for the recognition that differences and disability need to be considered in their broader social context. The original classification scheme (differentiating impairment, disability and handicap) in the 1980s was part of a broad social movement against discrimination. This campaign attempted to increase the public's awareness that medical problems did not inevitably handicap people in their everyday life, and that the degree of handicap experienced by individuals often related more to their social environment than the nature or extent of their problem. For example, a person might have an impairment involving spinal cord injury, which resulted in the disability of not being able to walk, but with wheelchair accessibility of public transport and buildings, this person need not experience any handicap in gaining employment. An example from the area of communication disorders might be someone whose impairment is due to surgical removal of vocal cords due to cancer (laryngectomy), resulting in the disability or inability to produce voice, but whose use of alternative voicing methods (for example, oesophageal voice, or electronically produced voice from a device such as a Servox) allows the person to continue working. The WHO reviewed and revised these descriptions at the turn of the century, with a substantial shift towards the recognition that these broad aspects of human functioning applied to all people, not just those with medical conditions, and so the terminology and framework was revised to capture a 'wellness' model of health (WHO, 2001). Currently, this biopsychosocial framework describes body functioning under 'impairment', and psychological and social functioning in terms of 'activity' (which may or may not be restricted) and 'social participation' (which may or may not be limited). The description of 'activity' and 'participation' does not always allow for a clear differentiation between these two domains, and they are often referred to as combined issues (WHO, 2000).

When researching communication disorders it is helpful to consider which of these aspects of functioning are being investigated, as meth ods of sampling and description will need to closely reflect the particular aspect in order to have face validity. To continue with the stuttering example (see also Yaruss, 1998), some researchers have been investigating impairment aspects through studies looking at the genetic basis of stuttering (Dworzynski *et al.*, 2007), and studies looking at how the brain function of people who stutter differs in important ways from people who do not stutter (Ingham, 2001). Other researchers have investigated how stuttering affects the communication activity of speaking, through studies of how the nature and frequency of stuttering varies under particular speaking conditions (Spencer *et al.*, 2005). Other researchers have investigated the impact of stuttering on people's lives, for example, looking at the types of jobs undertaken by people who stutter (Klein & Hood, 2004). This is not to say that research needs to be confined to one or other aspect of functioning in this framework. In particular, studies of intervention are strengthened by describing at least two of the three aspects of functioning (see aphasia intervention study in Section 3.2 below).

3.2   Treatment efficacy

Efficacy research looks at the relationship between therapeutic interventions and outcomes for individuals receiving those therapies (see
Concept 3.6). This research is concerned with establishing whether the
therapy caused any changes seen. When studies on particular disorders and their interventions are considered together, then this serves
to consider the extent of the 'evidence-base' for particular approaches.
Research into intervention typically involves at least two of the three
aspects of communication functioning – impairment, restrictions on
communication activity, limitations in social participation (described
in Sections 2.1.2 and 3.1.2 above). To take an example from aphasia
research, a particular approach to intervention for word-finding difficulty ('anomia') might implement therapy directly on naming,
hypothesizing that this therapy will alter brain activity (addressing
impairment), and also seek to establish that any changes seen within
therapy tasks carry-over into speaking tasks (which will be measured),
and arguing that any changes found may have an impact on social
participation in everyday life (which may or may not be measured
directly in the research process) – (e.g. see Copland *et al.*, 2006). This
type of broad-ranging research requires the development of a range
of descriptors and measures which are suitable for capturing function
and changes in function for each aspect. For example, computerized
imaging techniques are needed to capture changes in brain activity such as fMRI, while systematic and replicable tests of naming are
needed to describe this communication activity, and valid methods
of observing and describing discourse in everyday conversations is
needed to describe social participation.

Concept 3.6   Efficacy and effectiveness

Efficacy research seeks to establish whether a particular treatment brings
about a change. To do this often one needs to compare one treatment to
another in order to control for or to identify particular factors which might
or might not be contributing to that change.

Research into the relative *effectiveness* of interventions also necessarily compares one treatment to another, but this kind of research seeks to establish
whether one treatment works better than the other, with 'better' variously
defined, for example, in a shorter time, or at less cost, or with more carry-over
into everyday life. Research into effectiveness typically compares two treatments with previously established efficacy.

3.2.1 Establishing whether it was the therapy that caused the change

In efficacy research, the most fundamental issue for researchers to resolve is the control of any factors which are external to the treatment being provided which might bring about change, and thus potentially confound the interpretation of any changes seen at the end of the intervention. One of the difficulties faced by those researching communication disorders from brain damage, is that immediately following a stroke, a person's brain undergoes substantial biochemical changes which will settle spontaneously over the ensuing days, weeks and months. This period of spontaneous recovery varies from individual to individual, and will mean that any recovery of communication function during the first three to six months may or may not be attributable to therapy. Similar situations are involved for other communication disorders, for example, children's articulation, phonological, semantic and syntactic systems naturally mature and develop with age, and so interventions directed to children in the two- to three-year age-group in particular require particular design features to control for maturation effect.

How then can researchers design a methodology which allows them to investigate efficacy of intervention? Essentially, all intervention research requires some degree of what can be described as 'experimental' design (see Chapter 8 for some examples of this kind of design). Experimental design aims to control factors which might get in the way of knowing whether it was the intervention that made a difference or some other factor. A typical solution to the problems of maturation and recovery is achieved through two strategies. First is the incorporation of a period of repeated sampling prior to intervention to ensure that whatever is being targeted in intervention is either not changing, or is changing at some predictable rate ('establishing a baseline'). Repeating the period of baseline measures for some extended period of time following intervention further strengthens the study. The second strategy is the inclusion of another set of participants in the research who either do not receive treatment of any kind, or who receive a different kind of treatment which might be a placebo treatment or a treatment which is known to produce either different effects or lesser degrees of change ('control' groups).

Efficacy research can be conducted with groups of participants[2] or on individuals, with experimental control being able to be established for both group and single case research designs. Taking stuttering as the example, prolonged speech is a treatment approach which involves teaching an adult who stutters an altered speech pattern that initially sounds highly unnatural (with prolonged vowels and soft articulatory contacts for consonants, combined with a slow speech rate). When using this altered speech pattern, the individual will be able to produce speech fluently, and with practice and feedback the person who stutters gradually increases the naturalness of their speech while maintaining fluency. This sort of intervention is typically provided to groups of individuals (e.g., see O'Brian *et al.*, 2001). A very different sort of approach to stuttering intervention is the Lidcombe Program which is a behavioural intervention for young children who stutter, that involves training parents to identify both moments of fluency and dysfluency, and to deliver rewards (praise) and punishment (variously, provision of a fluent model, identification of difficulty, request to repeat fluently) contingent upon these moments. This sort of intervention was originally trialed on individuals (Onslow *et al.*, 1990), as an important first step prior to moving on to the development of small and large group designs (Onslow, 2001).

3.2.2   Establishing the evidence base for an approach to intervention

Each piece of research into the efficacy of an intervention provides another piece of evidence which informs the clinical decision-making of practitioners in the field. As previously introduced (see Section 1.4.2), the EBP paradigm has grown in influence over the last five years, arising initially from the recognition that often important advances in the field which were supported by good research evidence were not entering the common practice of clinicians. Instead, experienced practitioners often relied on knowledge gained in their original training, supplemented by their own experiences with patients in the intervening years. The EBP framework sets out to remind practitioners that not all pieces of evidence are equally strong, and to do this sets out a series of levels of evidence in a hierarchy of the extent of experimental control over relevant factors. The lowest level of evidence is expert opinion and descriptive single case studies and the highest level of evidence is derived from meta-analysis of results from many large randomized controlled trials (see Table 3.1).

The EBP paradigm is open to critique in its focus on quantitative and experimental research methodology (Trinder & Reynolds, 2000), and the use of summaries of current evidence (as for example found on the Cochrane library website http://www.cochrane.org/) can lead to questionable decision-making on the part of those funding services. For exam-

Table 3.1 Levels of evidence

Level of evidence	Description
1	Meta-analysis of systematic reviews of research
2	Randomized controlled experimental studies
3	Controlled cohort comparisons
4	Descriptive group studies; single case studies (including experimental single case studies)
5	Expert opinion, e.g. scholarly guidelines

Source: Levels as described in Oxford Centre for Evidence-Based Medicine Levels of Evidence, May 2001 (Phillips *et al.*, 2001).

ple, drug trials for common diseases are well suited to large randomized controlled trials, and can include additional controls such as keeping both the researchers and patients 'blind' to whether the active drug or placebo control is being administered. On the other hand, trials of therapy services which require communicative interaction for their effect are difficult to control in terms of the making sure that the same type of therapy is given to each person (given that patients' responses will affect the interaction, and that generally multiple therapists will need to be involved), and that therapists and patients need to be aware of therapy goals as an integral part of doing therapy (and hence cannot be effectively blinded to the therapy condition). Many researchers working within qualitative research paradigms have criticized the formulation of the levels of evidence, but it is important to note that these researchers stress the importance of recognizing the differing levels of 'rigour' in qualitative research, which could equally assist practitioners in clinical decision-making based on such research. Such issues are not reasons to deny the importance of continued attempts to research efficacy of therapy at the highest levels of evidence, but do provide some insight into why current therapy approaches within communication disorders have restricted evidence bases.

As previously mentioned (in Section 3.1), in the area of dysarthria, an approach to therapy for dysarthria associated with Parkinson's disease has been developed which provides a good example of an emerging evidence base. The LSVT works on the problems of reduced loudness and reduced intelligibility associated with Parkinson's disease. The main treatment goals for the LSVT are to increase respiratory support (RS) (through the 'Think Loud, Think Shout' instruction and practice), increase vocal fold closure (through isometric effort such as pushing or lifting during phonation, high/low pitch glides, sustained phonation at highest and lowest pitches), increase range of articulatory movement (achieved as an automatic by-product of 'shouting') and to increase awareness of intelligibility through repeated self-monitoring of perceived effort against effect achieved – one of the early randomized controlled trials for this study is described in Example 3.1.

In this section a number of the challenges faced by researchers investigating the effects of intervention have been outlined. Many of the challenges raised in intervention studies require the researcher to 'build' their research towards an intervention study, as they strive to establish sound measures and replicable procedures. As suggested at the end of Chapter 2, preparation is of major importance in research generally, and it can be seen that intervention research is an area where preparation is paramount if meaningful and worthwhile results are to be obtained.

Example 3.1　An example of a randomized controlled trial

Ramig and colleagues conducted one of the only two randomized controlled trials undertaken for treatment of dysarthria due to Parkinson's Disease (Ramig *et al.*, 1995). In their study they compared two forms of intensive treatment (16 sessions over 4 weeks) for 45 patients with mild-moderate idiopathic Parkinson Disease. They compared the LSVT to a treatment which was designed to increase Respiratory Support (RS). They found significant differences pre- vs post-therapy regardless of treatment group for measures of Sound Pressure Level during conversation, mean habitual fundamental frequency (pitch), fundamental frequency variability during reading, maximum duration of sustained vowel phonation and utterance duration during reading, and family ratings of loudness. They found significant differences pre- vs post-therapy for RS treatment only, for Sound Pressure Level during reading for females, and pause duration during reading for females. They found significant differences pre- vs post-therapy for LSVT only, for Sound Pressure Level during vowels, Sound Pressure Level during reading, fundamental frequency variability during monologue, and for family ratings of overall intelligibility.

They found that the younger participants did better, and that cognitive impairment was a factor, in that the more cognitively able did better. However, this study can be criticized in terms of its research design as the data analysis involved pre- vs post-comparison for each group, but the two groups were not compared with each other (Deane *et al.*, 2005)

3.3　Research 'around' the person with a communication disorder

Research in the field of communication disorders not only investigates the problems of the person with the disability, but also investigates related issues such as the effect of the disorder on families, ways to improve the communication between other people and the person with the disability, and ways to promote high-quality intervention through the education of professionals who work with individuals with communication disorders.

3.3.1 Education of community members

Research into the education of the broader community is often described under the general term of 'health promotion' and tends to fall into two groups, with the first group reflecting 'wellness' campaigns and preventive programmes, and the second group reflecting more specifically targeted information and training for family members or carers. The research that focuses on community wellness and preventive programmes is most typically centred on the importance of language stimulation in the early years of a child's development. Research into programmes providing information and training to the family and carers of already identified individuals with communication disorders generally resembles basic intervention research, involving some kind of comparison of pre- and post- intervention testing in order to evaluate the effect of a specified information and training programme. For example, Togher *et al.* (2004) developed and trialed a successful training programme for members of the police force designed to improve their confidence and competence in interacting with individuals with cognitive-communication disorder, for example, associated with head injury (Togher *et al.*, 2004) – see Example 3.2. Another example of this type of application of linguistics to therapy is in training the partner of an individual with aphasia, for example, Booth and Perkins (1999) reported their research on an individualized approach to training the partner, which was based on the use of CA to both identify intervention goals and to measure the outcomes of training.

Example 3.2 An example of intervention for communication partners

Togher *et al.* (2004) evaluated a training programme for police aimed at improving their ability to communicate effectively with individuals who had communication problems following TBI. Twenty police officers were randomly allocated to two groups, with only one of the groups receiving the training. Both before and after the intervention, interactions during telephone enquiries by individuals with TBI to all police officers were analysed for the presence of obligatory and optional elements of generic structure, based on principles from SFL. The study found that trained police showed more effective communication strategies than the untrained police, and also that the use of these strategies reciprocally promoted more effective communication behaviours in the individuals with TBI during these interactions.

3.3.2   Education of professionals

Research into the education of professionals involved in communication disorders is largely focused on the professional preparation of speech-language pathologists. Within the research into the professional preparation of speech-language pathologists, most of the research is focused on the processes of clinical education experiential learning, as opposed to learning in academic contexts, researching curriculum content or delivery.

Very little research has been conducted into learning in academic contexts addressing the evaluation of particular learning programmes, but there is some research which has looked at aspects of the student population at different learning stages (e.g. Chan *et al.*, 1994), and there have been surveys of what students need to know (e.g. Lincoln *et al.*, 2004).

Research into clinical education typically is conducted using small group research designs, with a focus on questions about the interactive variables that result in student learning. For example, in the relatively small body of research literature in the field of clinical education in speech pathology, some research has focused on the learning that occurs in discussions and feedback sessions between the student and the clinical educator – often termed 'supervisory conferencing' (McCready *et al.*, 1996; Shapiro, 1994).

3.3.3   Professional socialization

Implicit within research into clinical education are a number of assumptions about what it is to be a speech-language pathologist, for example, assumptions about how a speech-language pathologist should or should not interact with children or adults with communication disorders and their family or carers, and assumptions about the things that speech-language pathologists do which bring about changes in their clients' communication. These issues are important in describing what it is that makes a competent therapist and are useful for those developing academic and clinical education programmes. Also, describing such features allows for a critical consideration of whether or not particular aspects are in fact essential to the therapy process. For example, speech-language pathologists use the term 'rapport' to describe the establishment and maintenance of a relationship with the client which maximizes the client's learning and capacity for change, for example, such a relationship would typically be seen to be one in which the client trusts the speech-language pathologist.

However, the notion of 'rapport with client' is very much an unexamined feature of the therapeutic process. There is an assumption that such a notion would include aspects such as friendliness or ability to engage with the client about matters over and above the therapy process, however it is not known whether such behaviours are essential or irrelevant to rapport-building. Some preliminary research is under way which is beginning to engage with these types of issues (Ferguson & Elliot, 2001; Horton *et al.*, 2004).

3.4   Concluding comments

This chapter has introduced the main domains of research in the field of communication disorders as spanning research which investigates the nature of disorders and how they occur in society, research which investigates the approaches to intervention for different types of communication disorders, and research which investigates how people learn about communication disorders and intervention. As part of this coverage, this chapter has introduced the basic concepts in relation to validity and reliability.

The need for ongoing research into communication disorders can be seen within each domain. The nature of disorders needs more research at each level of functioning including impairment, communication activity and social participation, and there is a particular need for research to capture communication across these levels of functioning. Intervention research is complex in terms of research design given the need for balancing the need for careful control of salient variables against the need for meaningful and valid goals and nature of intervention. However, in order for the evidence base for interventions for communication disorders to increase, there is an important need for the systematic and comprehensive descriptions, both quantitative and qualitative, which can be developed from a range of diverse theoretical perspectives. Research into the wider issues around the ways other people are affected by communication disorders, and the ways in which others can contribute to improved interactions for people with communication disorders is in its infancy, with considerable scope for expansion.

Chapters 4 and 5 go on to explore these issues in more detail by examining the research into communication disorders in both children (Chapter 4) and adults (Chapter 5).

Notes

1. The term 'disfluency' is used to describe typically-occurring hesitation and repetition, while the term 'dysfluency' is used to describe behaviours that

most observers would consider to be stuttering or stammering. The terms 'stuttering' and 'stammering' are used synonymously in this book.

2. The term 'subjects' is usually associated with research paradigms which are quantitative and hypothesis driven, while the term 'participants' is typically associated with qualitative research paradigms. The terms stem from fundamental views about the role of the people in the study, so that 'subjects' are the object of study, whereas 'participants' are contributors to the development of ideas within the study.

Further reading

Irwin, D. L., Pannbacker, M., & Lass, N. J. (2008). *Clinical research methods in speech-language pathology and audiology.* San Diego, CA: Plural.

This book provides a grounding in each of the main aspects to developing a sound methodology in research in the area of communication disorders. The focus of the book is on clinical research.

Pring, T. (2005). *Research methods in communication disorders.* London: Whurr.

This book provides an accessible introduction to key statistical methods that are frequently used in the field of communication disorders research.

4
Researching Child Communication Disorders

This chapter will explore in greater depth some of the main issues that arise in researching child communication disorders. In this attempt, the focus will be on research which primarily involves the assessment of children's language and serves to illuminate both theoretical understanding of language as well as to deepen the understanding of particular communication disorders. By looking at three particular studies in detail (Fisher *et al.*, 2005; Paradis *et al.*, 2003; Thomson, 2005), it will be possible to explore the ways in which different research methodologies can be used to illuminate specific aspects of language. The first of these studies, discussed in Section 4.1, derives its theoretical base from the discipline of psychology in looking at the concept of Theory of Mind and its relationship to the development of language. The other two studies both investigate aspects of SLI from perspectives informed by the psycholinguistic and sociolinguistic paradigms. As previously discussed in Chapter 1, the psycholinguistic/cognitive paradigm is concerned with questions about the inner workings of language, for example, with how the abstract conception of language develops and is processed within the brain. On the other hand, the sociolinguistic/social-semiotic paradigm is concerned with questions about the outer, interactive aspects of language, as one speaker communicates with another (see Section 1.3). In the present chapter, the second study is informed by the psycholinguistic/cognitive paradigm in looking at issues related to bilingualism and the development of language. The third study looks at SLI from within a sociolinguistic/social-semiotic paradigm, through the application of a SFL perspective. All three studies primarily involve the assessment of children's language and serve to illuminate both theoretical understanding of language as well as to deepen the understanding of particular communication disorders. The basic concepts which arise in research in the field of communication disorders will be described as they occur. Readers interested in exploring further into the area of child language disorders are strongly recommended to read some of the comprehensive reference works available (e.g. Owens, 2008; Paul, 2007)

4.1   Language and mind

One of the contributions from the discipline of psychology to the area of language development and disorders over recent years has been the construct of Theory of Mind (ToM) – see Concept 4.1. Disorders which have been identified as affecting ToM include autism, and brain damage involving frontal and right cerebral hemispheres. The major work in ToM has been concentrated within what are often described as Autism Spectrum Disorders (ASD), which are disorders ranging from severe autism, high-functioning autism, and including Asperger's syndrome (Cohen & Volkmar, 1997). The main features of Autism are generally described as including,

- Qualitative impairment in social interaction
- Qualitative impairment in communication
- Restricted patterns of behaviour, interest and activities
- Delays or abnormal functioning before three years

Concept 4.1   Theory of Mind

Theory of Mind refers to the ability to recognize the thoughts and intentions of others, and so this is a framework about the way people themselves theorize about the thoughts of others. ToM allows a listener to gauge whether someone means what they say, for example, are they lying or joking perhaps? The ToM allows the speaker to tailor what is said to the needs of their listeners, for example, providing information which the listener is presumed not to know. ToM is acquired over the developmental period during childhood, for example, children's lies at three years will be fairly transparent, but by four or five years of age may be more skilful! Without ToM a person will take communication very much at face value, and have difficulty interpreting or conveying social nuances. For a very readable overview of the research on ToM see the work of Baron-Cohen (1995), and for an accessible fictional account of what life might be like without ToM, see Mark Haddon's novel, *The curious incident of the dog in the night-time* (Haddon, 2003).

Case study 1

The research of Fisher *et al.* (2005) provides a good example of research which tries to unravel the relationship between language and ToM in children and adolescents with ASD. This study looks at language and ToM in 176 children, 58 of whom had been diagnosed with ASD (ranging in age from 5.5 to 16.2 years) and 118 of whom were classified as having Moderate Learning Difficulty (MLD) and who were in special education classes (ranging in age from 5.2 to 14.6 years). The inclusion in this study of the MLD group allowed for a comparison group which has similar reduced language function to the ASD group in the context of cognitive impairment, but for whom difficulties with ToM is not a major defining feature. From previous research in the field, the researchers were aware that overall language ability and vocabulary was often correlated with ToM performance. However, they argued that this relationship does not allow any interpretation as to the cause and effect, in that it is just as likely that certain levels of vocabulary are required in order to grasp ToM as it is that a certain level of ToM is required in order for vocabulary to develop. So, joint attention could be considered to be an early precursor for the development of ToM, and for the development of referential naming. For example, a parent might draw the attention of a child to an aeroplane flying past and say, 'plane'. Thus, attention is jointly shared between the parent and child and directed to the same object, and an opportunity is thereby provided for learning vocabulary. On the other hand, they argued that previous research has not clarified the extent to which grammar is related to ToM performance, and this relationship might shed light on possible causal directions. They suggested that some grammatical development might be required in order for ToM to develop, for example, the ability to understand and use complex clause structures such as projection ('He thinks that she has the doll', 'He said that they left this morning'). However, it is hard to see how ToM would be a necessary precursor for the grammatical development of complex sentence structures. These two issues motivated the researchers to ask the following research questions: Are there significant differences between the ASD and MLD groups in terms of vocabulary and grammar, and is there any difference in the relationships between ToM and language between the two groups?

In order to describe the vocabulary and grammar of the participants, the researchers chose two standardized assessment tools: the British Picture Vocabulary Scales (BPVS) (Dunn *et al.*, 1999), and the Test of Reception of Grammar (TROG – 1989 version used in this research) (Bishop, 2003). The value of using standardized assessment tools for this research was that it allowed for direct comparison between the two groups doing exactly the same tasks, and provides for quantitative measures of language performance. Both assessment tools assessed receptive language only, not expressive language, and this is a commonly used research strategy in the area of communication disorders when research-ers are seeking to ascertain linguistic competence, and want to avoid any extraneous performance variables (e.g. reduced ability to interpret participants' responses due to reduced intelligibility associated with concomitant articulatory or phonological disorders). The BPVS requires the participant to point to one of four pictures presented when named, and the TROG uses a similar format in requiring the participant to point to one of four pictures that goes with a sentence that uses a particular grammatical form.

In order to describe the extent to which participants have developed ToM, the researchers used two 'False Belief' tasks which have been used across most ToM research, and which most typically developing four-year-old children are able to do. The first False Belief task was a version of the 'Sally-Anne' task which for this study involved 'Sally-David', and the second False Belief task was the 'Smarties' task (see Example 4.1).

Example 4.1   Examples of experimental tasks

Sally-Anne task: This task involves an unexpected location of an object, in that the children are shown a scene with the dolls where Sally moves Anne's marble from Anne's bag to her own (i.e. Sally's) bag while Anne is away. As the False Belief question, the participants are asked where Anne will look for her marble when she returns. Without ToM, the participant will answer 'Sally's bag', but with ToM the participant will recognize that Anne does not know about the unexpected transfer, and so will answer 'her bag'. The participants are also asked two control questions about other matters in the scenario to check for memory and understanding of events.

Smarties task: The 'Smarties' task involves unexpected contents of a tube of Smarties. The children are shown a tube of Smarties and shown that in fact the tube contains a pencil. They are then asked the first False Belief question as to what someone else might think was inside the tube and what they had thought was inside the tube before being shown. In answer to these ques-tions, children without ToM will answer 'a pencil', while children with ToM will answer 'Smarties', recognizing that someone else will be deceived as to the contents, just as they were. The children are also asked a control question to check for understanding of events.

Both these tasks are described as '1st order Theory of Mind', and represent a sampling of the simplest level of ToM. Tasks that sample more complex '2nd order' ToM involve a higher order of double-think, for example, 'where does X think Y will look for a particular object?', and beyond this level, higher order ToM abilities would involve the understanding of complex mental states and motivations, such as 'Does X mean what she says?', or 'What is X thinking or feeling?'.

Fisher *et al.* (2005) were able to establish that the two groups (ASD, MLD) were comparable in terms of language ability, since there was no significant difference in the average scores for receptive vocabulary or grammar (using Analysis of Variance statistics). The two groups did not differ on the Sally-David task, but the ASD group had on average greater difficulty on the Smarties task. Of the ASD group, 54 per cent passed the question about their own beliefs on the Smarties task, 49 per cent passed the question about someone else's beliefs on the Smarties task, and 49 per cent passed the False Belief question on the Sally-David task. For the MLD group, there appeared to be an order of task difficulty associated with these tasks (confirmed using McNemar statistical test), as 86 per cent passed the question about their own beliefs on the Smarties task, 78 per cent passed the question about someone else's beliefs on the Smarties task, and 63 per cent passed the False Belief question on the Sally-David task. These tasks are well established as testing a similar level of ToM, and so the researchers queried whether the appearance of an order of difficulty raised the question as to an increased memory processing load across the tasks, which provided more challenge for the MLD group. However, what is seen here is that the design of the study allowed the researchers to clearly pull apart the language performance of the groups from the ToM performance, as the ASD and MLD groups were similar in terms of language performance, but very different in terms of ToM performance. In other words, the difference in ToM was attributable to the nature of ASD, rather than the level of language performance per se. However, the research did find that language appeared to play a particular role vis a vis ToM for the ASD group in contrast to the MLD group, as discussed below.

Significant correlations were found between language performance and performance on the False Belief tasks for both ASD and MLD groups, and while there was no significant difference in how strongly correlated vocabulary was with ToM, there was a significant difference between the ASD and MLD groups for grammar and ToM, in that grammar was more strongly correlated with performance on the False Belief tasks for ASD than for MLD. Logistic regression (with individual performance confirmed through examination of scatter plots) showed that language (in particular receptive grammar) was a stronger predictor of False Belief performance for the ASD than the MLD group. For the ASD group, a receptive grammar performance which was under that

Table 4.1   Summary of Case Study 1

Aim		To investigate whether the previously observed relationship between the stage of language development and ToM is causal.
Method	Participants	58 children between 5.5 and 16.2 years with ASD
		118 children between 5.2 and 14.6 years with MLD
	Data collection	Testing for receptive vocabulary and grammar
		Responses to Sally-David and Smarties tasks
	Data analysis	Analysis of Variance (2 groups x 4 test/task responses) Plus McNemar, and logistic regression
Results		No significant difference between groups for receptive language, nor for Sally-David task
		MLD group showed an apparent effect of more difficulty associated with the increasing memory load across tasks
		ASD group had significantly more difficulty with Smarties task
		Receptive grammar was a stronger predictor of False Belief performance for ASD group
Researchers' conclusions		Since there was no significant difference in language performance between the groups, the observed difference for the Smarties task would appear to reflect ToM difficulties associated with ASD. However, the findings support that some degree of grammatical development may be a necessary precursor to the development of ToM – the extent to which this is a causal relationship remains unclear.
Critical appraisal		Well-designed and conducted Level 3 study. Methods of testing and response sampling allow for high control, but restricted ecological validity. (see Chapter 3)

Source: Fisher *et al.* (2005).

expected for a 5.75-year-old predicted failure in at least one of the False Belief tasks, while a receptive grammar performance over that expected for a 10-year-old predicted a pass in all three False Belief tasks (remember that typically developing children pass these tasks by four years of age). Remember also that these False Belief tasks tap into only first-order ToM, and that even those participants who pass these tasks may well still experience social interaction difficulties associated with difficulties at higher order ToM levels. This study is summarized in Table 4.1.

The interpretation of Fisher *et al.*'s (2005) findings suggested that there was some support for considering that some degree of grammatical development is a necessary precursor to the development of ToM. However, it remains a moot point as to whether the explanation of the relationship between these two is in fact causal, or if perhaps the relationship reflects some mutual dependence on additional cognitive factor(s). An important possibility discussed by Fisher *et al.* (2005) is that for typically developing children receptive grammatical abilities provide a pathway which allows for increasing degrees of social participation in activities which offer learning opportunities to become increasingly aware that others think and feel differently. For children with ASD, whose autistic impairment severely restricts their ability to participate fully within social interactions, language abilities may not be able to be used in the same way. Instead, the researchers raise the possibility that language becomes a surrogate strategy for decoding social interactions. If language is used in this way, as almost 'a way around' not knowing ToM, then individuals with ASD might be highly reliant on their language abilities to manage ToM tasks. Given that this study found such a close relationship between ToM and language, the researchers suggest their findings support this strategic possibility.

In reflecting on this research study, it is important to note the prime role played by a range of statistical methods which were used to gauge whether observed differences were substantial enough to be attributed to an effect of the variable in question, or might instead be attributable to chance, that is, whether the differences were 'significant'. In Chapter 6 the management of such analyses is discussed as one of the practical challenges faced by researchers who may have a limited background in statistics, but at this point it is worth noting that quantitative comparisons (e.g. frequencies or percentages) are usefully graphed as a first point of consideration (as presented in the Fisher *et al.*, 2005 study), with scatter-plots of individual performance providing another useful way to identify the apparent patterns in results. Armed with specific research questions (and ideally a set of hypotheses), graphs and scatter-plots, the applied linguist will find that statisticians can begin to grasp how they can best make their contribution to the next stage of analysis of results. It is also worthwhile considering the inbuilt limitations of research – see Concept 4.2 for a guide to critical appraisal.

Concept 4.2   Critical appraisal of research

Some questions to consider:

To what extent does the research design adequately address the aim of the research? (e.g. Does this research need to involve a large group design, or would a small group suffice? Does this research aim to look at qualitative and/or quantitative aspects of what is being studied?)

To what extent were the participants in the study typical of the larger group of individuals with similar problems in the community?

Were there sufficient participants in the study to be able to draw more general conclusions, or if this is a single case study, to what extent does the design of the study enable us to draw more general conclusions?

Did the methods of data collection allow for valid observation of the participants' performance?

Did the methods of data analysis provide an opportunity to adequately explore the research questions?

To what extent did the researchers constrain their interpretation of findings and discussion to the evidence yielded by their research?

What level of evidence is provided by this research?

For Study 1, we could begin by asking whether the tools and measures successfully sample aspects of both language and ToM. For example, ToM is a complex set of cognitions requiring a complex set of abilities across attention, perception, memory and executive function, and the False Belief tasks may reflect only dimly the complex interaction of these factors. Also, standardized tests of receptive vocabulary and grammar offer a very constrained look at how individuals can use language, and may potentially over- or under-estimate how the same individuals manage language interactively. Research which attempts to investigate higher order levels of ToM (such as attribution of mental or emotional states) faces the challenge of needing to sample increasingly complex language in discourse contexts. Interpretation of results from such studies raises issues intrinsically associated with these design necessities of how to separate problems experienced due to ToM difficulties from problems experienced due to linguistic complexity of tasks. Researchers need to be constantly aware that tools and measures are but methods of sampling, and data are essentially always in some degree a reduction or partial glimpse of the phenomenon being investigated.

4.2   The bilingual brain and language

The study presented above examined language disorder associated with another primary medical diagnosis, that is autism (ASD) and moderate learning difficulty (MLD) which are associated with a range of global developmental impairments. However, in the population of children who are referred by their parents or teachers as having worryingly delayed or disordered language it is estimated that only 5 per cent of this group have an identifiable primary medical diagnosis which would provide an explanation for the problem. By far the greatest proportion of children referred for language delay or disorder has no other problem, that is, their problem is specifically with language, and in this book the term 'Specific Language Impairment' has been used to describe this group (see Section 2.1.1). There is widespread use of an operational definition for SLI which was developed by Stark and Tallal (1981). The two central parts to this definition are that there should be

- evidence of general cognitive development within the expected range as indicated by test scores for performance IQ of greater than 85, and
- a significant difference (6–12 months) between either chronological age or mental age and indicators of receptive and/or expressive language age.

While this operational definition has been both expanded upon, and criticized over the years, the central tenets remain a recurring feature of research and practice in the area of child language disorders (see Plante, 1998).

Specific Language Impairment occurs worldwide and in all languages (see Section 1.8). When difficulties or delay in acquiring language occur in children who are bilingual this raises practical difficulties of identification for their parents, teachers and speech-language pathologists. It is often difficult to ascertain when 'difference' constitutes disorder. For example, are the difficulties observed by a teacher in English indicative of a wider problem with language development, or do they reflect lack of experience in the second language? One of the most compelling sources of evidence that SLI is the problem for such a child is the identification of similar problems in both languages, and so speech-language pathologists rely heavily on detailed reports from parents and interpreters to analyse the specific nature of difficulties in both languages. Added to this complexity is the fact that the language of children is constantly developing and so it is not just a question of identifying the presence of errors or divergence from the adult pattern, but a question of identifying the extent to which patterns of specific aspects of language use reflect those usually expected of children of the same age in the particular language. As yet one more layer of complexity, the grammatical structures of the two languages may be entirely different and the expected developmental pattern may also be different. Hence, it will rarely be possible to look for direct correspondences of patterns observed in one language with the other. Cross-linguistic research from a psycholinguistic perspective provides a way forward through these complexities, serving both to illuminate the nature of SLI in bilingual children, but also providing some light on key theoretical issues with regard to bilingualism itself in the process.

Case study 2

The work of Paradis *et al.* (2003) serves as a good illustration of work in this area. Bilingualism in their study was defined as the simultaneous acquisition of two languages (rather than sequentially acquired languages, as found when children learn their first language at home, and then their second language at school). Previous studies had suggested that bilingualism was associated with increased difficulties for children with SLI, but these studies had included children with dual languages acquired both simultaneously and sequentially, and so the amount of experience in different languages was a potentially confounding variable which may have affected proficiency in the second language. Paradis *et al.* (2003) posed the question of whether the problems would be of a similar nature and severity when the French of the bilingual children was compared with the French of the monolingual children, and when the English of the bilingual children was compared with the English of the English monolingual children. They hypothesized that if SLI is a fundamental impairment of the language faculty (whether or not such a faculty manages dual languages separately or together), that the impairment should be the same for each group for each language. Table 4.2 provides a summary of Study 2.

The study focused on the children's expressive language (in contrast with the previously discussed Study 1 which looked at receptive language), and focused very particularly on their use of specific grammatical morphemes in relation to what the researchers describe as the 'Extended Optional Infinitive phenomenon'. In typical language development children go through a stage where they use the infinitive form rather than marking for tense or verb agreement (e.g. 'Boy kick ball' for 'Boy kicked ball' or 'Boy kicks ball').

Previous research has shown that children with SLI have particular difficulty with tensed grammatical morphemes, which is both delayed

Table 4.2 Summary of Case Study 2

Aim		To investigate the extent to which SLI affects both languages for bilingual French/English children
Method	Participants	8 children with SLI, bilingual French/English
		21 children with SLI, monolingual in English
		10 children with SLI, monolingual in French (Children in each group matched for age and degree of SLI based on standardized test data)
	Data collection	Testing for SLI
		Transcribed 30–45 minute play interactions at home with parent and research assistant
	Data analysis	Linguistic analysis of grammatical development, particularly the acquisition of tensed grammatical morphemes as an indicator of SLI.
		Determination of language dominance through comparison of Mean Length of Utterance in words, longest utterance, number of unique word types over 100 utterances, and number of utterances in 30 minutes.
		(Reliability above 80% established over 30% of data) Statistical analysis – Wilcoxon Matched Pairs, Mann Whitney U-test
Results		More difficulty with tensed vs non-tensed grammatical morphemes within each group, and for both languages in bilingual children.
		No significant difference for each language when comparing the bilingual vs monolingual speakers.
Researchers' conclusions		Researchers argue that findings support SLI as a central problem of the language faculty, not tied to particular language.
Critical appraisal		Well-designed and conducted Level 3 study although with relatively small participant numbers. Methods of sampling allow for ecological validity while sacrificing some degree of control of comparability of interactions. (see Chapter 3)

Source: Paradis *et al.* (2003).

and disordered (see Concept 4.3). Not that difficulty with tensed grammatical morphemes is the only indicator of SLI, but this specific problem is a highly useful indicator for SLI, as research has established that problems with these grammatical morphemes are not tied to the surface form, since non-tensed grammatical morphemes such as plural (-s), for example, are more readily acquired.

Concept 4.3   Delay and disorder

In the field of communication disorders, some researchers and clinicians draw a distinction between delay and disorder.

Delay: Speech or language which is typical of a younger child

Disorder: Speech or language is qualitatively different from either same age or same language-age peers

This distinction prompts useful considerations for researchers in describing speech and language disability, and for clinicians in identifying the presence of disability. However, in practice, the distinction is not always possible to make, and some argue that the distinction is not useful, given that predictions for prognosis may not be tied to one or other label.

In order to sample the children's expressive language, the researchers used spontaneous language samples, which involved transcription of recorded 30–45-minute play interactions at home with the children and a parent and the research assistant in each language. This naturalistic sampling is a very different methodology to the use of standardized tests for elicitation used in the study discussed previously, and interesting to see in a study within the psycholinguistic paradigm. The researchers argue that it was important for sampling to be unconstrained given the preliminary nature of the research, in that not enough is known about the areas of possible difficulty to be able to develop experimental control over stimuli used to elicit responses from the children. Also, the small number of participants allowed for greater depth of analysis of individual data, making transcription-based data more feasible. However, one of the drawbacks of spontaneous language sampling was that the frequency of occurrence of the particular morphemes of interest varied across the samples, and so the researchers used the percentage correct in obligatory contexts as their comparative measure. The tensed grammatical morphemes identified in English were *be* as auxiliary verb and as copula, third person singular (-s), past tense (-ed), and irregular past tense, and in French were *etre* as copula, *etre/avoir* as auxiliary verb when in *passe compose* tense, *aller* when auxiliary verb in *future proche* tense.

Researching Child Communication Disorders 73

The non-tense bearing morphemes identified in English were progressive (-ing), prepositions (in/on), and plural (-s). Direct translation of these is not possible in French, so the non-tense bearing morphemes identified in French were definite and indefinite determiners (*le, la, les; un, une, des*), and prepositions *a, de* (to/of/from). In order to determine language dominance, the researchers used an operational definition of the dominant language being that for which the higher measure was obtained for four of five of the following: Mean Length of Utterance in Words, longest utterance, number of unique word types in a 100 utterance stretch, and number of utterances in 30 minutes. The use of spontaneous language sampling also necessitated the need to establish the reliability of measurement, by double checks on the transcription and coding for grammatical morphemes and other measures (with these researchers re-transcribing and re-coding 30 per cent of the samples, checking that percentage of agreement was above 80 per cent, and re-coding and discussing each individual point of difference to arrive at a consensus decision) – see Chapter 10 for transcription resources.

Paradis *et al.*'s (2003) findings were that within each group, and for both languages used by the bilingual children, there was more difficulty with tensed as compared with non-tensed grammatical morphemes (as confirmed using the Wilcoxon signed rank test). In other words, the researchers' hypothesis that the Extended Optional Infinitive phenomenon would be observed across groups was supported. There were no significant differences between the groups in the level of difficulty shown in the use of the tensed grammatical morphemes (as confirmed using the Mann Whitney U-test), so that the difficulties shown in French by the French–English bilingual children were similar to those shown by the French monolingual children, and the difficulties shown in English by the French–English bilingual children were similar to those shown by the English monolingual children. These findings support the researchers' argument that SLI is best viewed as a central problem of the language faculty, and that dual language handling does not appear to cause additional problems for children with SLI.

The findings of Paradis *et al.* (2003) with regard to dominance and deceleration are somewhat less convincing. Of the eight bilingual children with SLI, five were considered to meet the operational definition of one language being dominant, while the others were 'balanced' in their bilingualism. Three of these children showed better (as in less impaired) tense marking in their dominant language, and Paradis *et al.* interpreted this finding by arguing that this was insufficient to support problems associated with bilingualism. However, the point of comparison here is really that three of the five children who showed a dominant language showed some effect of dominance, so the point must, at least, be considered a moot one. On the other hand, there was no evidence to suggest that bilingualism had a decelerating effect, in that the bilingual children with SLI showed no greater difficulty than did their matched monolingual language counterparts. The researchers argued on this basis that on a practical level this provided some evidence to reassure parents of children with SLI that a bilingual language environment and expectations are unlikely to be any more problematic. They also suggested that this finding raised the possibility that where therapy is only possible in one language, then this therapy might still assist the child with SLI in their language processing for both languages. However, this suggestion relies on the possibility of language transfer (of underlying abstract grammatical features from one language to another), and this is not directly addressed by their research.

In summary, exploration of the research reported by Paradis *et al.* (2003) has shown how linguistic theory and analysis is applied to increase the understanding not only of the problem of SLI, but also of bilingualism in general. Their research is also a good example of the relatively less frequently seen combination of formal psycholinguistic theory coupled with naturalistic sampling methodology, demonstrating the way in which researchers go about selecting methodology based on the types of questions being asked (e.g. in this case questions about language production), and the state of previous knowledge in the area (in this case, experimental design would have been premature), and also on practical grounds (in this case, small numbers allowed for in-depth coding of specific grammatical forms).

4.3   Language outside the brain

Up till now in this chapter SLI has been viewed chiefly through a psycholinguistic/cognitive perspective, which has allowed a look at the ways in which research has been conducted to consider language as internal to the individual. However, sociolinguistic/social-semiotic perspectives offer a complementary perspective (see Section 1.3), looking at language in use between individuals, in social interaction.

Case study 3

There are many different perspectives that look at language in use, but one of those which has been applied to research into SLI is SFL

Table 4.3   Summary of Case Study 3

Aim		To identify differences in language use for production of narratives between children with and without SLI
Method	Participants	25 children with SLI
		25 children with typically developing language
		Matched for age between 5 years 1 month and 8 years 8 months
	Data collection	Transcribed recordings of children retelling a story from a picture book, and a story from their own life (e.g. exciting or frightening events)
	Data analysis	Analysis based on SFL – analysis of 'Theme' (simple/multiple; marked/unmarked; thematic progression)
		Reliability of analysis established for 16% of sample.
		2 x 2 factorial analysis
Results		Children typically developing language made more use of multiple theme (particularly in the story retell). No statistically significant differences in relation to frequency of use of marked theme, but more typically developing children used this linguistic resource in the story retell. Qualitatively, typically developing children observed to use different resources for thematic progression.
Researchers' conclusions		Findings support the main difficulty for SLI with use of lexicogrammatical resources of language.
Critical appraisal		Comparative descriptive study providing level 3 evidence. Sampling control achieved using semi-structured naturalistic tasks.

Source: Thomson (2003).

(Halliday & Matthiessen, 2004). Thomson argues that previous research in SLI from sociolinguistic perspectives has offered much in illuminating global aspects of the discourse of children with SLI, variously capturing elements of structure in particular types of discourse, and features in the discourse which show how speakers design their utterances for their listener (Thomson, 2005). However, she argues that such perspectives neglect the use of wording and grammar ('lexicogrammar') that we know to be a major difficulty for children with SLI. Thomson proposes that SFL is a theoretical approach to describing language that allows for consideration of both aspects of language use (Thomson, 2003), and her research illustrates this through an examination of textual organization – see Table 4.3 for a summary.

Thomson (2005) compared 25 children who had been diagnosed with SLI (in line with the definition previously discussed in this chapter – see Section 4.2), with 25 children reported to be developing typically by their teachers and parents. The two groups were matched for age, with all children being between 5 years 1 month and 8 years 8 months old. This study looked closely at narrative, as this type of discourse has been suggested to be an important developmental step as children move from discourse types that are about the 'here and now' (as in general play and associated with activities of daily living), and start to move towards discourse types that are about 'there and then', which are increasingly demanded through their academic development (e.g. expositions, explanations of procedures, arguments). Previous research has established the importance of narrative skills as a predictor of literacy development, and given the known problems with literacy experienced by children with SLI, narrative has been a major focus for research in this area (Bamberg, 1997).

Thomson asked the children to produce two narratives, one through retelling a short story from a picture book, while the other was elicited by seeking their own stories about, for example, exciting or frightening events from their lives. The samples were audio-recorded for transcription and analysis purposes. The retold story allowed the researcher to look at the children's potential for movement towards the literary narrative, with the prior model of the story acting as a scaffold for their attempt, while the elicited story provided a naturalistic sample with sufficient constraints (in terms of length, situation of elicitation) to allow for detailed transcription, analysis and comparison.

After transcribing the recordings, Thomson analysed the texts for specific aspects of what is described as 'Theme' in the SFL framework (Fries, 1983; Ghadessy, 1995; Matthiessen, 1995). Theme refers to the part of what is being said that is 'new', or to be highlighted for the listener. Two aspects of Theme were selected as reflective of the ability to handle the more global aspects of discourse, namely markedness and progression, and the aspect of Theme selected as reflective of the lexicogrammatical aspects of discourse was use of multiple themes.

In English, the 'default' thematic structure is that Theme is what comes first in an utterance. Markedness refers to the use of the non-default structural arrangement, and in English this relates to the foregrounding of information, for example, 'I will go there tomorrow' is the default. However, if the utterance were 'Tomorrow I will go there', then it is not my going there that is the main point of what I am saying, but rather it is 'tomorrow' that is important. With regard to progression, the earliest developing thematic progression involves repetition of the *Theme* in successive clauses (e.g. '*I* ate my breakfast, *I* played with my toys, *and then I* had lunch, ...'), and this type of progression is referred to as 'iterative'. The more literary development of thematic progression involves the systematic movement of the *Theme* to the 'Rheme' (or remainder of the clause) and the Rheme to the *Theme* in successive clauses (e.g. '*I* ate my breakfast. *My breakfast* was good fun. *Also good fun* was playing with my toys. *After playing with my toys* I had lunch ... ..'). This type of thematic progression has been described as 'linear' or 'zig-zagging'. Thomson hypothesized that if previous claims in the research literature were correct about children with SLI having particular difficulties with the more global aspects of discourse, then the typically developing children should produce more marked themes, and more linear thematic progression. Also, the children with SLI should relatively make more use of the earlier developing iterative thematic progression than the typically developing children.

Simple Themes in English comprise only the information about the 'topic', such as 'The *boy* ...'. Multiple Themes may also involve, for example, a conjunction linking this clause/sentence to the last one, such as '*And* the boy ... .', as well as other information that lets the listener know about the viewpoint of the speaker, for example, '*And perhaps* the boy ... .' which serves to engage the listener. Given the known reduced vocabulary and grammatical resources associated with SLI, Thomson hypothesized that typically developing children would show more use of multiple themes than the children with SLI.

With regard to the macro-structural aspect of marked theme, no significant differences were observed between the groups, but Thomson noted that the numbers of marked theme were low overall, with considerable variability across individuals. Qualitatively, points of interest included the observation of the use of circumstantial adjuncts as marked theme ('One day ... ..'). Those typically developing children who used such marked themes in the retell were more likely to use these in the elicited story (12 of 17), but children with SLI were not observed to do this as frequently (4 of 12). For thematic progression, the hypothesis was partially supported in that while there was no significant difference between the groups for the earlier developing iterative progression, the typically developing children made significantly more frequent use of the later developing linear progression. Qualitatively, this finding was supported through the observation that while some typically developing children were seen to be using the existential subject ('There was....') which allowed them to introduce more information, none of the children with SLI were observed to use this linguistic resource for narrative. These findings overall raise questions regarding the previous literature that suggests that there are specific difficulties with discourse organization in SLI. The sole point of difference between the two groups with regard to linear progression points equally to the possibility of reduced grammatical resources hindering the ability of the children in SLI to adjust their clausal structures for this purpose.

With regard to the aspect of multiple theme, the hypothesis was confirmed in that typically developing children made more use of multiple theme, and this was particularly seen in the retell narrative. This finding underscored the known problems with lexicogrammar for children with SLI, and also highlighted their disadvantage as they attempt to tackle types of discourse of the sort required within academic contexts, and which relate closely to developing literacy skills.

Methodologically, Thomson faced similar challenges to those faced by Paradis *et al.* (2003) in the use of naturalistic language samples. Thomson established the reliability of her identification of the aspects of Theme through comparing her coding (on a point-by-point agreement basis) with that of two independent coders for 16% of the sample, prior to establishing final coding by consensus. Thomson was also dealing with samples of unequal length, and so used proportional measures (e.g. marked themes as a proportion of total themes). Similar to both Fisher *et al.* (2005) and Paradis *et al.* (2003), Thomson used statistical analyses to confirm the significance of differences observed between the groups (using 2 x 2 factorial analysis). In line with other research into language in use, this study included qualitative description of patterns emerging in the data both to illustrate key findings and to probe more deeply.

The implications of Thomson's (2005) study inform an understanding of the problems evident in the language used by children with SLI, as well as informing the recognition of the social learning consequences of SLI. For speech-language pathologists, the study also points to the value of the inclusion of different types of discourse as part of the assessment of children with SLI, and the value of analysing a range of aspects of discourse. For researchers, the study also highlights that different types of discourse provide different opportunities to consider different aspects of language use.

4.4   Concluding comments

These three studies have been selected to illustrate some of the features that are to be found across all research in the area of communication disorders. In each of the three studies selected for in-depth description in this chapter, the researchers relied on previously published research literature of their own and others' studies in order to develop their research questions. Further to this, each researcher identified particular aspects or issues from the previous research and mounted a clear line of argumentation to justify why their research questions were important to further this line of enquiry. Beyond this, each researcher then developed the research question into an 'answerable' question, that is, one which was sufficiently constrained and operationalized to be testable through the consideration of data. The research presented in this chapter has been largely quantitative and hypothesis driven. However, even when researching from a qualitative paradigm, decisions will need to be made regarding what to observe, and how to observe. Through addressing these issues, researchers will inevitably find themselves increasingly able to make explicit their assumptions and render their research open to scrutiny, which is, after all, a primary aim for researchers from both quantitative and qualitative paradigms (as previously discussed in Section 1.5).

Of course, this chapter has only just touched very briefly on the knowledge and research in the area of child language disorder and its consequences for child communication. However, from these three studies it is possible to see the complex interplay between cognition and language, and between language and social interaction. Both of these synergies require a wide-ranging approach to research which is essentially interdisciplinary in nature. For example, in Fisher *et al.* (2005), psychological understandings were crucially linked with psycholinguistic understandings of language development, while in Paradis *et al.* (2003) psycholinguistic understandings required a strong grasp of both bilingual mental representation and the bilingual social environment, and in Thomson (2005) it was evident that knowledge from education, linguistics and speech pathology informed an understanding of the educational implications of SLI.

Further reading

Owens, R. E. (2008). *Language development: An introduction* (7th edn). Boston: Pearson Education.

This book provides a comprehensive introduction to the area of child language development and the key research that informs an understanding of communication disorders.

Paul, R. (2007). *Language disorders from infancy through adolescence: Assessment and intervention*. St Louis, Missouri: Mosby Elsevier.

This book has a strong clinical focus on child language disorders, and provides an up-to-date coverage of key research across this complex area.

5
Researching Adult Communication Disorders

This chapter explores research approaches and issues surrounding adult communication disorders. Research in this area has tended to focus on adult communication disorders of an acquired nature, that is, occurring as a result of some trauma such as brain injury or stroke. However, developmental disorders such as stuttering can persist into adulthood, and language restrictions as a result of global developmental delay are obviously present throughout life and present ongoing communication difficulties and challenges. Some of these are further complicated by the ageing process itself. In addition, disorders of voice production caused by such pathologies as vocal nodules (a benign growth on the vocal folds often related to vocal abuse such as prolonged shouting/raising of the voice behaviours) can be either short- or long-term in nature. However, discussion in this chapter will be restricted to acquired disorders of a neurological nature, that is, stroke or TBI.

As discussed in previous chapters, research into communication disorders can take place within different paradigms. The purpose of this chapter is to provide examples of approaches adopted in such paradigms, highlighting the sort of questions asked in this broad area, and the ways in which researchers attempt to answer such questions. Research which investigates the impairment level of acquired neurological communication disorders is outlined in Section 5.1. Research from a psycholinguistic perspective is discussed in Section 5.2, and the following section looks at the added understandings obtainable through a sociolinguistic perspective (Section 5.3). In the final section (5.4), wider considerations with regard to the individual's social interaction and quality of life are looked at through research from both psychosocial and narrative frameworks.

5.1   Neurological approaches

As noted earlier (Section 1.4.1), some of the earliest studies in adult communication disorders emanated from an interest in how and where
language was processed in the brain. More recently Positron Emission
Tomography (PET) and fMRI studies have increased interest further as
sophisticated technology can now explore brain function in more detail
than was previously the case. Areas investigated include the role of the
right hemisphere in language processing as opposed to the traditional
role of the left hemisphere, neurological correlates of processing of
particular aspects of the language, for example, grammatical forms such
as past tense (Desai *et al.*, 2006), nouns and verbs (Shapiro *et al.*, 2005),
the nature of language recovery after stroke (Saur *et al.*, 2006) and the
neurophysiological effects of rehabilitation (Peck *et al.*, 2004). The following case study provides an example of investigations into this area.

Case study 1

In a study on the effects of aphasia therapy on neurological organization,
Peck *et al.* (2004) investigated the performance of three right-handed
individuals with aphasia on a naming-related task while undergoing an
fMRI examination, before and after eight weeks of therapy (see Table
5.1). They were primarily examining the participants' haemodynamic

Table 5.1   Summary of Case Study 1

Aim		To examine the participants' haemodynamic response to language treatment, exploring right hemisphere involvement
Method	Participants	3 right-handed individuals (2 female, 1 male) with non-fluent aphasia who had suffered strokes at least 6 months prior to study (to avoid effects of spontaneous recovery); ages 46, 79 and 48 3 right-handed non-brain damaged control participants; 3 females; ages 42, 74 and 59
	Data collection	• Tests of naming ability and word generation before and after treatment • fMRI data on TTP values of haemodynamic response of a variety of cortical areas

Continued

Table 5.1 Continued

Data analysis	• Comparison of naming scores pre- and post-treatment using z scores and probability values • Comparison of TTP and time delay measures using Pearson correlation co-efficient
Results	• All aphasic participants demonstrated improvement in naming ability after treatment • All participants demonstrated a decrease in TTP in right hemisphere cortex after treatment, reflecting faster verbal output • One participant demonstrated an increase in TTP in some right hemisphere areas • Less effect on TTP was noted in the left hemisphere cortex • High correlation between TTP and time delay measures
Researchers' conclusions	• Language therapy increased the speed of word-finding in aphasic speakers • The right hemisphere does play a role in language rehabilitation • TTP is a useful measure in exploring language function • Single case studies are important to address individual variability
Critical appraisal	This is a Level 4 study (see Chapter 3) using single case design to explore effects of language therapy on the brain; in particular, the role of the right hemisphere. The establishment of stable baselines for the naming behaviours was important. Probe stimuli were described in terms of numbers – although more detail could have been provided so that probe and treatment stimuli could have been compared. Control participants were not matched well. Restricted ecological validity due to the experimental nature of the tasks involved.

Source: Peck *et al.* 2004.

response to treatment, that is, the blood flow to different areas in the brain depending on what and how an individual is required to do. In this study, the therapy was aimed to stimulate right hemisphere activity, as previous research has demonstrated the increased activation of the right hemisphere following left hemisphere damage. The participants had all suffered strokes more than six months prior to the study, the period of time after which spontaneous neuronal re-organization is said to be less likely to occur. Hence, any improvements noted, according to the researchers, could be attributed to the therapy. Two of the participants received the 'intention treatment' and one received the 'attention treatment' – see Examples 5.1 and 5.2 for details of premises underlying these treatments and tasks involved.

Example 5.1   Theoretical premises motivating hypotheses and tasks

The intention treatment:

(1) that intention mechanisms for hand movement and spoken language overlap enough that language initiation can be facilitated when preceded by hand movement, (2) that using a left hand movement specifically activates right hemisphere initiation mechanisms, and (3) that activating right hemisphere initiation mechanisms facilitates participation of right hemisphere mechanisms in word production. (Peck *et al.* 2004, p. 555)

The attention treatment

(1) that the hemispace to which one attends (left vs right) will tend to engage attention mechanisms in the contralateral hemisphere, (2) that attention as well as language mechanisms may be damaged in aphasia, and (3) that engaging intact contralateral attention mechanisms will improve performance on concurrent language tasks when ipsilesional attention mechanisms are damaged. (Peck *et al.* 2004, p. 555)

Example 5.2   Examples of different treatment tasks

For the *intention treatment*, participants were required to use their left hand to open a box and push a button that elicited a picture of an object on a computer monitor in front of them. They were then required to name the object, with some correction and cueing involved (e.g. being given the first letter, a semantic category).

For the *attention treatment*, the participant had to turn her head to the left following an auditory tone signal, in order to see a computer monitor containing individuals' pictures of objects, which she then had to name.

Baseline measures were taken of the participants' accuracy of naming, and treatment commenced once a stable baseline was reached, in order to ensure that any changes could be attributed to the therapy and not to individual variation on different testing occasions.

Apart from taking behavioural measures of accuracy of response over time on naming tasks, fMRI studies were undertaken, but using a modified word generation task, that is, the participant was given a category (e.g. farm animals, tools) and asked to provide the name of one member of that category. This task was performed while the participant was in the fMRI machine having the brain scanned. Three control participants also underwent fMRI for comparison purposes. The participants with aphasia all showed an increase in performance on both the naming task and the word generation task after treatment. The study's primary measure involving haemodynamic response time, known as time to peak (TTP), demonstrated a significant decrease in two of the participants in the right auditory cortex, Broca's homologue (the area of the brain in the right hemisphere corresponding to Broca's area which is in the left hemisphere), the right motor cortex, and the right pre-supplementary motor area, indicating more rapid response times following therapy. Some decrease in response times was also noted in the third participant. Average response times after treatment corresponded to those of the control participants.

Such a study highlights the kind of issues currently being investigated from a neurological perspective. Technology is now providing ways to see how the brain works dynamically during certain language behaviours and to explore neurological correlates of language in ways that were not available to use 20 years ago. However, in order to study language behaviours using this technology, it remains necessary to strictly operationalize them in a way that is relatively controlled.

Quote 5.1 Reflecting operationalization of tasks and the need for experimental control

As Peck and colleagues note

> It is well known that brain activation obtained during a covert language task is different from that obtained during overt verbal responses. In addition, artifacts due to task-correlated motion, head motion, prolonged responses, and unpredictable responses, produced when aphasic patients speak out loud during an fMRI scan, are a serious technical issue. (Peck *et al.*, 2004, p. 558)

For these reasons, relatively restricted and decontextualized language tasks such as naming often constitute the most viable tasks at this point in investigations, and more naturalistic sampling awaits technological developments.

Envisaging the neurological correlates of language function has been one of the ongoing challenges in research into communication disorders. As noted above, observing behaviours following brain damage can tell much about normal brain functioning. However, a parallel path of exploration exists in this area of research as scholars postulate processes involved in language functioning within the brain, not focusing on actual neurological correlates, but on developing models based on cognitive concepts such as decoding, encoding, top-down and bottom-up processing, and mental representations. Such concepts do not necessarily have definite neurological correlates (at least, in the current state of knowledge), but provide an abstract conception of how information is processed. Research in this context into acquired communication disorders has occurred within a psycholinguistic paradigm, and this is explored further in the following section.

5.2   Cognitive neuropsychological approaches

In the psycholinguistic framework (previously introduced in Section 1.3), cognitive models previously proposed to account for different types of memory, for example, are now accounting for detailed language behaviours and associated processes. A sub-discipline of this paradigm known as cognitive neuropsychology has emerged specifically to model such behaviours in individuals with neurological impairments. Research in a cognitive neuropsychological framework has, to date, predominantly focused on single word processing, although much work has been done at sentence level, and more recently, processing at discourse level has also received increasing attention. While top-down processing is acknowledged as an important feature of these models, incorporating the effects of context, language is seen in a hierarchical way so that words are the basic unit of processing, followed by the sentence, then discourse as the most complex. Words make up sentences, sentences make up discourse, and hence processing is primarily explored on this hierarchical basis. One of the primary deficits noted in aphasia, for example (language impairment after neurological damage such as stroke – see Section 2.1.1), is word-finding difficulty. A multitude of studies has investigated this deficit via naming tasks in which the individual has to name a variety of pictures, based, for example, on factors such as word frequency and imageability. More recently, there has been an increasing interest in verb retrieval, again with investigations requiring people with aphasia primarily to name actions depicted in pictures. It is postulated that treatment of individual words with such speakers can facilitate word retrieval in discourse contexts. Another premise involved in this research is that the different linguistic levels (posited as involving processing of pragmatics, semantics, syntax and phonology) can be differentially affected.

Case study 2

A good example of studies using this approach is a study by Howard and Gatehouse which investigated the naming difficulties experienced by three individuals with aphasia in order to differentiate naming impairments occurring at the semantic level as opposed to the lexical output level (Howard & Gatehouse, 2006). In the cognitive neuropsychological approach it is proposed that naming difficulties occurring in aphasia can occur because of different kinds of impairment. Impairment at the semantic level can result in naming difficulty across modalities, that is, spoken and written, where the central referential meaning is actually compromised regardless of the modality utilized. Individuals with this kind of difficulty demonstrate semantic errors (e.g. substitution of *glass/cup, cat/dog*) and are affected by the variables of imageability and concreteness. In contrast, individuals with an impairment at the lexical level only may show differential naming abilities across modalities, for example, the person may be able to name the object verbally, but be unable to write the name, or vice versa. Semantic errors are not as common, and degree of word-finding difficulty will be affected by such factors as frequency and familiarity of the word being sought.

In Howard and Gatehouse's study, the three participants underwent a series of tests to determine the level or source of their naming deficit. It was over two years since each of the participants had suffered strokes, hence they were expected to have relatively stable performances. Results of the tests were taken in combination in order to diagnose the disorder. The pattern of their responses was said to reflect the level of impairment. One participant JGr demonstrated semantic errors on a naming task and was also influenced by imageability and concreteness of the target words, that is, the more abstract the word, the less likely it was that the participant produced it accurately. It was hypothesized that JGr had a semantic impairment. Participant LM, on the other hand, demonstrated few semantic errors, but gave lots of 'other' responses such as a gesture, or tracing the first letter of the word when attempting to name. LM's performance was influenced by the familiarity and frequency of the target word, and was felt to be more reflective of a lexical level deficit. Participant KS demonstrated both semantic errors and effects of concreteness, as well as effects of word length, usually characteristic of lexical output difficulties. In order to further assess the participants' skills, the authors proposed further tasks (see Table 5.2). One such task involved the use of phonemic cues – one being the correct initial sound of the word, and the other being a mis-cue, prompting a semantically related word. The authors hypothesized that the participants with the semantic problem, that is, JGr and KS, would benefit from correct cues, and would be adversely affected by the mis-cues. On the other hand, LM should also benefit from the correct cues, and yet be unaffected by the mis-cues. These predictions were upheld by the participants' performance, with the exception that

Table 5.2   Summary of Case Study 2

Aim		To investigate whether a series of tasks assessing different aspects of language can assist in providing a 'coherent account' of the basis of word-finding difficulties in aphasia.
Method	Participants	3 individuals with aphasia: 2 males aged 56 and 64 respectively – both with Broca's aphasia; 1 female aged 64 with mild fluent aphasia
		All were at least 2 years post-stroke
	Data collection	Picture naming with no cues Picture naming with phonemic or mis-cueing
		Tests of semantic comprehension: • Auditory and written word-picture matching • Auditory synonym judgments • Pyramids and Palm Trees test • Picture-name verification
		Tests of grapheme-phoneme knowledge: • Written naming • Reading aloud • Letter to sound conversion • Indicating initial letters

Continued

Table 5.2 Continued

	Data analysis	Descriptive statistics – percentages and proportions correct.
		Results compared using variety of tests of significance e.g. Fisher exact test, McNemar's Test
		Error types noted
Results		Testing revealed that each participant demonstrated a different profile reflecting different underlying impairments – semantic deficit, lexical output deficit and mixture of both
Researchers' conclusions		• Hypothesis testing and the tests used in this study can reveal different underlying impairments for the same behavioural phenomenon, that is, naming problems
		• Relying on similar output patterns can be misleading in terms of the nature of underlying impairment
Critical appraisal		This is a Level 4 study (see Chapter 3) using single case design. The participants are well described. Testing is well controlled. The study is replicable in terms of methodology. This is a clear study demonstrating the usefulness of hypothesis testing and of single case analysis in order to explore theoretical bases of disorders such as naming.

Source: Howard and Gatehouse (2006).

KS did not respond to initial phonemic cues, although she did respond to more phonological information.

Another task involved comprehension of single words – see Table 5.2. In addition, participants were required to complete the Pyramids & Palm Trees Test (Howard & Patterson, 1992) in which the participant has to match one picture to a choice of two others that are either semantically related or not (e.g. a pair of glasses to match with either eyes or ears; a curtain to match with either a door or a window).

JGr's performance was outside the normal range for all of these tests, while LM performed normally on all of them. KS scored outside the normal range for all tests except the synonym judgment test. Errors on the tests were all semantic in nature. For example, when hearing the word '*dog*', KS pointed to '*cat*'. The synonym judgment test requires less-detailed semantic analysis than the other tests, hence the researchers discounted this result, particularly in light of the clear semantic deficit on the other tests.

The final test given to participants was one involving written naming. On this task, JGr performed very poorly, as did LM, however KS performed better than the others, but produced close graphemic errors, for example, *culinder* for *colander*, and *dinscore* for *dinosaur*.

The researchers concluded that JGr demonstrated an impairment of word-finding at the semantic level, as opposed to LM who had difficulties at the level of the phonemic output lexicon. Of interest is the fact that both JGr and LM presented as having what could be classified as a Broca's aphasia. However, the testing involved in this study revealed different underlying impairments. KS presented a slightly more complex picture and was diagnosed as having difficulties at both the semantic and the phonemic output levels.

Such studies provide an hypothesis-driven approach to the investigation of language disorders, with the framework also being applied to the disorders of dementia (Noble *et al.*, 2000; Rogers *et al.*, 2006; Silveri *et al.*, 2003), apraxia (Rodriquez *et al.*, 2006; Rose, 2006) and dyslexia in both children and adults (Cole-Virtue *et al.*, 2000; Coltheart, 2005). These studies also operate within a framework of modularity that suggests that different components of language can operate independently from each other to some extent, as evidenced in the kinds of specific linguistic breakdown observed after brain damage. They focus on a constitutive and hierarchical approach to language, that is, that sounds make up words, words make up sentences, sentences make up discourse, and that a lower level will predict performance at the higher level.

Case study 3

Another study demonstrating a more specifically psycholinguistically oriented approach is one undertaken by Thompson *et al.* (2003) (Table 5.3) . This study focused on the sentence level, and rather than being an investigative study only, was a treatment study, applying psycholinguistic theory directly to intervention potential. Their research question focused on individuals with agrammatic aphasia, and examined the hypothesis that 'training production of syntactically complex sentences results in generalization to less complex sentences that have processes in common with treated structures' (Thompson *et al.*, 2003, p. 591). Using the Chomskyan notion of wh-movement, important for constructing non-canonical sentence forms, participants were

Table 5.3 Summary of Case Study 3

Aim		To test hypothesis that training syntactically complex sentences will result in generalization to less complex sentences containing similar processes
Method	Participants	4 individuals with chronic Broca's aphasia post-stroke
		Native English speakers
		Right handed
		Completed high school
	Data collection	Pre- and post-treatment administration of:
		• Western Aphasia Battery
		• Northwestern Verb Production Battery
		• Northwestern Sentence Comprehension Test
		• Narrative samples of Cinderella story
		Baseline measures of sentence production and comprehension
		During treatment, probes of production and comprehension measures as per baseline measures
	Data analysis	Descriptive comparison of pre- and post-treatment scores
Results		• All participants showed improvements in Verb Production, Sentence Comprehension and narrative production
		• The two participants who were treated on the complex forms demonstrated generalization to less complex forms
		• The two participants who were treated on the complex forms demonstrated no generalization to more complex forms
Researchers' conclusions		Treatment results supported the hypothesis that treating more complex syntactic structures would result in generalization to less complex structures.
		Narrative improvements demonstrate a more general than specific treatment effect, possibly resulting from general focus on syntactic and semantic properties of sentences.
Critical appraisal		This is a Level 4 study: Single subject, multiple baseline design
		Good description of participants
		Good reliability of measures demonstrated
		Replicable methodology

Source: Thompson *et al.* (2003).

trained in the comprehension and production of sentences of different complexities. A single subject multiple baseline design was used as the progress of each participant was tracked on one particular measure, while other measures of untreated sentence types were monitored during the treatment. Baselines consisted of individual sentence tasks, however performance on a narrative task was examined pre- and post-treatment, in order to explore the generalization of the sentence level treatment to the discourse context. Two of the four participants were trained on the more complex object-relative clause structures, while the other two participants were trained on wh-questions. It was hypothesized that training the object-relative clause sentences would generalize to improvements on object-cleft sentences and wh-questions, while the training of wh-questions did not generalize to the more complex structures. All structures were baselined (on four occasions for two of the participants, and on two occasions for the other two). Probes were also completed post-treatment, to examine maintenance effects. Predictions were borne out in the results. Generalization occurred from the most complex structures to those of lesser complexity, but the reverse did not occur.

This study provides a good example of explicit integration of a specified linguistic theory in order to develop an intervention which itself added to the support for the theoretical concepts involved.

5.3   Sociolinguistic approaches

An alternative approach to communication disorders involves working within a sociolinguistic perspective. Such approaches focus on social discourse as the phenomenon under consideration, and incorporate the notion of context into fundamental hypotheses about behaviours. Research in this paradigm investigates the way a speaker with a communication disorder engages with other individuals in a variety of situations. Unlike cognitive neuropsychological approaches which focus on language constituents in 'decontextualised' tasks such as naming, sociolinguistic approaches *only* focus on language as it is used in everyday social contexts. Within this framework there have been two primary approaches used to date applied to acquired neurological communication disorders – functional approaches arising from functional grammatical theories such as SFL (Armstrong *et al.*, 2005; Halliday & Matthiessen, 2004) and CA (Beeke *et al.*, 2007; Ferguson, 1998). In this section examples from both these approaches will be discussed.

5.3.1 SFL and acquired neurological communication disorders

Functional linguistic approaches use a grammatically based theory, but one that is focused on language in context. SFL, for example, incorporates all the traditional linguistic levels of phonology, syntax and semantics (although conflates the lexical and syntactic aspects under the heading of 'lexicogrammar', and prefers to see semantics as meanings occurring at the text level). However, it includes further levels of context into the model, and sees all of the 'levels' as interacting, rather than modular in nature. Unlike a psycholinguistic approach, a dialectic relationship is seen to exist between the levels. Meaning is seen as multidimensional – it is not derived from individual word meanings alone. Ideational meanings (e.g. relating events) are created through a combination of lexical items (lexicogrammar). But interpersonal meanings (e.g. speech functions such as argue, rejoin, contradict; evaluative terms such as *bastard, fantastic, awful* etc. expressing a variety of emotions) also exist and are related to the way in which contextual factors such as familiarity, relationship status in terms of power, influence choice of wording. The notion of genre is very important in such a framework, as the purpose of the discourse will determine the kinds of communication taking place, as well as the communication choices determining the genre. See Quote 5.2 for elaboration of this term.

Quote 5.2 Definition of Genre (Martin & Rose, 2003)

[D]ifferent types of texts that enact various types of social contexts. (Martin & Rose, 2003, p. 7)

[A] staged, goal-oriented process. Social because we participate in genres with other people, goal-oriented because we use genres to get things done; staged because it usually take us a few steps to reach our goals. (Martin & Rose, 2003, pp. 7–8)

For studies in this framework, multiple discourse samples are required if generic, that is, contextual factors are to be accounted for. See the Special Issue of the journal *Clinical Linguistics and Phonetics*, 19(3), 2005, for examples of recent applications of this approach in the field of communication disorders. These include studies of the language of adults suffering from a variety of acquired neurological disorders including aphasia after stroke, so-called 'cognitive' communication problems following TBI and communication disorders occurring as part of dementia.

Case study 4

A study by Armstrong provides an example of a functional account of aphasic language in a monologic context, where meanings are related to discourse and genre abilities, rather than focusing on a particular linguistic 'level' (Armstrong, 2001). Armstrong examined the discourse of four aphasic speakers (see Table 5.4) in terms of the variety of meanings they could convey, focusing on different verb types. The recount genre was the focus of the study, with participants producing four different texts within this genre. The verb or 'process' types analysed (Halliday, 1985; Halliday & Matthiessen, 2004) included material processes (depicting some action e.g. *run, eat*), relational processes (involving the verb 'to be' and attributes, location, identity), mental processes (of perception e.g. *hear, see*, feelings e.g. *love, hate*, and cognition e.g. *believe, know*), verbal processes (e.g. *talk, argue*) and behavioural processes (physiological in nature e.g. *cough, perspire*). These processes realize different kinds of meanings that predominate in certain patterns in different genres. For example, in a recount, one would expect material and relational verbs to predominate as the speaker describes an event to the participants involved. To a lesser extent, mental processes may be involved as the speaker provides his/her opinion on the event, or feelings involved. Verbal and behavioural processes will probably be the least involved. On the other hand, in an argument genre, mental and relational processes should predominate as the speaker gives his/her opinion and uses many attributes as an assessment of the topic at hand. In examining the different kinds of processes used by the aphasic speakers, Armstrong aimed to see to what extent people with aphasia could fulfil such functions as opinion giving, expression of feelings, recounts of events. In addition to process type, lexical frequency and variety were also examined.

In the study, aphasic participants were asked to provide a variety of recounts (see Table 5.4). Four individuals without brain damage were used as controls. They were also asked to supply four texts, the only difference being that the stroke recount was replaced with a recount of a serious illness they had experienced.

Percentages of different process types were compared across the four matched pairs, with results suggesting that while two of the four aphasic speakers had similar patterns of process type usage as the control speakers, two relied primarily on material processes, demonstrating little use of relational or mental processes for evaluation purposes, that is, to provide their opinions, feelings on the potentially emotional event

Table 5.4   Summary of Case Study 4

Aim		To investigate the impact of aphasic difficulties with verbs on the discourse of individuals with aphasia; specifically recount genre
Method	Participants	4 individuals with aphasia
		2 males aged 57 and 70 respectively with fluent aphasia; 2 females aged 65 and 80 respectively with fluent aphasia
		4 non-brain-damaged control participants matched for age, gender and education
	Data collection	Recounts obtained from participants:
		• What happened when they had their stroke (controls: serious illness)
		• A happy event
		• Their employment history
		• A wartime experience (the participants were all alive at the time of World War II)
	Data analysis	Process analysis (Halliday, 1985)
		Descriptive analysis using percentages of different process types used
Results		Restricted variety of process types used by two individuals with aphasia
		Restricted lexical variety used by all participants with aphasia
Researchers' conclusions		Restricted variety of process types affected discourse functions such as evaluation/opinion giving
		Restricted lexical variety leads to restricted discourse meanings
Critical appraisal		This is a Level 4 descriptive group study (see Chapter 3). The participants are well described. Numbers are small. No statistical analysis undertaken. The study is replicable in terms of methodology. Ecological validity is high.

Source: Armstrong (2001).

being recounted. The two participants with aphasia who produced a similar pattern to the non-brain-damaged control speakers used less lexical variety, again contributing to a restricted variety of meanings expressed.

Similar to other studies which involve in-depth discourse analysis, this study involved only a small number of participants. This mainly reflects the large amount of analysis involved in discourse studies, however it obviously limits generalization to whole populations. Nevertheless, such studies provide a basis for future studies – either larger in participant number, or studies that replicate the methodology whose aim is to support or negate the previous findings. The lack of statistical analysis in this study is also noted. In such small studies, statistical significance can be queried, and primarily the focus is on description. Armstrong provides excerpts from participants' texts which illustrate different semantic functions and suggest strengths and weaknesses that contribute to a speaker's ability to participate in a variety of functions. For example, in the recounts obtained, some of the aphasic speakers predominantly discussed the events but rarely provided opinions or evaluations of these. It was proposed that the aphasic speakers may have had less access to the more abstract notions involved in relational processes, or perhaps even less access to particular lexical items such as adjectives. For such speakers, expository or persuasive discourse may be difficult, as these genres tend to utilize such processes often to a larger degree than material processes. Hence, while the speaker can produce a recount of events (impoverished though it may be), participation in other genres may be restricted. In such studies, frequency of occurrence of particular functions is not so much the focus; rather it is whether or not the speaker has the ability to realize certain meanings, and how they do this that is of interest in determining potential social participation.

Case study 5

An example of a study focusing on interactions using a functional model is that of Togher *et al.* (2004) who undertook a training programme with communication partners of individuals who had suffered a TBI (Togher *et al.*, 2004) (Table 5.5) . Cognitive-communication problems (see Section 2.1.1) following TBI differ from those observed in aphasia as the lexicogrammar itself is usually less involved. The primary problems are manifested in conversational interactions in which the person with the TBI is often able to speak fluently, in grammatical utterances, but the discourse is often tangential, verbose and socially inappropriate. Individuals after TBI often do not observe social rules of politeness and turn-taking, and are often unable to stay on topic. On the other hand, some may be able to passively respond to questions, but not initiate or continue a conversation. Togher *et al.*'s (2004) work has looked specifically at such interactional phenomena, characterizing primary features in interpersonal terms, and has attempted to test intervention techniques based on sociolinguistic principles.

Table 5.5 Summary of Case Study 5

Aim		To investigate the effectiveness of a partner training programme to facilitate communication with individuals with TBI
Method	Participants	20 police officers, matched for age and education
		20 males with TBI matched for age, severity and time post-injury – diagnosed with a pragmatic communication problem, but intelligible speech
	Data collection	• Random assignment of participants to treatment and control groups • Pre-treatment performance on telephone conversation (person with TBI talking with police officer) followed by post-treatment telephone conversation
	Data analysis	• Number of moves • Percentage of moves for each structural element in the discourse • Duration of structural elements • Number of aberrant moves
Results		• Mean number of moves reduced overall – more efficient interaction • Increase in proportion of time spent by police in establishing reason for the call, and in-service compliance – again increasing efficiency and satisfaction • Increase in closing element – indicating solidarity
Researchers' conclusions		Training of communication partners improved quality of interactions during service encounter
Critical appraisal		Level 2 study: Randomized Control Trial
		Participants well described and well matched
		Replicable methodology
		Good reliability of analyses
		Ecological validity high

Source: Togher *et al.* 2004.

In the study, Togher *et al.* (2004) investigated the effectiveness of 'a training program designed to improve communication partners' responsiveness to people with TBI during routine service inquiries with a community agency. (p. 313) – in this case, the police service. It had been found previously (Togher *et al.*, 1997) that compared with non-brain-damaged matched control participants, individuals with TBI were disadvantaged in such encounters, as they 'were more frequently questioned about the accuracy of their contributions, asked to repeat information more often, and their contributions were followed up less often' (p. 318). In addition in their 1997 study, 'police officers gave less information, and used patronizing comments, flat voice tone, and slowed speech production when talking to people with TBI'. The 2004 study focused on the communication partners in this case, rather than the person with the TBI. Twenty police recruits were randomly assigned to two training groups – one focusing on communication and the control group receiving standard weapons training. The communication group received six two-hour sessions focused on educating participants regarding the nature and consequences of a TBI, and strategies to be used to facilitate communication in a telephone service encounter, based on concepts of generic structure potential for a service encounter, that is, structural elements of greeting, address, service initiation, service request, service enquiry, service compliance, closing remarks and goodbyes (Eggins & Slade, 1997/2004). This study was classified as a randomized control trial, since it involved randomization of participants to either a treatment or a control (no-treatment) group. Recordings of interactions before and after training were made, transcribed and analysed. The training (consisting of role plays, and real interaction practice with people with TBI), resulted in a shorter length of interaction – less interactional moves performed by the police recruits. However, the amount of time spent establishing the purpose of the inquiry (service request) and service compliance increased which meant that more of the telephone call was actually devoted to the inquiry at hand. Fewer moves were spent on unrelated comments, and more were spent on closing the interaction, said to reflect solidarity between participants. Overall, the call was felt to be more efficiently and effectively handled post-training.

This study demonstrates how complex interactional behaviours can be meaningfully quantified in order to provide measures of the effects of intervention. The study also provides an example of how theoretically driven sociolinguistic analyses can be usefully integrated within a more quantitative paradigm.

5.3.2   CA and acquired neurological communication disorders

Conversation Analysis (CA) is also focused on interactions, based on the premise that all discourse is co-constructed, and has been applied over recent years to the study of interactions involving individuals with acquired neurological communication disorders (Goodwin, 2003). However, unlike an SFL approach to interaction, CA is less focused on the more traditional layering of language function, and more focused on particular communication behaviours such as repair strategies observed when communication breaks down. This framework has been used in numerous areas of research for many purposes, but in the field of communication disorders has mainly been used to date in the investigation of neurogenic disorders such as aphasia, and communication problems resulting from TBI or other cognitive disorders such as dementia. For example, some researchers have sought to describe conversational interactions (Ferguson, 1994, 1998; Friedland & Penn, 2003; Laakso & Klippi, 1999; Perkins, 1995; Perkins *et al.*, 1999; Wilkinson, 1999), while others have been working with CA to develop methods to measure the outcomes of therapy programmes (Booth & Perkins, 1999; Booth & Swabey, 1999; Locke *et al.*, 2001; Whitworth *et al.*, 1997). A focus of these areas has been on turn-taking and repair strategies used by communication partners when communication breaks down due to the communication impairment involved. One of the differences in CA studies from more traditional investigations is that instead of focusing on the individual with aphasia alone, the person's conversational partners become a focus, as noted in Togher *et al.'* (2004) study above.

More recent work has examined particular linguistic patterns and their function in conversation. Case Study 6 illustrates such work.

Case study 6

In a single case study of a 39-year-old woman, Connie, who had a non-fluent aphasia (Beeke *et al.*, 2003a), 20 minutes of conversation between Connie and a friend were analysed in terms of grammatical patterns used. Two distinct patterns which emerged from the data were that of 'fronting' of information, and sequential construction of a proposition. Fronting occurred when noun phrases and/or temporal phrases were produced at the beginning of a turn in order to thematize or highlight a particular meaning or orient the listener, for example, 'last week….you go out?' (refer also to the discussion of thematizing in the child language study presented in Section 4.3). While this pattern can also occur in the discourse of non-brain-damaged speakers, the authors discuss the non-standard ways in which such phenomena occurred in the aphasic discourse and their function. In the example above, fronting was often a substitute for tense marking on the verb which is difficult in non-fluent aphasia. Fronting also means that the speaker can then use a pronoun in the full clause following the initial noun phrase, rather than having to process the noun phrase along with the verb phrase and other elements – also difficult in non-fluent aphasia, in which syntactic processing is problematic.

The authors suggest that rather than being symptomatic of the aphasic deficit and hence a predetermined category expected in the data, fronting in particular may 'represent an attempt to manage the sequential demands of turns at talk in the light of aphasic language limitations'. (Beeke *et al.*, 2003a p. 87). The pattern found in this study was not looked for initially, but rather emerged from the data as a particular strategy/pattern this speaker used.

The second pattern was that of a sequential construction of a proposition, which occurs when a proposition is construed from a series of 'contextually linked referents' (ibid., p. 98). Such a pattern is exemplified in Example 5.1 and demonstrates the ways in which utterances can be linked semantically without the presence of intact grammatical constructions.

Example 5.1 Sequential construction of a proposition: the aphasic speaker Connie discussing making a wedding cake for her friend, and having to buy particular hexagonal cake-tins for this task

Jane:	oh what sort are they havin'
Connie:	m tuh hexagon shape m tuh [I
Jane:	[you got tins
	for that
Connie:	no no uh – I have the tins
Jane:	you gotta get 'em
Connie:	yeah yeah
Jane:	oh right. (
Connie:	m Edgerton Green cake shop
Jane:	oh is there one there?
Connie:	yeah

Source: Beeke *et al.*, 2003a, p. 98

Such studies involving CA have often focused on one or two couples' conversations, as well as group conversations (Klippi, 2003), as the description is rich and detailed. In many of these studies, relatively small segments of conversation are chosen for analysis, and as with all such studies, the representativeness of the sample is always an issue for discussion. Studies employing CA demonstrate again how complex behaviours can be quantified, but also how qualitative information is essential in the description of the limitations on communication activities and the restrictions on social participation.

Table 5.6 Summary of Case Study 6

Aim		To investigate the notion that aphasic grammar can be understood at least partly in terms of conversational constraints/contexts
Method	Participants	Female with non-fluent aphasia, aged 39 years 4 years post-stroke Broca's aphasia with accompanying dyspraxia and mild dysarthria Good comprehension
	Data collection	• 20 minute conversation between aphasic participant and friend
	Data analysis	• 12 minutes of sample analysed – beginning one third into transcript to minimize effects of initial self-consciousness • Conversation Analysis used
Results		2 grammatical phenomena emerged: • Fronting • Sequential construction of proposition
Researchers' conclusions		Non-standard grammatical patterns in aphasic conversations may represent attempts to manage turns at talk. They can function to facilitate interactions.
Critical appraisal		This is a level 4 single case study
		Good description of participants
		Replicable methodology

Source: Beeke *et al.* (2003a).

5.4   Other approaches

Another important area of research in the area of adult communication disorders is that dealing with the *psychosocial* effects of a communication disorder on the individual and his/her family (Code & Muller, 1992; Code *et al.*, 1999; Elman & Bernstein-Ellis, 1999). Such studies tend to focus on the emotional state of the individual and their family, and have a particular interest in adjustment over time to chronic disability. Similarly, studies of quality of life and recovery of social function after stroke and head injury provide a fuller understanding of the impact of the impairment on the life of the person with the communication problem and on those around them (Cruice *et al.*, 2003; Engell *et al.*, 2003; Ross & Wertz, 2003).

Case study 7

Cruice *et al.* (2003) examined quality of life in 30 people with long-term aphasia after stroke. Using a total of 12 different measures, including both specific communication measures as well as measures of psychosocial aspects such as depression, they addressed the issue of the extent to which communication impairments affect general quality of life. Not surprisingly the researchers found a clear relationship between quality of life and communication impairment. They performed a series of correlational analyses to look for relationships between specific factors such as scores on standardized aphasia tests and social activity, emotional health, and a sense of self-acceptance. They also used the WHO framework of Impairment, Activity and Participation (see Chapter 2) to discuss the communication characteristics of participants (Table 5.7).

While the field of communication disorders has up until recently seen narrative discourse as a source of data to be analysed for evidence of disorder (see previous discussion in Section 4.3), the narrative has been recognized by other disciplines as a rich source of information about the understandings of the individual about their experiences and as a source of therapy (Bower, 1997; Coupland & Coupland, 1998). Adults with neurological communication disorders have undergone a life-changing experience, and so their narratives are seen as a window into that experience (Faircloth *et al.*, 2004; Frank, 1995). In the field of communication disorders, such narrative therapy approaches are still in their infancy, perhaps because of the difficulties that people with communication difficulty experience in the very process of talking about their problems, although they are beginning to emerge (Hinckley, 2007).

5.5   Concluding comments

This chapter has looked at just a fraction of the research in the area of acquired neurological communication disorders, and as stated at the outset, left aside the equally important areas of research into other disorders that affect the communication of adults, including those that affect speech, voice and fluency. However, it should be clear that there are many directions open for further research which will serve to improve the understanding of communication disorders and ways in which the lives of adults with such disorders might be improved. In Chapter 6, ways to commence research in the field of communication disorders are discussed.

Table 5.7   Summary of Case Study 7

Aim		To investigate the relationship between communication impairment and different aspects of quality of life
Method	Participants	30 individuals with chronic aphasia (more than 12 months post-stroke); 16 male, 14 female
		English as first language
		Moderate level of comprehension
		Reliable yes/no response
		No concomitant neurological disorder
		Normal to moderate mobility
		Living independently in the community
	Data collection	Assessment battery included: • Geriatric Depression Scale • Western Aphasia Battery • Short Form – 36 Health Survey • Social Activities Checklist • Dartmouth COOP Charts • Hearing and vision tests
	Data analysis	Pearson *r* correlation between test scores
Results		• Overall, communication scores predicted well-being and social health • Other sensory impairments e.g. vision, hearing, also related to quality of life and social health • Impairments such as depression related to quality of life as well as the aphasia itself
Researchers' conclusions		Functional communication ability, and to a lesser degree, language function, are involved in quality of life
		Some difficulties in measuring quality of life in aphasia due to language limitations of participants
Critical appraisal		This is a Level 4 descriptive group study.
		Well designed, replicable.

Source: Cruice *et al.* (2003).

Further readings

Chapey, R. (2001). *Language intervention strategies in aphasia and related neuro-genic communication disorders* (4th edn) Philadelphia: Lippincott, Williams & Wilkins.
This book provides an excellent overview of different acquired communication disorders and the variety of both evaluative and treatment approaches taken to each of them.
Goodwin, C. (ed.). (2003). *Conversation and brain damage*. Oxford: Oxford University Press.
This book provides a good introduction to the examination of communicative interactions between individuals with communication disorders and their communicative partners. It focuses on co-construction of communication and ways to investigate this.

Part III
Research Projects Related to Communication Disorders

6
Practical Issues in Planning Research

This chapter discusses a number of the key practical issues which arise when researching in the field of communication disorders, particularly focusing on the issues that arise for interdisciplinary research. A number of these issues centre on ethical and professional considerations. Notions of ethics and professionalism are interlinked, in that a guiding set of ethical principles is one of the central defining features of a profession, and guidelines for what constitutes professional behaviour form part of the descriptions of ethical practice. In reading the previous research literature, it is clear that ethical considerations and the preservation of the rights of participants with communication disorders has been a product also of the historical culture over the course of time (e.g. see discussion in Ambrose & Yairi, 2002). The issues raised in this chapter are currently recognized in the international research community, although different countries and institutions will have their own procedures for addressing these issues. This chapter sets out to raise the most common issues for consideration, and researchers will need to identify how such issues are proceduralized within their own communities in order to ensure that they meet their professional and ethical responsibilities within their research context. In particular, it is important to note that generally speaking, researchers also need approval from their own institution before approaching another institution or individual potential participants. For many researchers, the university may be the researcher's institution if the research is undertaken as part of a coursework or research degree. In such cases, a submission would typically be made to the University Human Ethics Committee or equivalent outlining the proposed project.

The first section (Section 6.1) of this chapter is chiefly concerned with ethical issues, as we explore the situation when the researcher is an 'insider', that is when a close personal or professional relationship exists between the researcher and the individuals whose communication is being researched. In the second section (Section 6.2) we explore the professional issues involved when the researcher is an 'outsider', a situation commonly experienced within interdisciplinary research.

6.1   The researcher as 'insider'

Ethics is more than a simple set of rules of conduct or codification of social mores, rather it is a way of thinking that involves critical reasoning, reflection and judgment which is finely tuned to the particular demands of the social and cultural context. Codes of ethics and guidelines for good practice developed by professional associations typically are non-prescriptive, instead seeking to set out frameworks for consideration and decision-making, for example those set out by Speech Pathology Australia (SPAA, 2000), and the British Association for Applied Linguistics (BAAL, 1994). Within the field of applied linguistics, such guidelines have raised some debate, highlighting the importance of individual researchers taking responsibility for the ethical design and conduct of their research (Boyd & Davies, 2002). Guidelines for ethical conduct and good practice in research published by governmental institutions are typically more prescriptive in terms of particular ways in which general principles are to be observed (e.g. National Medical Health and Research Council, NHMRC, 1999, 2002, 2003; World Medical Association, WMA, 1964–2004).

Whether broadly or specifically described, rarely would a researcher find a perfect fit between guidelines and the particular needs and issues arising from the researcher's project, and so researchers are always seeking to apply general principles to specific issues, while conforming to specific requirements. For example, it is relatively straightforward to recognize the importance of the ethical principle that potential participants in research have the right to be fully informed about the nature of the research and their involvement in it before they give their consent to participate. The institutional requirements to ensure informed consent include the provision of detailed written information accompanied by any required verbal explanation, and often this includes some particular pieces of information to be provided in very specific wording. However, researchers face considerable challenges in obtaining consent from people whose English proficiency is compromised (by English as a second language, or by communication disorder). In these situations, researchers attempt to ensure that their participants' communication is taken into account through providing adequate translation of materials,

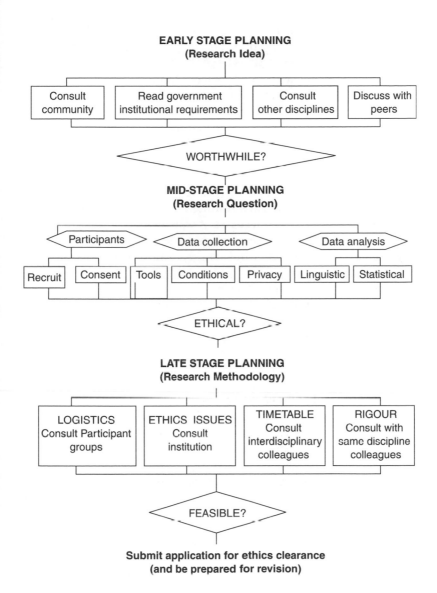

Figure 6.1 Planning for ethical research

or rendering of material into more accessible language. In the field of communication disorders, researchers in the area of aphasia have developed guidelines for what they describe as 'aphasia friendly' formats, involving, for example, the provision of simplified wording and pictorial and gestural support (Rose *et al.*, 2003). In other words, professional and ethical research involves more than the simple application of guidelines, as it involves consideration of the unique set of ethical issues which each project involves. Figure 6.1, outlines the key steps and processes in planning for ethical research, and the following discussion of the issues for the researcher as 'insider' follows these stages.

6.1.1　Impact of research

As can be seen in Figure 6.1, the early stage planning for ethical research involves a process of extensive reading and consultation in order to establish that the proposed research is worthwhile. As previously discussed in Chapter 3, not all researchable matters are necessarily worth the expenditure of resources (time, energy, funds) that will be required of the researchers, participants and funding bodies. For this reason, most ethics clearance committees will want to see some evidence that the research is worthwhile, in terms of its impact either on theoretical knowledge in the area or on the community. This is not to say that all research must have far reaching impact, and indeed most research contributes in relatively minor ways, but it does mean that researchers need to be able to answer the basic question, 'So what?'.

Researchers need to have not only reviewed the relevant research literature, but would also be well advised to consult (informally at this stage) with relevant community groups. For example, self-help or advocacy groups for people with communication disorders are an important resource (as previously discussed in Section 2.2.3). In the case where the researcher is an 'insider', for example, connected to the population to be studied through a professional or personal relationship, it is still important to consider wider consultation. For example, a speech-language pathologist may be very aware of issues facing people with aphasia during their rehabilitation due to frequent close contact during this stage, but less aware of issues relevant to the research which may arise in the longer term past the period of active rehabilitation, and so would benefit from establishing a 'reference group' of people with aphasia and their carers to provide input in the development of research if relevant to this group.

At this stage, it is useful to discuss the research idea with professional peers (i.e. in the same discipline) as well as with colleagues from other disciplines. Sometimes researchers are already working within an established interdisciplinary team in which such discussions take place either informally or at team meetings, but if no such team has been established, preliminary telephone, email and face-to-face enquires and consultations often serve to inform the shape of the research and sometimes lead to ongoing development of a research team.

In most research on communication disorders, it is an assumption that the purpose of the research in the longer term is to benefit people affected by the problem, but as applied linguists will be aware, research findings can potentially be misconstrued or misapplied. Shohamy (2004) argues that researchers have to consider their responsibilities with regard to the ethical use of findings, for example, in ensuring that research testing language proficiency does not end up as a discriminatory political tool (McNamara, 2000; Shohamy, 2004). Efficacy research into particular interventions is particularly at risk here, since poorly designed research which leads to equivocal findings can result in reduction of services to the populations concerned. In other words, researchers also need to take the time to consider, 'So what if....?', and do all that they can to design research sufficiently clear in its purpose that findings are not open to misuse.

6.1.2 Freedom of consent and conflict of interest

In mid-stage planning for ethical research (see Figure 6.1), the researcher sets about solving a myriad of practical procedures that are going to be required to get the project done. One of the first tasks is the identification of potential participants and the development of the method for their recruitment into the research. Continuing consultation with relevant participant groups and interprofessional colleagues will assist in devising a method suitable for the population, but researchers who are 'insiders' face the potential of threatening the principle of freedom of consent for participants. Examples 6.1 and 6.2 are provided to provide the reader with an opportunity to consider how such issues might be dealt with. We have provided our thoughts in relation to these examples at the end of this chapter.

Example 6.1 Ethical dilemma regarding conflict of interest

A speech-language pathologist wants to conduct a research study using a single-case-study design with a current client to determine the effect of a particular treatment method. If the speech-language pathologist asks the client directly to consent to be involved in the research, then the client may feel some degree of coercion to consent, since perhaps ongoing treatment or the harmonious relationship with the clinician might be endangered by refusing. What could this clinical researcher do in order to provide for the client to be free to consent?

Example 6.2   Ethical dilemma regarding freedom of consent

A teacher wants to research a particular teaching approach, for example, in the teacher's second language learning classroom. How 'free' are the students to consent to participate in this research? What could this researcher do in order to provide for the students to be free to consent?

It is not uncommon for a particular research interest to have been sparked through the researcher's personal experience, and within the field of linguistics there has been a long tradition of acceptance of researchers conducting research on individuals or groups with whom they are affiliated in some way. This research strategy has been a highly productive way to conduct research through in-depth descriptive case studies conducted longitudinally, with data drawn from natural and authentic communication interactions. For example, much of what is known about child language acquisition and development comes from studies of linguists working with their own children's language (e.g. Brown, 1973; Halliday, 1975). In the area of communication disorders, one of the contributors to the study of aphasia from a conversation analytic perspective is the sociolinguist Charles Goodwin, whose work includes highly detailed description of his father's communication following the onset of severe aphasia (Goodwin, 1995). Also, research informed by ethnography (Hammersley & Atkinson, 1983) seeks specifically to adopt an insider perspective through such methods as participant observation, and has been very influential in sociolinguistics for many years (Hymes, 1974), and has also influenced research in communication disorders (Ripich & Spinelli, 1985; Simmons-Mackie & Damico, 1999).

However, where insider status arises from the researcher being a parent or relative of the individual with a communication disorder, a number of particular and important ethical issues arise. In the case of children, one of the issues is that the parents of a child participating in a research project are required to give consent, and so the researcher who is also a parent faces a conflict of interest in providing that consent, and the freedom of the other parent to provide consent for the child's participation is constrained by the relationship with the researcher-parent. The child might indicate readiness to participate, but their freedom to withdraw from the research at any time is questionable, for example, would a child be really free to withdraw consent for use of their data for a parent about to submit their doctorate using that material, given the consequences to the parent–child relationship? Where the potential participant is an adult relative or close friend, then the participant has the ability to consent, but the freedom of that consent is threatened by the consequences for the relationship with the researcher if the potential participant should wish to refuse. This situation might be addressed, for example, through the relative or friend being one of a number of potential people invited to participate, being allowed time for consideration, and through consent being actively provided (i.e. at the relative or friend's later initiative, not expected immediately in response to researcher's enquiry).

Hand-in-hand with the freedom of consent issues in these situations is that of conflict of interest in relation to the research process itself, in that it is difficult to ensure neutrality during the processes of data collection and analysis. Researchers familiar with qualitative research paradigms such as ethnography will recognize the dilemma here, since rigour can be achieved through the researcher's 'participant observation' allowing high validity, and there needs to be recognition of the essential subjectivity of the analytic process and its importance in interpretation of data and theoretical formulation. However, external accountability is also part of rigorous research, and the recognition of conflict of interest is important since it prompts the researcher to set in place methods designed to increase the validity of the research, for example, through designing checks on the reliability of data collection (through independent coding of recorded data), and the use of independent analysers 'blind' to whether participant data are from the intervention or control group, for example.

As a final note on researchers with a close insider status, it is worth considering developing the research so that data will be collected on participants who are not immediate relatives, close friends or current clients. There continues to be considerable value gained from important role of personal and professional experience in assisting the researcher in understanding the nature of the communication disorder and its consequences, in informing the development of worthwhile research questions, and in assisting in the design of research which is feasible to implement. However, this knowledge can form the background for making informed decisions about design and procedures for research to be undertaken with other individuals with the same communication disorder who are free to consent or refuse to participate, and in situations which allow the researcher to feel confident that data collection and analysis can be conducted with rigour.

6.1.3   Recognition of limits of expertise

Another issue which arises in mid-stage planning for the researcher is the decision about the kind of tools or sampling methods that will be used to elicit data, and also the kind of analytic methods that will be used. Decisions about sampling and analytic methods give rise to the ethical issue of recognizing the limitations of the expertise of the researcher, and ensuring that all procedures carried out in accordance with the highest standards of professional practice. For example, even in studies for which the main data of interest to the research will be natural language sampling, there will be a need to describe the nature and severity of the communication disorder in ways that are clear to other researchers and practitioners in the field. For most communication disorders, researchers have developed a number of assessment tools which are standardized in the sense that they obtain data using a set of pre-established elicitation guidelines and they analyse the data obtained according to predetermined methods. Such tools vary in terms of the extent of their empirically established validity and reliability, and usually have some stated requirements regarding the expertise needed for the test administrator. Some tools are open for any user given familiarity and practice with the test, while others state, for example, the requirement for the user to be a qualified speech-language pathologist or psychologist, and others require substantial and formal training requirements over and above formal qualifications. Researchers needing to describe their participants' IQ, for example, should recognize that a qualified psychologist is needed to do this testing, and this will have implications for who is involved in the research team, and for funding if a psychologist needs to be employed.

In a similar vein, most linguists would recognize the need for statistical advice for research involving quantitative comparisons, but it is important to recognize (as indicated in Figure 6.1) that initial statistical consultation ideally is conducted in early to mid-stage planning. The nature of data collected and the conditions under which it is collected will fundamentally alter the options available for statistical analysis (see Table 6.1). For example, many linguistic analysis systems involve categorical data (such as, grammatical categories, or types of language behaviour) for which non-parametric statistical analyses are best suited, however, for some research it may be possible to consider the extent to which interval or ratio data might be a better descriptor (such as, occurrence of linguistic

Table 6.1 Types of data

Types of data	Description	Communication example
Nominal	Category	Pronouns: he, she, his, her...
Ordinal	On a continuum	Perceived loudness on a rating scale
Interval	Increases in equal amounts	Number of errors
Ratio	In an amount proportional to another amount	Percent syllables stuttered (i.e. number of stutters as a proportion of number of syllables x 100) – %SS

item per utterance), which would allow the greater power of parametric statistical analyses. Early statistical advice can save the researcher considerable time in the later stages of the research, as many pitfalls can be avoided.

The importance of recognizing limits of expertise becomes a particular issue for researchers who are insiders in situations where participants may look to the researcher for advice or counselling in relation to their communication disorder. The pre-established personal or close professional relationship may place a considerable sense of emotional responsibility on the researcher, and it is important to recognize that the best support the researcher can offer is to provide information and resources for the participant to enable them to seek the appropriate professional assistance. For this reason, many ethical clearance applications ask the researcher to prepare lists of such resources for the sorts of issues which might be anticipated to arise in the context of the research.

6.1.4 Conditions of data collection and storage

As part of mid-stage planning, the researcher will be developing plans for how the data will be collected and stored, and the main ethical issue involved here is that of ensuring the privacy of the individual participant throughout the entire course of the research, from recruitment through data collection and analysis to data storage and destruction. To respect the privacy of the participants, researchers adopt strategies which involve maintaining anonymity or confidentiality.

This is an issue for all researchers, but particularly for those with insider status. For example, researchers who are related to their participants may thereby identify the participant if that relationship is known, in that the child of the researcher even when given a pseudonym is identifiable through their relationship to the researcher. Also, research which is conducted within small communities (such as cultural minorities, or say, the deaf community within a particular city, or even within a particular school) runs the risk of identifying participants either at the time of data collection or in later presentations or publications of the research if the community is identified. Example 6.3 provides an opportunity to consider these issues.

Example 6.3   Ethical dilemma regarding confidentiality

An opportunity has arisen for the researcher to conduct a longitudinal single case study with a child who has a relatively rare disorder – Landau-Kleffner syndrome – and who is living in a small country town. What could threaten the privacy of this child and their family? How could this be managed?

Researchers who want to be able to use clips from recordings of interaction in presentations of the research need to be aware that since the person's identity is apparent from recordings, specific consent needs to be given for this type of use of data. With regard to the use of the data beyond the period of the particular research project, researchers who are considering the development of a corpus of data for ongoing research and potential collaboration with other researchers, need to obtain specific consent for such 'archival' use of data (and particularly if identifiable data will be part of that corpus, such as recordings).

Although not tied to the insider status of the researcher or otherwise, recording is one of the most commonly encountered ethical issues in relation to invasion of privacy for researchers in the field of communication disorders, and recording raises related issues of the covert or overt nature of the data collection. As a general ethical principle, covert data collection or deception of the participants is to be avoided, but there are instances where arguments arise on why covert data collection is needed. For example, in the area of stuttering, individuals who have undergone treatment are frequently observed to show a reduction in stuttering when being recorded (suggested by some to reflect behavioural modification where fluency becomes associated with conditions of recording in therapy). Researchers in the area of stuttering often obtain consent from their participants to be covertly observed, for example, through pseudo-market research calls over the telephone, at some time in the future, with the proviso that they will be debriefed following the data collection. As clarified in the guidelines for good practice of the British Association for Applied Linguistics (BAAL, 1994), while covert data collection or deception is to be avoided, distraction is an acceptable strategy when required. For example, while recording needs to be overt, most participants will relax within a relatively short period, particularly if no undue attention is paid to the recording equipment by the researcher, and other tasks or conversational activities are engaging.

6.2 The researcher as 'outsider'

Applied linguists researching in the field of communication disorders find themselves 'outside' the professional and government systems and practices in which most access is available to the individuals in whom the researcher is interested. Similarly, speech-language pathologists may be undertaking research within institutional cultures which differ in substantial ways from their more familiar work environment. This section looks at a few of the most commonly experienced challenges for the researcher as an 'outsider'. Much of the following discussion relates to the late stage of planning outlined in Figure 6.1.

6.2.1 Collaboration

A recurring thread through this book has been the usefulness of consultation with reference groups, specialist consultations, and with colleagues from the same and other professions. At the same time, collaboration brings with it challenges to disciplinary and professional territories, and considerable demands on clear communication. However, territorial boundaries and miscommunication associated with differing paradigms and mutually incomprehensible terminology are essentially negotiable in a situation in which there has been the establishment of trust, commitment and mutual respect. To establish such a situation, Candlin suggests that it is important to recognize the need for an ongoing relationship with those involved at the site of data collection (Candlin, 2003) (within the boundaries established by all concerned, of course) – in a sense, establishing that this research is about the people with communication disorders rather than about the researcher's goals. Roberts and Sarangi (Roberts & Sarangi, 2003) suggest a similar commitment when they point out that applied linguistic research in medical settings is not just about applying linguistic theory to the context of medical encounters, but equally important is that such research needs itself to find an application in the sense of being useful for the individuals concerned (be they practitioners or patients). As a practical step toward facilitating these goals, it is useful for all members of the interdisciplinary research team to have read and contributed to the development of written documentation of research plans and methodology, such as are required in the development of the ethics clearance application. Such written documentation should include documentation of the potential outcomes of the research, that is, not just the findings as such, but the potential (or, even better, proposed) applications of the findings. This written documentation is the major outcome of the late stage planning as represented in Figure 6.1.

Working in a team brings with it the need for clear delineation of the roles and responsibilities of each of the individuals involved. Interdisciplinary teams in particular need to spend the time to clarify what is expected of each member of the team at each stage of the research, since assumptions held by one professional are not necessarily shared by another (Roberts & Sarangi, 2003). As with all research, fair dealing in attribution of the work of others, and the contributions of each team member, including student researchers, needs to be recognized. One way to achieve this practically is to include on a logistical planner or timeline (see Section 6.2.2 below), who is responsible for the achievement of each task or activity outlined, as well as to include specified times when role allocation and attribution are to be discussed and reviewed.

Clarke provides some useful pointers to novice researchers entering medical settings, from his experience both as a researcher and as a 'researchee' (Clarke, 2003). He notes that outsiders can feel awkward in their observation role, and perhaps feel that they need to be withdrawn from the interaction with the patient in order to achieve the 'fly-on-the-wall' neutrality. However, he notes that such behaviour draws attention to itself and makes patients and clinicians very conscious of being observed, so that a better strategy is to establish and maintain a relaxed yet unobtrusive rapport with participants in the interaction, for example, greeting patients warmly, feeling comfortable interacting with small children who may engage the researcher in play, sitting in the circle of chairs, but just slightly back from the circle (but not outside the circle). He also notes (as 'essential trivia' p. 380) the importance of an appropriate standard of dress and personal grooming in medical settings, to again ensure that the researcher 'blends in' with the institutional environment. Such practicalities seem minor, but can make a great difference in the extent to which the outside researcher is accepted within the setting in which they are conducting research.

6.2.2   Recruitment of participants

In Section 6.1, we discussed some of the insider aspects of recruitment of participants. However, for the outsider, recruitment of participants in the area of communication disorders can be particularly challenging. One of the most logical ways to access people with communication problems is through an institution where it is most likely that several people meeting the researcher's particular criteria might be found. For example, if interested in autism, a special school for children with autism might be the most appropriate venue. If interested in communication problems following stroke, a speech pathology department within a major hospital would be a logical place. In order to approach individuals with communication disorders, however, several issues must be given consideration. For example, most institutions require that the researcher does not directly contact potential research participants. First, this is because the institution cannot provide any details of patients/clients to others without their consent. Second, there must not be seen to be any opportunity for coercion on the part of the researcher. The potential participants must receive objective information about the research project before they are asked to consent to participation. They must also be assured that failure to participate in, or withdrawal from the project will have no ramifications for their care at that institution. They must also be made aware of any possible negative effects of participating in the project prior to giving consent. For these reasons, it is usual for the researcher to contact a profession working with potential research participants if they are approaching an institution. As noted, in the case of hospitals, the speech pathology department is the most appropriate place. In the education system, the school principal may act as the conduit, although approval may be required from the over-arching body, for example, the relevant government department. The researcher needs to be aware that there may be different levels of administration and he/she needs to investigate the appropriate procedures thoroughly.

Similarly, support groups can be a good source of referrals to research projects. Again, however, the researcher must approach the relevant administrative officers within groups, clubs and so on before approaching members individually. An alternative recruitment strategy is through advertising (e.g. local newspapers, internet, or in community group newsletters).

One of the most important pieces of information the outside researcher can obtain in the planning stage is an estimate of likely participant numbers through discussion with speech-language pathologists or other professional involved with the group to be researched. In the logistical plan or timeline (see Section 6.2.2 below), recruitment is an essential aspect to be considered in detail, as the flow of potential participants will determine when data collection and analysis can be productively scheduled.

6.2.3   Logistical planning

As a major part of late stage planning, the researcher develops some form of timeline providing details about when key stages of the research will be conducted and who is responsible for which stage. This sort of timeline is a requirement of most ethics clearance applications, and an essential basis for any budgetary planning in funding applications (since it allows the researcher to know when the difference resources are required). An example of such a timeline is provided in Figure 6.2.

Research Activity	Jun	Jul	Aug	Sep	Oct	Nov	Dec	Jan Jun 2008	Jul Dec 2008	Jan Jun 2009	Jul Dec 2009
Ethics	CI	CI									
Literature review	CI	CI RS	RS	RS	→						
Team Meetings (CO chair)			12th	12th			12th	Bi-monthly			
Review Progress (CI chair)							12th		Dec	Jun	Dec
Recruit			CO →								
Collect data				CO RS	→						
Prepare data				RS	→						
Analyse data					CI, CO, AI			CO, RS	→		
Present							Pilot presented at Department seminar (CI)	June conference (CI, CO, AI); Present preliminary work to participants (CI, AI, RS)	Prepare	June conference (Team); Interdisciplinary presentation (Team); Present to participants (Team)	
Report							Pilot (CI)	Proceedings (CI, CO, AI)		Summaries (RS)	Journal (Team)
Key: CI = Chief Investigator, CO = Co-Investigator, RS = Research Student, AI = Associate Investigator (interdisciplinary colleague)											

Figure 6.2   Example of a research timeline

As part of planning with regard to research in the field of communication disorders, it is important to recognize the additional time requirements that are going to be needed at every stage of the research. Recruitment of participants is likely to take time given the multiple consents often involved (parents, carers), the need to access participants via other institutions and through other personnel, and the need for careful provision of information in order to obtain informed consent. Data collection itself is likely to take a long time for each individual participant, often involving multiple occasions of data collection in order to minimize fatigue or any distress on the part of the participants, and in order to reduce the imposition on the families and others involved.

Preparation of any transcription is likely to take longer than transcription of typical language production, for example, in a general estimate for transcription of interactions involving speakers with communication disorders is to allow four times as long as when non-disordered speakers are involved (i.e. allow four minutes of transcription time per one minute of recording for interactions involving speakers with communication disorders). While many researchers discuss the potential for using automated voice recognition software to reduce some of the time taken from transcription, currently, such software does not manage disordered speech and language well, as such speakers typically have high variability and are not able to participate in the set-up tasks to enable recognition. Other, more sociolinguistic, transcription guidelines provide for ways to capture additional features of the interaction (see Psathas & Anderson, 1990, for a discussion). It can be useful to consider the amount of transcription needed, for example, consider the following questions.

- Does the interaction need to be transcribed? Can meaningful and reliable data be collected online (at the same time as the interaction), or from the recording in some other way? For example, checking off observational categories, sampling at systematic intervals (see Damico *et al.*, 1999, for an example).
- Does the entire interactional sample need to be transcribed? To what extent might a section of the sample be representative of the whole sample, or of particular relevance to the research question at hand. For example, in Labov and Fanshel's (1977) work on a psychiatric interview, the first five minutes was considered to be the most crucial as it involved the setting up of the therapeutic relationship.
- What specific features of the interaction need to be transcribed? For example, if the analysis will not be including non-verbal features

(e.g. hand gestures, or pause times), then the transcription conventions adopted for the research need not necessarily capture these in detail.

Similarly, any sort of coding for analysis purposes takes longer due to the increased difficulty of making coding decisions when usage is problematic (e.g. as discussed in Section 1.6, where for a text of a speaker with aphasia, when might a particular instance of word omission be an 'omission' or an instance of 'ellipsis'). Example 6.4 provides another example of the challenges of analysing problematic language usage.

Example 6.4   Problem usage and the challenges for analysis

M is a 50-year-old woman who speaks English as her first language, and who worked as a primary school teacher until a left cerebrovascular accident (stroke) two years prior to this conversation. M's language problems can be described as 'agrammatic aphasia'. In this sample, she is describing a recent fall while walking in which she hurt her knee and head.

M: Is a, is a hurting my...that one...and is is rest shattered, and is uh eye big, is a, is, is um, bruised. Is a, "oh wow" is big and is lump is is is egg.

In transcribing this sample, it was difficult to determine utterance boundaries, as her prosody was disrupted by considerable pausing in the effort of speaking, and the sentence structure was not complete. M makes use of the words 'is a' repeatedly and these appear to be used as a form of 'filler' or perhaps as a self-cue to assist with the initiation of the utterance, rather than as necessarily representing a grammatical formulation. Thus, while the listener can gather the meaning from this agrammatic sample, for the analyst there are a number of quandaries.

Time spent on logistical planning is time well spent, even if it raises considerations that send the researcher back to the drawing-board, and results in major reformulation of the research question itself. One of the fundamental goals of the researcher is to arrive at the 'researchable question', and a very large part of what makes a particular question is just how feasible it is to research. Feasible research means that the research can be successfully carried through to its completion, and the findings of the research are sufficiently sound to generate the anticipated outcomes.

The participation in research by individuals with communication disorders and their carers is of great importance to increasing the understanding of these problems and to developing ways problems can be better managed, but their participation is also a major undertaking given the other demands on their lives. When research is logistically difficult for participants, or when it appears to them to not achieve its goals, then they are unlikely to participate in subsequent research. Thus, given that research participants are a valuable and scarce resource, then this chapter has attempted to raise a number of questions that researchers might reflect upon during their planning:

- From my reading and discussions with others, is this research direction likely to bring worthwhile benefits (e.g. to knowledge, to the general public or professional discipline)?
- In my planning for this research, have I done all that I can to respect the rights of the participants?
- Having considered the logistics involved in doing this research, what might threaten its timely completion?
- So, in light of the above three questions...Can this research be done?

6.3   Discussion of previously provided examples

In Example 6.1, a speech-language pathologist wanted to conduct a research study using a single-case-study design with a current client to determine the effect of a particular treatment method, but was aware that the relationship with the client might pressure the client to consent. Clinical research typically deals with this sort of issue through a clear invitation made prospectively to potential participants to participate in research on therapy, with that invitation provided 'at a distance' from the treating clinician (e.g. by mail, or through another person), and allowing for time for reflection and active consent on the part of the participant. Where treatment services would normally be provided to the individuals concerned, then alternative provision must be made to ensure that treatment is available for those who do not wish to participate in the research. In cases of so-called 'serendipitous' research, where an unexpected case has arisen in which either the diagnosis or therapy is of research interest, this is typically dealt with by retrospective consent sought by someone other than the treating clinician and allowing for time for reflection and active consent, ideally after all active intervention has ceased.

In Example 6.2, a teacher wanted to research a particular teaching approach, for example in the teacher's second language learning classroom. In these situations where prospective consent is not practicable, teacher-researchers typically provide the teaching programme to all class participants, but the approach for consent is handled by a third-party, keeping the teacher-researcher 'blind' to which class members have agreed that their data can be used in the research.

In Example 6.3, the researcher was conducting a longitudinal single case study with a child who has the relatively rare disorder of Landau-Kleffner syndrome, and who is living in a small country town. In such situations, researchers need to take special care to preserve confidentiality, for example, through not identifying their relationship with the participants in publications or presentations, through de-identifying places of data collection such as particular schools or hospitals, and of course through the use of pseudonyms or codes to refer to participants. In cases where confidentiality cannot be preserved (e.g. when there may be only one or two cases of a rare medical condition in the country) then it needs to be clear that the participants are aware that their privacy cannot be assured and they need to be able to give free and informed consent to their identity being known.

Further reading

The special issue of *Applied Linguistics, 23*(4) provides a series of papers (a number of which have been discussed briefly in this chapter). These papers and the others in this issue provide coverage of many of the key issues that shape interdisciplinary research involving the field of applied linguistics.

Kerridge, I. H., Lowe, M., & McPhee, J. (2005). *Ethics and law for the health professions* (2nd edn). Annandale: Federation Press.

This book provides more in-depth coverage of the issues presented in this chapter. While it does not deal with communication disorders specifically, the many examples drawn from the healthcare context provide useful points to consider.

7
Communicating Research from Start to Finish

An important aspect of doing research is disseminating the findings. Tied to the ethical responsibilities of conducting research is the notion that any study undertaken contributes in some way to relevant questions in society – be they purely theoretical in nature, or of direct practical consequence. Theoretical studies add to the knowledge base in a particular area. In the case of the humanities, such an addition may inform a society about, for example, communal values or cultural practices that may be of historical or anthropological significance. In the sciences, findings will lay the bases for theories that may result ultimately, but not directly, in practical developments in technology, medicine and so on. 'Applied' studies either take a particular theory and use it to address a particular practical issue or work in the opposite direction, that is, derive theories from phenomena observed in real settings. In the case of clinical practice, the results directly relate to implementation of change. When undertaking research, one of the aims is to affect knowledge/social practice in some way, and in order to do this, the researchers must examine the optimal way(s) to disseminate their results.

When undertaking research involving human beings, the onus on the researcher to publish is perhaps even greater than in other types of research. Individuals who have been participants in research have usually given up their time for the prime purpose of improving knowledge in an area which will improve the social good of others. Dissemination of the results is an integral part of their understanding of what will occur, and hence is an integral responsibility of the researcher. In particular, medical/allied health research involves individuals with a variety of illnesses and conditions for whom participation in a research project often involves significant inconvenience and sometimes stress.

As research should ultimately result in improvements in management of such illnesses/disorders, timely dissemination is vital.

This chapter explores the options open to researchers to communicate their research findings and some of the factors involved in making the decisions regarding suitable audiences, formats and outlet vehicles. Many of these decisions will be informed by the kinds of issues discussed throughout the previous chapters, for example, theoretical paradigms and methodological frameworks. Benefits surrounding publication and dissemination of research results will be discussed, as well as details of the publication process itself, and the paths involved.

7.1   Why publish?

As noted above, an implicit tenet of research is that the results will be shared for the greater good of communal knowledge and communal practice. In having the results of a particular study in the public domain, the results can be analysed and critiqued in order to inform both current theoretical thinking and practice, and to inform future research. Studies may be replicated, developed further, or serve to stimulate a completely different approach to a problem raised in the initial study. In sharing results, researchers also often become part of a network of those interested in a particular area. Such a network often stimulates collaborative research, and provides productive ongoing support.

New researchers often feel reluctant in contacting established researchers perhaps in another country, but should be aware of the benefit in doing so, that it is common practice, and that the ensuing collegiality is often lifelong and invaluable to one's research (as previously mentioned in the context of planning research in Section 6.1.1). Contact with an established researcher can result in finding out new directions which the researcher is pursuing, and obtaining copies of work prior to publication, so that the new researcher is in touch with the most current knowledge (publication can often lag behind actual knowledge because of the processes and ensuing time lags involved). The new researcher can also often ask advice or opinions, or share findings which will lead to further development of their own research.

In research into the field of communication disorders, there are often explicit or implicit implications for treatment. Hence, another reason to disseminate results of research is to improve and expand avenues for treatment of the disorders.

7.2   Where to publish?

7.2.1   Journals

The multidisciplinary nature of research enables studies in the field of communication disorders to be published across a wide variety of journals. These range from local newsletter/magazine formats often published by professional organizations largely for a local membership audience to international journals whose circulation is wide-reaching and often interdisciplinary. In addition, journals range from specialist journals focusing on particular disorders or aspects of communication to journals relating to a specific discipline, but more general in nature in terms of material covered (see Chapter 10 for examples).

Choosing a journal will depend on the relevant audience for the research. As noted throughout this book, interest in communication disorders relates to several disciplines. The theoretical background that informs the research will largely determine the relevant audience. If the research is clinically oriented, then one of the journals targeting particular professional audiences is the most relevant, for example, speech pathology, psychology and medicine. If the research is more theoretically oriented, one could target either specific professional journals relevant to the topic (e.g. *Aphasiology, Voice*) or perhaps one of the more interdisciplinary journals (e.g. *Brain and Language, Journal of Applied Linguistics*).

Another aspect that differentiates journals is the key methodological paradigms that characterize the work presented. For example, as noted in Chapter 5 (Section 1.5), there are quantitative and qualitative methodologies used in the study of communication disorders. While qualitative research is becoming increasingly used in this area (quantitative frameworks being the most traditionally utilized), some journals still tend to focus on either one or the other. For this reason, it is recommended that those preparing to submit an article become familiar with the journals being considered, in terms of both content and the methodological frameworks contained therein, and choose one that will be at least familiar with and sympathetic to the theoretical stance of the researcher.

Beginning researchers are well advised to commence disseminating their findings at conferences, many of which publish conference proceedings, some of which are peer reviewed (see Section 7.4.1 below). In addition, the smaller professional magazines and national scholarly journals are also good venues for preliminary research. Large established international journals are often highly competitive and inexperienced researchers may not have reached a sufficiently high standard of writing or methodological sophistication to merit publication in these journals. This is not to suggest, however, that the research itself is not of value and should not be published. It simply means that publication is a competitive endeavour and researchers should be aware that the most prestigious journals that have a heavy submission rate are more likely to have a higher rejection rate than smaller journals.

Increasingly the notion of journal 'impact factor' is seen to be important, although remains controversial to some extent as a measure of the significance of a journal. The impact factor of a journal refers to a measure of citations of articles contained in that journal to other science and social science journals over a three-year period. However, it must be also noted that while journals with high-impact factors suggest a wider audience, the audience may not in fact be the most relevant audience for the work submitted. For example, papers on communication disorders can be published in high-impact factor journals such *The Lancet*. However, in reality, the reader interest in this particular area may be very low, compared with that of a more specialist journal from a professional field such as speech pathology, where communication disorders are of interest to all readers of the journal.

Suffice to say that choice of place to submit research is dependent on a number of factors – experience of the researcher, relevance of the research topic to a particular audience, breadth of the audience tapped, circulation of the journal and relative competitiveness involved in selection for publication.

7.2.2   Books and book chapters

Another option for publication is to write a book or book chapter. Sometimes, dissertations are published as monographs, often by a university publisher, or as a book published by a commercial publisher. However, in the field of communication disorders, publication of such initial research is relatively rare. Books are usually compilations of an experienced researcher's work over a number of years or consist of a number of chapters contributed by experts usually on a particular topic and edited by a leading expert in the field. Book series are also common, where different aspects of a particular theme are expanded upon by a series of authors. Edited books are common in the field of communication disorders, and are becoming increasingly specialized as the field develops. Authors with particular expertise are usually invited to contribute a chapter to such books. Such chapters can take a variety of forms, but are less likely to involve empirical data related to one particular study. They tend to be reviews of an area, or an author's thoughts on a topic. They can also be instructive as in a textbook, where the book aims to introduce readers to a field or sub-topic, and instruct on particular methods of practice within that field.

Certain publishers specialize in different areas (see Chapter 10 for some examples). Publishers generally provide information for prospective authors on their websites, and this information generally includes their disciplinary or interdisciplinary focus, as well as more specific guidelines for the preparation of book proposals and manuscripts.

7.3   Peer review

Many of the journals and books mentioned above, and the conference submission process (described below in Section 7.4.1) involve peer review, which is considered the highest form of review. When a publication has selected papers on the basis of peer review, then it is said to be a 'refereed' publication. Publication in a refereed journal is considered to be more prestigious than a non-refereed publication. Peer review is the process by which researchers in a particular field review each other's work. Reviewers are usually experts in a particular field and are asked to assess an article or chapter for aspects such as significance and potential interest to readers of the particular journal, originality, the author's familiarity with the literature in the area, the appropriateness of the study's design and methodology, including statistical interpretations, and the organization of the information and overall quality of writing.

While the peer review process can be daunting, it provides an excellent opportunity for the researcher to receive feedback and beginning researchers should not shy away from this procedure. Much is gained from having work reviewed by experts in the field – whether the researchers are starting out or are already experienced researchers.

Journals usually consist of an Editor, or Co-editors, Associate Editors, an Editorial Board, Editorial Consultants and Copy Editors. The Editor oversees the whole process, and has the final say on whether an article is to be published. The Editorial Board, chaired by the Editor, decides on the overall direction of the journal. Associate Editors usually oversee particular sub-areas. For example, there may be Associate Editors for areas such as Neurogenic Language Disorders, Voice Disorders, Speech Disorders and so on if the journal deals with the range of communication disorders. Editorial Consultants do the actual reviews and journals usually require up to 3 reviews of each article submitted. The Associate Editors send the article to the Editorial Consultants for review. Most journals provide a listing of their Editors, Board members and Editorial Consultants in the journal itself, however, typically, the author will not be told who provided the peer review. Upon completion of the peer review, the Associate Editors read the reviews, and make a recommendation to the Editor for publication or rejection. Where conflict of opinion arises, further review may be sought (see Example 7.1).

Example 7.1

A researcher submitted a single case study for publication. The study involved providing a treatment aimed at improving an aphasic speaker's ability to produce S-V-O sentences. Reviewer #1 recommended the article be rejected on the grounds of insufficient baseline data (the study reported 2 data points). Reviewer #2, however, recommended publication and regarded the baseline data as acceptable in light of particular constraints discussed in the study. The Editor then sent the paper to a third reviewer in order to resolve the issue.

The review process should ideally take between four weeks and six weeks, but in reality, it can take up to three months or longer for authors to receive reviews back. Many journals provide a footnote to their published articles that states the dates received and accepted, and this provides some indication of the typical time-lags involved for any particular journal. It is important to realize that few papers are accepted outright on first submission. However, many are given the opportunity to make revisions and re-submit. Some are accepted with minor revisions only, some with major revisions, and some are simply offered the opportunity to re-submit once significant changes have been made. In the latter case, no publication is guaranteed and full review is again sought before decisions are made for publication. If rejected outright, authors can choose to send the article to another journal for further review. Beginning researchers should look for guidance on actions to be taken after review. Usually, reviews are extremely constructive and can be used to significantly improve a paper. However, rejections can also result when the article does not conform to the particular journal where it was submitted. It is not uncommon at all for one journal to reject a paper, and another to accept it. So, persistence is *always* required!

Example 7.2

A researcher submitted a qualitative research study involving relatives' perspectives on the experience of living with someone with aphasia. The study consisted primarily of interview data. It was submitted to a journal that specializes in experimental studies of aphasia. The study was rejected. After re-considering in more detail the guidelines given to authors in this and several other journals, the researcher decided to submit it to another journal which has a more social focus and has published studies using similar methodologies.

When re-submitting an article, the author is expected to respond to the reviewers' comments. This can be done by addressing the comments individually in a letter to the Editor, highlighting where either changes have been made as a result of the comments, or reasons why the author disagrees with the reviewer's comments.

While the peer review process aims to maintain a high standard of published research, the process itself is arguably flawed in several aspects. For example, as Ferguson writes, 'One of the biggest challenges is the contention that the peer review process actively promotes conservative research and prevents publication or funding of innovative research – for example, publication of qualitative research has until recently been difficult' (Ferguson, 2002, p. 61). The field of communication disorders stems largely from the medical field, and research has subsequently predominantly been published in journals from the 'science' rather than the 'humanities' or social sciences paradigms. Hence, 'good' research has traditionally been seen to involve quantification and the notion of significant statistical differences in data obtained (e.g. between a group receiving treatment and those not receiving treatment) rather than being qualitative and interpretive in nature. Similarly, large group studies have been favoured over smaller case study designs. While such narrow parameters are slowly being modified, it is important to understand that such biases may well exist within the peer review process, and that choice of journal for publication may affect reviews (see Example 7.2).

7.4   Preparing research for dissemination

There are many general resources available to assist in the processes of writing and presenting research (e.g. Thody, 2006). It is useful to keep in mind that writing and presenting interdisciplinary research often requires shifts in the way the research is talked about and the formats that are considered acceptable (Hyland, 2004). This can mean that researchers who have previously considered their writing/presenting styles to be well developed can find they need to learn new approaches. For example, clinicians moving back into a research context may need to consider the differences between report-writing and writing for academic purposes (Higgs *et al.*, 2005). For those from a linguistic background, there may be less familiarity with the style requirements for the research in the field of communication disorders, which is typically strongly influenced by the discipline of psychology (see Beins & Beins, 2008). Many of the barriers to writing and presenting such as 'writer's block' or anxiety are commonly experienced regardless of disciplinary background, and other researchers have developed ways to manage these (Locke *et al.*, 2007; Silvia, 2007).

In the following sections, some of the practical processes involved in the preparation of research for dissemination are discussed.

7.4.1   Preparation for a conference paper

Conferences are excellent venues for dissemination of research findings, and an excellent place to 'test the waters' prior to submission for publication. They provide opportunities to meet colleagues interested in a similar field of investigation, establish networks, and discuss ideas and methodologies. As with journals, conferences can be very general in nature, or very specific. For example, the annual conference for American Speech, Hearing and Language Association (ASHA Convention) encompasses all aspects of communication disorders, but with a clinical focus, and the number of delegates sometimes reaches 15,000. The triennial international applied linguistics conference (AILA World Congress) is not focused solely on communication disorders, but is interested in any application of linguistic theory, be it educational, clinical, social, and the numbers of delegates may reach 5,000. Alternatively, there are several smaller conferences that focus on particular communication disorders, for example, the Clinical Aphasiology Conference which focuses on aphasia. This is restricted to researchers in the field and all attendees must submit a paper (not all get to present, however). Number of delegates for such small conferences is usually about 100. (See Chapter 10 for further examples.)

Most conferences send out a Call for Papers up to 12 months prior to the conference. Many require some form of abstract. This can be anywhere from 100 to 1500 words in length. The shorter ones require a brief summary of the paper, but the summary or 'abstract' should be written in such a way that it highlights the originality of the content, and its relevance and interest to the specific conference. The longer submissions usually involve a relatively detailed summary of all findings and implications. When designing the programme of a conference, the programme committee will select the papers that are at the cutting edge of the field, and have the potential to be of interest to the conference audience. The programme is usually published prior to the conference and is an incentive for people to attend, hence the papers must be seen to be in touch with current issues, innovative and interesting. Acceptance is usually competitive, involving critical examination by a panel of experts, or possibly peer review.

Some conferences publish Proceedings. It is wise to inquire about this before submitting, as publication is desirable and indeed mandatory in some universities if students/staff are to receive any financial assistance to attend the conference. Proceedings may either be peer-reviewed or not. Guidelines for submissions will be available from the conference organizer. Some conferences publish Proceedings after the conference, while some may require submission for proceedings prior to the conference.

As well as preparing for the written proposal and proceeding submissions, the researcher will also be involved in preparing for presenting through either a poster or platform method. Poster presentation is often preferred for research which is preliminary in nature, or for beginning researchers. Most conferences allocate a time in which researchers are expected to stand by their posters, and be available to discuss the work with conference participants. Such discussions often provide very useful feedback, and may serve as the basis for further contact with other interested researchers in the future. Similarly, platform presentations also provide the opportunity for both presentation of the paper and a discussion time where questions and comments from the audience are encouraged. Presenters can make excellent contacts at conferences with colleagues interested in the same areas and can establish networks for ongoing dialogue which is always valuable to the development of a research area (see Concept 7.1 and Concept 7.2 for further information).

Concept 7.1   Preparing for platform presentations

- Write full paper/prepare notes
- Make decisions about audio-visual accompaniments, e.g. slides prepared using Microsoft Office® PowerPoint; DVDs
- Rehearse presentation focusing on:
  - o   time constraints
  - o   preparation of back-up strategies for managing timing
- practice of responses to anticipated questions from the audience

(Beins & Beins (2008) provide resources that are of assistance in preparing for oral presentations; Locke *et al.*, 2007).

Concept 7.2   Preparing for poster presentations

- Carefully read conference organizer's details about format and presentation requirements (e.g. size)
- Talk with others who have previously presented posters about style (e.g. use of colour, lamination), expense and ease of travel (e.g. in a rolled tube, or in separate A4 sheets)
- Be prepared to be available and to discuss poster with conference participants at time allocated

---

7.4.2   Journal article

It is very important to decide to which journal you are intending to submit before writing the article. As noted in Section 7.2.1 above, journals have different missions. Each journal has a different style and different readership, and the audience will very much determine how the article needs to be written. For example, for a clinical journal, clinical implications of the research are essential, and theoretical premises and framework may have to be defined more explicitly than in a more theoretical journal. For a more theoretically oriented article, the researcher needs to be aware of the degree of explicitness of references/ definitions required for the readership. For example, if the readership consists predominantly of linguists, then clinical/medical terms need to be defined. Basic linguistic terms do not need to be defined, but terminology specific to a particular theory may have to be explained.

There is a variety of article types that are published in journals, for example, individual case studies, literature reviews, experimental studies, qualitative studies, and each journal provides information for contributing authors that outlines the types preferred by that journal (see Concept 7.3). The types of articles often reflect the different types of research methodologies used (see Chapter 8, Section 8.1). Every journal has Guidelines for Authors outlining their particular style in terms of length, referencing, titles and headings, abbreviations, figures, tables, spelling and so on. Authors must be very familiar with these prior to submitting the article. These guidelines can usually be found on the journal's website.

Concept 7.3   Types of journal articles

Issues Paper/Literature Review: This paper would provide a detailed overview of a particular aspect of communication disorders, describing current theories and the most relevant and recent studies applying these theories. The paper would usually highlight unanswered questions and propose avenues for further research in the particular area under discussion in order to progress the knowledge base.

Tutorial paper: This paper serves to instruct readers on how to conduct a particular analysis, or use a particular theoretical framework for research or clinical purposes.

Experimental or descriptive investigations: These papers would be data based and present data from several participants, sometimes including control groups, gathered to address a particular question or questions. They may or may not focus on predetermined hypotheses.

Case study: This paper would provide data from one participant in order to highlight a particular point, interesting phenomena, or provide evidence for or against a particular theory.

All journals require an abstract of the article that summarizes its content. Abstracts vary in structure, and potential authors should review the Guidelines for Authors carefully in this regard. However, an abstract should highlight a general context for the research, the motivation for the article, and in the case of empirical studies, should report methods, findings and implications.

It is important, regardless of the type of article submitted, that the author organizes the information clearly, highlighting main points, and making clear connections between points in the article. A common problem identified by reviewers is that the author has presented a lot of information relevant to the topic, but that there is a lack of continuity and argument throughout the paper. In addition, excessively long sentences are also common problems.

In the case of research involving individuals with communication disorders, as in other related pathological conditions, it is important to provide a detailed account of participants. It is essential that other researchers reading the article have sufficient information so as to be able to replicate the research in order to support or refute the original findings, and generalize the results to individuals with similar profiles. In clinical fields, and using a psycholinguistic paradigm, there are standardized tests that can be used to establish certain language skills of an individual as compared to a set of normative data. If used in the research study being described, such findings should always be included, as well as age, gender, socio-economic status, educational background and any number of other relevant defining characteristics, although these represent the standard ones included.

It is recommended that authors obtain feedback from colleagues prior to submission in order to be able to submit the best possible version of the research paper. In the case of a research higher degree student, supervisors should always be consulted as well as other experienced researchers with whom the student has contact, for example, someone working in the same area with whom the student has corresponded regarding the project. New researchers are sometimes reluctant to engage in this process, but must be aware that this is common practice, and is part of the peer review system in which good research flourishes. Manuscripts should be spell-checked prior to submission, and references checked to ensure that the references in the text match the reference list.

All journals insist on original material and so authors should not submit the same article concurrently to two different journals. As discussed previously in this chapter (see Section 7.3), the process of submission for publication takes time, but the preparation process itself brings its own rewards in terms of enhancing the quality of the research.

7.5   Ethical issues

There are a number of ethical issues associated with the dissemination of research, including the issues of ethics clearance for the research itself, and the attribution of work of others.

7.5.1   Ethics clearance issues

As noted in previous chapters (see Chapter 6 for detailed consideration), when undertaking research dealing with people, particular ethical issues arise and must be acknowledged when disseminating findings. Most journals, for example, will require an inclusion of a statement regarding the institutional ethical clearances obtained.

As noted at the beginning of this chapter (Section 7.1), individuals with communication disorders have usually given their time to the research at some inconvenience, for the purpose of assisting the advancement of knowledge in the area. For this reason, it is now standard practice in most research to provide feedback to participants, in summary form, as to the findings from the research and also how these findings have been disseminated. In the case of individuals with language and/or cognitive impairment, such feedback may have to be simplified to assist comprehension. This may involve what has been described as 'aphasia-friendly language where sentences are brief, no use of jargon, print may be large, and sometimes pictures may be used (Worrall *et al.*, 2005).

Also, the issue of maintaining confidentiality is also of paramount importance. Any published data must be totally de-identified, that is, participants should not be able to be identified. Different names from the participants' real names can be used (first name only), or more often initials (not the participant's real initials).

7.5.2 Attribution of the work of others

When referring to the work of other researchers which has been previously published or presented, researchers need to follow the conventions of the particular journal or book publishers with regard to the amount and sequencing of information. In the field of communication disorders, one of the most widely used set of guidelines with regard to attribution is provided through the American Psychological Association, available through university libraries, and through numerous websites offering guidelines and examples, and publications of concise guides (e.g. Perrin, 2007).

When submitting work for publication, there are times when an author would like to reproduce a particular diagram or model from the previously published work of others, for example, because that model may underpin the empirical research presented. Through the publication process, in most cases the copyright (i.e. ownership) of the diagram has come to rest with the publisher rather than the author (if this is not the case, then some note regarding retention of copyright by the author will usually be evident). Thus, permission to reproduce this material needs to be sought from the owner of the copyright, and sometimes a payment may be required. Prospective authors need to discuss obtaining such permissions with their publishers. Such permission will include the requirements for the way in which the material needs to be referenced in order to correctly attribute the copyright.

A more complex set of issues regarding attribution often arises regarding intellectual property rights where multiple researchers are involved. So, for example, many universities will have some stated policies regarding default assumptions regarding the intellectual property of the institution, academic supervisors/researchers, and students, and it is important for researchers to be familiar with these assumptions. In some research settings, there are conventional attributions as to the roles of the researchers, so for example, for many researchers in the field of communication disorders, the name listed first in the list of authors will be the individual with the greatest input across all aspects of the research, while the last listed author will often reflect the role of the leader of the research team who may be the supervisor of the first-named author.

However, authorship conventions vary, and in particular instances researchers may differ regarding how their relative contributions are acknowledged. A guiding principle is to recognize that open discussion of authorship is a legitimate topic for discussion, and that authorship can be provisionally agreed upon, but can be reviewed as the research process unfolds.

7.6   Concluding comments

This chapter has focussed on the practicalities of the processes involved in presenting and publishing research. The number of steps and possibilities which arise at each step may sometimes act as a stumbling block, and at times worthwhile research stays 'in the drawer' in the face of the work required for dissemination. As stated at the outset of this chapter, in the field of communication disorders dissemination is not just about the researcher however, but about the people whose lives stand to benefit, and this can make the process of dissemination one of the most rewarding aspects of undertaking the research.

Further readings

Beins, B. C., & Beins, A. M. (2008). Effective writing in psychology: Papers, posters, and presentations. Malden, MA: Blackwell.
  This book provides a background for disseminating research findings in a variety of ways, and hints for maximizing clear communication of these findings.
Higgs, J., McAllister, L., & Rosenthal, J. (2005). Learning academic writing. In J. Higgs, A. Sefton, A. Street, L. McAllister & I. Hay (eds), Communicating in the health and social sciences (ch. 4) (pp. 29–41). Oxford: Oxford University Press.
  This chapter focuses on academic writing as a specific genre and highlights the particular characteristics that are of significance to researchers in the health and social sciences.

8
Project Development

The principles that guide research in the field of communication disorders (Maxwell & Sataki, 1997; Pring, 2005) are common to those more generally in the field of psychology and in health-related research (Kazdin, 2003; Minichiello *et al.*, 2004). This chapter explores in more detail various types of research design that are used commonly in investigating communication disorders, and which can be conducted as stand-alone projects. The projects we discuss in this chapter would suit applied linguistic researchers as well as speech-language pathologists and other practitioners in the field, either working alone or in a small interdisciplinary research team (say, two to three researchers). In the next chapter (Chapter 9), we will discuss how such projects may be developed into what we describe as a 'programme' of research as the ideas and methodologies mature. However, in this chapter, we have looked to provide examples of types of research to suit a relatively fast turnaround, in that they might feasibly be developed and implemented within a year, or alternatively, other types of research that may take longer, but which could still be feasible within an institutional setting as an integral part of ongoing service provision. Generally speaking, the types of research explored in this chapter involve relatively small numbers of research participants, and so there are clear limitations to the extent to which findings from this sort of research can be generalized to the population as a whole. This chapter serves to introduce the types of projects which might involve one or at most two different research methodologies, while the next chapter looks more at how researchers use a range of different types of research methodology, across larger population samples. In the present chapter, examples of research from the published literature across a range of different communication disorders are presented in order to demonstrate some of the issues faced by researchers in this field, and to demonstrate how further projects can potentially be developed from such research.

8.1 Types of research

As previously discussed in Chapter 3, the commonly used research designs in the area of communication disorders generally involve either single case studies or small group studies, and can involve either cross-sectional or longitudinal data collection. Both single case and group studies can be descriptive in nature in that the data and the environment in which it is collected is described in terms of factors and influences observed but no deliberate or systematic manipulation of these factors is involved, or may employ experimental research designs in which key factors and influences are identified prior to the commencement of the research and are manipulated in order to gauge their effects on the data. Surveys and questionnaires are methods for data collection which can be used in small or large group study designs which involve some very particular research design features, and so are singled out here for further discussion. Action research is a relatively under-used design in the area of communication disorders, and offers great potential for further exploration. It is important to recognize that no particular type of research is intrinsically better than another, rather it is the rigorous conduct of research that differentiates research which yields valid data and interpretations which are useful

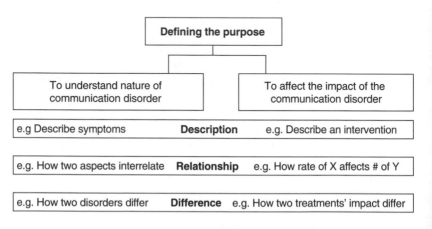

Figure 8.1 Research options

for theoretical or practical developments. Choosing a type or combination of types of research design depends largely on the purpose of the research, and Figure 8.1 provides an overview of some of the main options to be considered.

The rest of this chapter will discuss some examples of each of the main types of research design which have been published in the research literature in the field of communication disorders. The examples have been chosen with a particular view to allow a glimpse of some of the intrinsic constraints of real-world research in the area of communication disorders, and their potential for opening up ongoing lines of practitioner research.

8.2 Single case studies

Single case methodology is particularly well suited to research in the field of communication disorders as the highly heterogenous nature of the different types of problem often prevents meaningful grouping (McReynolds & Kearns, 1983). For example, as previously discussed in Chapter 5, researchers working within the cognitive-neuropsychological paradigm argue that patterns of aphasic deficit are so individualized that treatments need to be tailored individually, and thus treatment efficacy studies need to be conducted through tightly controlled series of single case studies. On a practical level, single case methodology is often the most feasible for clinicians, since it reflects the nature of clinical practice, and is the most feasible for the beginning researcher, and more since it allows an opportunity for the development and piloting of research skills and methodology.

8.2.1 Descriptive case studies

Descriptive single case research involves qualitative and/or quantitative detailed description of a range of aspects of the communication disorder. Typically this sort of research design is used when describing unusual or rare cases about which there is very little reported in the published research literature. Another motivation for this type of research is in exemplifying or testing a theoretical point.

A study of the development of phonology in two Cantonese-English speaking children (Holm & Dodd, 1999) provides a good example of research using single case research design to provide both case description and a test of theory – see Table 8.1 for a summary. Holm and Dodd looked at two cases of typically developing children whose first language was Cantonese, and who commenced their exposure to English at the commencement of the study when they were about two and a half years old. Their development of their phonological system in each language was compared at monthly intervals for ten months. Findings suggested that their phonological systems developed separately after an initial period of some interference between the language phonological rule systems.

The depth and detail of linguistic description needed to address these clinical and theoretical questions tends (necessarily) to restrict such

Table 8.1   Summary of Holm & Dodd (1999)

Aim		To consider the question as to whether bilingual speakers develop separate phonological systems for each language, through comparing the phonological development of two bilingual children
Method	Participants	Two typically developing children (two years three months, two years nine months) who were Cantonese speaking only till commencement of the study
	Data collection	Natural speech samples in separate play interactions with English and Cantonese speaking partners at monthly intervals for ten months
	Data analysis	Analysis of phonetic inventories and phonological processes. Quantitative and qualitative description; provision of graphed data for visual inspection
Results		In Cantonese, at commencement of data collection, errors were consistent with those expected for Cantonese speaking children, but as English developed, errors became atypical. Most atypical productions reflected rule overgeneralization, and with increasing exposure to English, phonological rules became more specifically applied to each language.
Researchers' conclusions		Findings suggest that second language acquisition may cause slight disruption to speech acquisition in first language, but that this appears to be temporary in typical developing children. Findings support development of separate phonological systems.
Critical appraisal		Descriptive longitudinal single case studies. Level 4 evidence.

investigations to single case studies, and so there is a continuing need for such case studies to be replicated in order to provide firmer evidence for the extent to which findings can be generalized to the wider bilingual population (see Tables 8.2, 8.3 and 8.4 which provide ideas for further research; see also, Hua & Dodd, 2006).

8.2.2 Experimental case studies

Experimental single case research involves the identification, control and manipulation of variables deemed to be of significance to test specific research questions and hypotheses. The strength of experimental case studies is enhanced by lengthy baselines, multiple points of data collection in each phase, the collection of a range measures on aspects of communication (including aspects of communication hypothesized NOT to change as a function of the intervention or condition, which allows for control of spontaneous change) and by incorporation of a reversal phase (where the intervention is withdrawn, and the untreated condition re-sampled) (Barlow & Hersen, 1984; Kazdin, 1982).

Table 8.2 Summary of potential project 1

Aim		What is the effect of concurrent bilingualism on phonological development? While Holm & Dodd (1999) looked at two cases of successive bilingualism, would the same picture emerge in cases of concurrent language development?
Method	Participants	Two typically developing bilingual children, exposed to two languages (e.g. bilingual parents, environments)
	Data collection	Natural speech sampling, controlling for language context though language used by communication partner
	Data analysis	Phonetic inventory and phonological process analysis could be expanded to include other phonological analyses
Results		Comparison of development longitudinally across two languages
Possible implications		Implications for identification of disorder in children who are queried as showing problems in development
Critical appraisal		Case study designs allow for in-depth linguistic description, but limited generalizability of findings

Table 8.3   Summary of potential project 2

Aim		What is the effect of bilingualism on phonological system in adults? While Holm & Dodd (1999) looked at two cases of successive bilingualism in children at the critical period for phonological development, would the same picture emerge in cases of consecutive language learning in adults? That is, to what extent is the phonological system in the first language immutable once developed? (See also literature on language attrition, Seliger & Vago, 1991).
Method	Participants	Two adults, with first exposure to second language at commencement of the study (e.g. recent migrants).
	Data collection	Natural speech sampling, controlling for language context though language used by communication partner.
	Data analysis	Phonetic inventory and phonological process analysis could be expanded to include other phonological analyses.
Results		Comparison of change longitudinally across two languages over at least a 12-month period.
Possible implications		Implications for theories of language attrition, and for second language learning methods.
Critical appraisal		Case study designs allow for in-depth linguistic description, but limited generalizability of findings.

Taylor and Iacono (2003) provide a report of a process of intervention for a three-and-a-half-year-old boy who had mild intellectual disability with severe communication impairment with no known cause – see Table 8.5 for a summary.

The 3-and-half-year-old boy who participated in the study by Taylor and Iacono (2003) had a receptive vocabulary that was estimated at 237 words, while his expressive vocabulary was 49 words, of which 47 were produced through the use of manual signs. The study used a single case multiple baseline design in that the effects of intervention were measured across 3 different play contexts. Each play context was highly structured using a scripted story telling format, with different themes: zoo, house, playground. The design allowed for rapid introduction of

Table 8.4 Summary of potential project 3

Aim		What is the effect of bilingualism on the development of selected aspects of language (e.g. morphological, syntactic, semantic)? While Holm & Dodd (1999) looked at phonological development in two cases of successive bilingualism, their descriptive methodology provides a potential model for the study of other aspects of language development.
Method	Participants	Two typically developing children (at critical period for language development i.e. between two to three years) who speak another language only till commencement of the study.
	Data collection	Natural speech samples in separate play interactions with different language-speaking partners at monthly intervals for ten months.
	Data analysis	Analysis of aspects of language development (e.g. quantitative and qualitative description; provision of graphed data for visual inspection).
Results		Comparison of change longitudinally across two languages over a 12-month period.
Possible implications		Contributes to understanding the extent to which bilingualism facilitates and/or interferes with second language development. Findings contribute to theoretical understandings of the language system.
Critical appraisal		Descriptive longitudinal single case studies. Level 4 evidence. Case study designs allow for in-depth linguistic description, but limited generalizability of findings.

the intervention within one of the contexts, while continuing to take baseline measures (no intervention) in the other two contexts. This staggered introduction of contexts of sampling is often referred to as a 'time series' design (Matyas & Greenwood, 1996).

The intervention involved Alternative and Augmentative Communication (AAC) using manual sign with the highly scaffolded narrative script as therapy aimed to enhance the child's use of both pretend play behaviours (as a recognized precursor to language development) and symbolic communication (whether using manual sign or verbal communication). Over 24 sessions, the child attained success criteria in

Table 8.5   Summary of Taylor & Iacono (2003)

Aim		To investigate the effect of an intervention using narrative scripts and manual sign on child's use of language
Method	Participants	Single case – three-years-and-six-month-old boy with mild intellectual disability and severe communication impairment.
	Data collection	Multiple baseline with a staggered introduction of the intervention into three different play contexts (time series design).
	Data analysis	Observation of pretend play behaviours and symbolic communication behaviours.
Results		While pretend play behaviours increased only when the therapy was introduced into each context, it was concluded that the therapy was responsible for the effect. Additionally, a non-controlled introduction of the use of an electronic Alternative and Augmentative Communication (AAC) system was noted to co-occur with an increase in symbolic communication behaviours.
Possible implications		The narrative script with manual sign therapy was found to be effective in increasing pretend play behaviour (an important precursor to language development).
Critical appraisal		Single case study providing Level 4 evidence. Due to the lack of control over the introduction of the electronic communication system, it was not possible to know whether it alone was responsible for the changes seen in symbolic communication, or whether there were effects related to the concurrent therapy.

each context in between 7 to 11 sessions, and pre- and post-measures indicated an increase in pretend play behaviour. No significant increase in the use of symbolic communication occurred until the addition of a (non-experimental) phase using an additional AAC device, an electronic system where a recorded voice produces the word(s) when pictures are pressed. Thus, the researchers conclude that the controlled phase of the study demonstrated that change in pretend play was attributable to the therapy (since improvements were observed only when each context was treated, and not when untreated), but the findings from the additional, non-experimentally controlled, phase, highlight the need for further study to explore the effect of the electronic AAC system. In their study, it was not possible to know whether the increased use of symbolic communication during this additional phase were attributable to the change in communication modality, or perhaps reflected the cumulative effects of the preceding weeks of the therapy across each of the contexts.

Some ideas for further research using experimental single case study design are presented in Tables 8.6 and 8.7.

Table 8.6 Summary of potential project 4

Aim		What is the effect of different modes of AAC on the development of symbolic communication? (e.g. What is the effect of manual sign as compared with an electronic voice/picture system?)
Method	Participants	Single case – described in detail. Child needs to be at the threshold for development of symbolic communication and suitable for AAC modes to be investigated.
	Data collection	Multiple baseline, time series design. For example, at least three sampling occasions in at least three different contexts, with the same measures taken on all sampling occasions. The first phase should observe the child's natural communication, with the staggered introduction of the first AAC system, then the second system.
	Data analysis	Descriptive observational count data. Intra- and inter-judge reliability needs to be established particularly for coding 'on-line' (i.e. during the moment of the interaction). There needs to be control over the communication partner, e.g. familiarity, relationship.
Results		Visual inspection of graphed data to ascertain whether the introduction of each system was associated with particular changes in observed behaviour.
Possible implications		Contribution to an understanding of the components of effective intervention.
Critical appraisal		Single case study providing Level 4 evidence. Intrinsically limited in extent to which findings can be generalized to other cases or populations.

Table 8.7 Summary of potential project 5

Aim		What is the effect of different modes of AAC on the quantity and quality of communicative interaction in adults? (e.g. What is the effect of manual sign as compared with an electronic voice/picture system?)
Method	Participants	Single case – described in detail. Adult needs to be competent user of two different AAC modes to be investigated.
	Data collection	Multiple baseline, time series design. For example, at least three sampling occasions in at least three different contexts, with the same measures taken on all sampling occasions. The first phase should observe the adult's natural communication (i.e. using preferred modes or combination of modes), with the staggered introduction of the first AAC system, then the second system.
	Data analysis	Descriptive observational count data. Intra- and inter-judge reliability needs to be established particularly for coding 'on-line' (i.e. during the moment of the interaction). There needs to be control over the communication partner, e.g. familiarity, relationship.
Results		Visual inspection of graphed data to ascertain whether the introduction of each system was associated with particular changes in observed behaviour.
Possible implications		Contribution to an understanding of the components of effective communicative interaction using AAC.
Critical appraisal		Single case study providing Level 4 evidence. Intrinsically limited in extent to which findings can be generalized to other cases or populations.

8.3 Small group studies

Probably the first question to address in considering small group studies, is just how small is 'small'? For some research purposes a sample size of 100 participants might be deemed to be small, for example, in developing a normative sample for an assessment tool, but for other research purposes a sample size of 20 participants might be relatively large, for example, in the study of relatively rare disorders, such as 'pure' apraxia of speech in adults. Broadly speaking, a small group study might investigate the communication of between 5 to 20 individuals.

Since statistical analyses are frequently used in quantitative small group comparative studies, often the sample size is shaped by the need to ensure that there will be sufficient numbers for the statistical test to have adequate 'power' (Cohen, 1969; Jones *et al.*, 2002; Meline & Schmitt, 1997), and hence (as discussed previously in Chapter 6), it is important to consult with a statistician before making a final decision as to sample size. In qualitative research, often the sample size is determined through the process of research, as data collection and analysis are conducted concurrently, with data collection continuing until new themes cease to emerge from the data analysis (Liamputtong & Ezzy, 2005b; Morse & Field, 1995).

Small group studies are frequently described as either 'cohort' studies or 'case-control' studies. In a cohort study, data are drawn from the one population sample, and subgroups within this cohort are investigated with reference to some feature of communication. For example, a cohort of seven-year-old children might be studied with reference to their literacy levels on a particular test battery. High scoring children might be contrasted to low scoring children, with reference to some hypothesized contributor to literacy achievement, for example, phonological awareness. On the other hand, a case-control study would compare two groups selected for the feature of interest to the research. Using the same example, a case-control study might pre-select groups on the basis of the presence or absence of phonological disorder, and then contrast their literacy levels. In either cohort or case-control studies, participants in the subgroups may be unmatched, or matched – see Concept 8.1.

Concept 8.1 Matching participants

Matching participants between groups is a basic research strategy used to facilitate comparisons between groups. There are two main issues involved with matching.

First, the researcher needs to select the factors on which the groups need to be matched, since not every aspect can be matched, nor would every aspect be relevant to the research at hand. For much of the research in child language disorders, for example, chronological age is an important variable, with mental development age also being important for some studies, and equivalent language age being important for some selected studied. Basic socio-demographic variables of parents' (particularly mothers') education level, or parents' occupation, or suburb is often considered important where environmental influences may affect children's performance.

The second issue relates to how closely the groups are to be matched, with some researchers using a 'matched-pair' process in which participants are selectively matched from each group (which enables some particular types of statistical analyses), or a less restricted process by which the means (averages) for each group are compared statistically to check that there are no significant differences between groups for the variables in questions.

8.3.1   Cohort studies

Cohort studies are generally larger than the scale of research which is the focus of this chapter, but a study by Rescorla *et al.* (2001) provides a useful example – see Table 8.8 for a summary.

Rescorla *et al.* (2001) set out to establish a normative sample of the high- and low-frequency words first acquired by toddlers, and to compare this with the lexicon of late talkers. Late talkers are children who show

Table 8.8   Summary of Rescorla *et al.* (2001)

Aim		To investigate the differences in lexical development between typically developing toddlers with that of children identified as 'late talkers'.
Method	Participants	758 typically developing children aged between 22 and 26 months
		40 children identified as late talkers aged between 2 and 3 years with vocabulary of less than 50 words and no word combinations
	Data collection	Vocabulary checklist completed by parents
	Data analysis	Effect of other factors established – e.g. socioeconomic group
		Proportion of high- and low-frequency words
Results		Socioeconomic group affected proportional use of high- and low-frequency words
		Late talkers showed same proportion of high- and low-frequency words as typically developing children
Possible implications		Clinical implication is that children who do not show this normative pattern (allowing for socioeconomic status) need to be considered at risk for SLI (i.e. rather than just delay in terms of later development)
Critical appraisal		Cohort study with adequate numbers of participants, providing Level 3 evidence. Vocabulary checklist relies on report data.

a specific delay in their development of expressive language, in the context of typically developing receptive language and other cognitive and motor milestones. The findings of the first stage of the study involving 758 children indicated that there was overall a high correlation between the use of high- and low-frequency words and socioeconomic groups. The second stage of the study involved collecting data from a small group of 40 children who were identified as late talkers, aged between 2 and 3 years with a vocabulary of less than 50 words or no word combinations. The findings of the study indicated that the late talkers were

Table 8.9 Summary of potential project 7

Aim		To investigate the differences in lexical development between typically developing toddlers with that of children identified as 'late talkers', based on observational rather than reported data
Method	Participants	40 typically developing children aged between 22 and 26 months
		10 children identified as late talkers aged between 2 and 3 years with vocabulary of less than 50 words and no word combinations
		Socioeconomic group to be described to check groups are comparable
	Data collection	Vocabulary checklist completed by parents
		Observational data based on recorded natural play interactions with parent and researcher in home environment, with samples on a weekly basis over at least three recording sessions of at least ten minutes each
	Data analysis	Proportion of high- and low-frequency words
Results		Compare typically developing children and late talkers
		Compare the parent report data with the observed data
Possible implications		Provides a replication of key aspects of Rescourla and colleagues study, with consideration given to the validity of sampling.
Critical appraisal		Cohort study providing Level 3 evidence. Participant numbers are low, but necessarily restricted by time demands for the observational sampling.

Table 8.10   Summary of potential project 8

Aim		To investigate the differences in receptive semantic development between typically developing toddlers with that of children identified as 'late talkers'.
Method	Participants	100 typically developing children aged between 22 and – 26 months
		20 children identified as late talkers aged between 2 and 3 years with vocabulary of less than 50 words and no word combinations
	Data collection	A receptive test protocol would need to be developed for this study – tests designed for the observation of this age group should be consulted. (Note that the development of the test protocol would in itself constitute a useful study.)
	Data analysis	Effect of other factors established – e.g. socioeconomic group
		Proportion of high- and low-frequency words understood
Results		Data examined to consider the effect of socioeconomic group on proportional recognition of high- and low-frequency words, and to compare late talkers and typically developing children
Possible implications		Clinical implication is to find ways that allow identification of the expected patterns of development for late talkers (which potentially allows for greater confidence in the identification of children with SLI as opposed to late talkers).
Critical appraisal		Cohort study providing Level 3 evidence. Participant numbers are lower than Rescourla *et al.* (2001), but necessarily restricted by time demands for the observational testing protocol.

reported to use a similar pattern of high- and low-frequency words to other children, even though they were acquiring them at a later age. The research provides a useful normative sample against which clinicians can compare individual children's vocabulary acquisition, assisting in the identification of children whose pattern of acquisition differs from that of typically developing children, that is, who might be at risk of SLI.

There is a continuing need for studies which provide data on typical language performance, both in developing language, and in adult use, and even small cohort studies provide a valuable direction for further research – see Tables 8.9 and 8.10 for examples of potential studies.

8.3.2   Case-control studies

Case-control studies often involve the identification, control and manipulation of variables deemed to be of significance to test specific research questions and hypotheses. Unlike single case experimental studies, the role of baseline measures is not so important, since the greater number of

Table 8.11   Summary of Han *et al.* (2005)

Aim		Compared two teaching methods designed to facilitate the learning of vocabulary in typically developing children. Previous research had established the greater effect of one approach, so the question for this research was how the teaching methods differed between the approaches.
Method	Participants	Five classrooms (three using the more effective approach, and two using the other approach).
	Data collection	Ten-minute recordings of each classroom interaction at the start, middle and end of the three-and-half-month period of intervention.
	Data analysis	Interactions were transcribed and analysed for selected aspects of communication, including teacher's and children's meaningful talk (ratio morphemes to utterances), vocabulary diversity (number of different words), teacher's Type Token Ratios, and use of identified vocabulary instructional strategies (saying, asking, talking about letter/sound/meaning, defining, explaining).
Results		More effective approach was found to show greater children's meaningful talk, and more instructional episodes. Both approaches made most use of the 'say' strategy, but a greater number of additional strategies were used in the more effective approach.
Researchers' conclusions		That the different approaches were associated with different teaching methods, which may have contributed to the different outcomes of these approaches.
Critical appraisal		This is a qualitative study, asking a 'how' question.

participants provides a source of validity with regard to validity of measures. Hence, case-control studies most commonly use pre- vs post-testing, or comparison of group performance across a range of conditions.

As a way to provide examples of such research it is useful to look at two very different studies, again exploring the area of vocabulary. The first of these examines the effect of different teaching curriculum on vocabulary learning in typically developing children (Han *et al.*, 2005) – see Table 8.11, while the second study compares methods of teaching vocabulary to children with difficulties in this area (Nash & Snowling, 2006) – see Table 8.12.

These two case-control studies used relatively straightforward comparisons, with matching achieved through the use of children drawn from a similar educational stage and school location, and allowing

Table 8.12 Summary of Nash & Snowling (2006)

Aim		To compare two methods of teaching vocabulary for children with language learning difficulties. The two methods were teaching vocabulary through use of definitions, and through deriving meanings from written context (using semantic/ visual mapping).
Method	Participants	24 children aged 7–8 years, in the lower third of all children in their grade cohort for receptive vocabulary.
	Data collection	Divided into 2 groups and taught using the 2 different strategies twice a week for 30 minutes for 6 weeks in groups of 6 children with same teacher.
	Data analysis	Pre- and post-measures of vocabulary knowledge
Results		Both groups improved post-intervention, but at three-month follow-up, those taught by the semantic/visual mapping strategy showed the greater amount of continued vocabulary development.
Researchers' conclusions		That for this population, the semantic/ visual mapping strategy was more effective in promoting development of vocabulary.
Critical appraisal		Comparative study providing Level 3 evidence. The low participant numbers reduce ability to generalize from this evidence.

Table 8.13   Summary of potential project 9

Aim		Is there a difference in development of oral language skills required for academic settings in children whose learning is facilitated through informal (seated circle discussions of 'news') vs formal (standing at front of class presentation of 'news') methods?
Method	Participants	Children in two classes in their first term of schooling, within the one school, with equal distribution between classes of ability levels (as reported by parent information) and prior educational experience (e.g. pre-school attendance). One class to use formal and other to use informal methods in Term 1 (ten weeks).
	Data collection	Recordings of 'news' interactions throughout the term.
	Data analysis	Transcribed interactions analysed for the presence of elements of generic structure, and other selected markers of academic language use.
Results		Qualitative and quantitative comparisons between classes.
Possible implications		Identification of methods which facilitate particular aspects of academic oral language use.
Critical appraisal		Control is sacrificed in this design to achieve natural sampling. The data sample is large which may enhance validity, but will threaten feasibility.

for subsequent allocation to intervention subgroups. While there are stronger designs, this type of research design lends itself to 'practitioner' research as it allows the teacher or speech-language pathologist to evaluate the effects of everyday practices on aspects of language learning without unduly disrupting the day-to-day lives and experiences of the participants (or the practitioner). See Table 8.13 for ideas for further research using small group studies.

8.4   Longitudinal descriptive research

Both single case studies (discussed in Section 8.2) and small group studies (discussed in Section 8.3) can involve data collected at one particular period in time, and such small group studies are typically referred to as 'cross-sectional' in that they involve collection of data which samples across a particular population at particular points in time. However, both single case studies and small group studies can involve 'longitudinal' data, that is, collection and analysis of data sampled over a period of time in which there is change (for better or worse). The period of time might be lengthy, as for example in studies of child language development and in the case discussed in Section 8.1.1 (Holm & Dodd, 1999) or relatively short, as for example in studies of rapid language deterioration as a consequence of neurological disease (Sowman *et al.*, 2006). One way researchers overcome the logistical time constraints of longitudinal research is to

Table 8.14   Summary of Clegg *et al.* (2005)

Aim		To investigate the long-term outcomes for individuals diagnosed in childhood with language impairment.
Method	Participants	17 men aged between 33 and 38 years, diagnosed when children with severe receptive developmental language disorder in the context of normal intellectual development
		16 of their siblings (i.e. match for environment)
		17 controls matched for age, gender, performance IQ
		1,384 cases from a large national longitudinal study of development selected to match for social class in childhood, and performance IQ
	Data collection	IQ testing (performance and verbal)
		Literacy
		Theory of Mind tasks
		Indicators of social adaptation (employment history, friendship network, relationships)
		Psychiatric measures
	Data analysis	Group comparisons
Results		Participants continue to show severe and persisting language difficulties in the context of normal intelligence, with impact on all above measures.
Researchers' conclusions		Severe language impairment persists into adulthood, with substantial negative impact on quality of life.
Critical appraisal		Well-controlled study making use of a range of groups to ensure valid comparisons.

conduct retrospective studies, sometimes in conjunction with prospective studies. For example, the researcher may identify a group of participants in their middle school years, then look back at data collected before this time (obtained from their health records, and perhaps from concurrent parent report of past performance), and then collect the present data, with a view to a later, prospective, data collection at some later period in the participants' lives. An example of a longitudinal study can be found in the work of Clegg *et al.* (2005) – see Table 8.14 for a summary.

In their study, they followed up 17 men aged between 33 and 38 years who had been diagnosed with severe receptive developmental language disorder (in the context of normal intellectual development) when they were children aged between 4 and 9 years. The findings of the research overall underscore the persisting nature of severe language impairment and the substantial impact this disorder has on individuals' lives.

Longitudinal research has an important role to play in understanding the progression or persistence of communication difficulties. While cross-sectional studies can typically obtain a greater number of participants than are logistically possible to recruit and retain within a lengthy longitudinal study, longitudinal studies can serve to reveal issues that may be masked by cross-sectional studies. For example, in the study of the long-term psychosocial outcomes associated with TBI, cross-sectional studies at any point show reasonable employment rates and engagement within close personal relationships. However, longitudinal studies reveal a pattern of frequent loss of employment and relationship breakdown associated with this impairment (Anson & Ponsford, 2006; Devitt *et al.*, 2006).

Longitudinal studies require considerable commitment from individual researchers or teams, as well as a highly structured and well-planned organization of procedures to enable consistent and replicable data collection over time. However, longitudinal studies make a major contribution to the understanding of natural processes of progression in communication disorders. See Table 8.15 for further ideas using a longitudinal research design.

8.5   Action research

Traditionally, research aims to investigate and understand a phenomenon, and while the goal of applied research is that findings are designed to be useful in the real world, the research and its application form a series of separate stages. For example, traditionally, research might investigate the efficacy of a particular treatment method, the findings might then be applied in a particular service, and the outcomes obtained in

Table 8.15   Summary of potential project 10

Aim		What are the differences between (selected aspects of) narrative development in typically developing children at ages 5–6 years, 8–9 years, and 11–12 years?
Method	Participants	Children in their first, third and fifth year of schooling in the same school.
	Data collection	Data collection could be cross-sectional (i.e. all children in these cohorts at a particular point in time), and/or longitudinal (i.e. by collecting data on the same cohort as they proceed through the years). Note also that this study could alternatively be conducted as a single case study or small group design. Narrative data are suggested as particularly useful, given its close relationship with the development of literacy – so for example, oral and written narratives could form the data set, particularly in the later years.
	Data analysis	Analysis of selected areas of narrative development, e.g. structural elements, and/or use of lexicogrammatical resources.
Results		Quantitative and qualitative analyses.
Possible implications		This kind of normative research is an invaluable contribution to assist in the identification of when children are falling behind their peers in key aspects of their language development.
Critical appraisal		The greater the numbers of participants the greater the ability to draw more general inferences from such data. However, at the same time, larger numbers necessarily mean that data sampling will need to be more standardized and constrained in terms of validity.

that service might also be subject to research. In contrast, action research aims not only to investigate and understand a particular phenomenon, but also to change it, as an integral part of the research process itself. Action research has provided a very useful methodology for practitioners, with wide application within education, and more recently in health, where it is highly compatible with quality improvement activities as the findings from early stages of the research can be promptly put into place and evaluated in a continuous cycle (Reason & Bradbury, 2001). Action research typically involves the participants as researchers, so that they are integrally involved in the development of the research question, the design of the methodology, data collection, analysis and interpretation. Action research is very much an 'insider' research methodology (see Chapter 6), although such research often involves outside researchers, for example, in research driven by community workers aimed at empowerment of disadvantaged groups (McDonald *et al.*, 2002). When the involvement of participants is of key importance to the research, then it would be described as 'Participatory Action Research' (Kemmis & McTaggart, 2005). Action research is highly compatible with qualitative research paradigms, given the priority given to participant perspectives, but it is

Table 8.16 Summary of Munoz & Jeris (2005)

Aim		To develop a means by with interdisciplinary teamwork skills can be taught within the academic context
Method	Participants	Five academic staff (audiology, speech pathology, rehabilitation counselling) Eight graduate students (audiology, speech pathology, rehabilitation counselling)
	Data collection	Written reflections based on weekly readings and participants' life experiences Weekly discussion groups Web-based asynchronous discussions
	Data analysis	Thematic analysis
Results		Emergent themes included identification of ways to facilitate interdisciplinary teamwork were the need for acceptance of differing perspective, empowerment, self-awareness of the learning process for self and others.
Researchers' conclusions		First stage of action research process, to be used in the next stage to develop criteria for the assessment of teamwork.
Critical appraisal		An example of reflective process being used as a research tool within an educational context. The context seems considerably divorced from the authentic experience of interdisciplinarity in these disciplines, which could be addressed in later stages of the action research process.

important to note that both qualitative and quantitative methodologies can be usefully employed within an action research design.

Munoz and Jeris (2005) present an action research project which they undertook within the context of one short course of study – see Table 8.16. This project addressed the dilemma of how interdisciplinary teamwork skills can be taught within academic contexts, which traditionally provide separate disciplinary learning experiences (despite the requirement for interdisciplinary teamwork within employment settings).

Participatory action research holds considerable appeal for those seeking to empower people whose lives are affected by communication disorder, and seeking the ability to translate findings directly into changes allows for practitioners to integrate this type of research within everyday work, while providing for a systematic qualitative and quantitative empirical basis to the evaluation of such changes. Ideas for further research using this design are presented in Table 8.17.

Table 8.17   Summary of potential project 11

Aim		In what ways can applied linguists and speech-language pathologists provide a collaborative interdisciplinary approach to the assessment of children with language impairment? What might facilitate or hinder such an approach?
Method	Participants	Academic staff and graduate students from these two disciplines.
	Data collection	Written reflective journals and written assessment reports drawn from a problem-based learning environment working on a single case study.
	Data analysis	Thematic analysis
		Interpretive phenomenological analysis
Results		While the case study could be hypothetical, involving written and recorded data, this learning experience and research would be more powerful if based on an actual case.
Possible implications		Research would serve to inform interdisciplinarity in the workplace, and also in educational and research contexts.
Critical appraisal		Note that involvement of the client as a full and active participant in this research would contribute to empowerment and changes in service delivery.

8.6 Questionnaire/surveys

Questionnaires and surveys are not types of research design, but rather methods that can be used within a range of research designs, for example in small group studies and action research. Questionnaires and surveys can be qualitative or quantitative in nature, and often form part of a series of projects exploring a particular research question. For example, in-depth qualitative interviews with a few single cases might allow for the development of a preliminary questionnaire or survey, which might be then exposed to the critique and feedback of a small group of participants in a qualitative focus group, further developed, and then piloted using a small group study, prior to its use as one of a large number of data collection devices in a large-scale project. Questionnaire methods are attractive to researchers seeking large sampling within a relatively short period of time. However, generally speaking, studies which employ only questionnaire methods tend to be only able to address very restricted research questions, and the strength of studies using questionnaires depends very much on the process of rigorous questionnaire design and development (De Vaus, 1995).

Questionnaires are very useful in adding additional explanatory information when combined with other methodologies. A good example of this is with the two studies by Glosowska *et al.* (2000, 2002). In their (2000) study, they evaluated the outcomes of speech and language therapy for 159 children under the age of three and a half who were randomly allocated to 'routine' therapy or 'watchful waiting'. The treated group showed a significant improvement in auditory comprehension, but otherwise there was no difference between the groups, and while there was overall improvement in both groups, at the end of 12 months, 70 per cent still had significant problems. The researchers noted the less-than-ideal regime for therapy (up to 17 sessions over a 12-month period), and were able to explore the issues arising from this study further through an examination of questionnaire results. See Table 8.18 for a summary of their (2002) study.

The questionnaire study (Glosowska *et al.*, 2002) points to important directions for further research using a similar randomized controlled study design, for example, the need for an alternative treatment control group (rather than an untreated control), the need to investigate the factor of the amount of therapy required to effect change, and the need to investigate the role of parent-provided practice in the efficacy

Table 8.18   Summary of Glosowska *et al.* (2002)

Aim		To investigate parents' perspective of the outcomes of speech and language therapy.
Method	Participants	147 of 159 parents responded (93% response rate)
	Data collection	Questionnaire included quantitative and qualitative questions In-depth interviews with 16 parents
	Data analysis	Quantative and qualitative analyses
Results		Parent reported similar outcomes to that obtained by test findings
		Parents in treated group were surprised at the extent to which parental involvement in the provision of therapy was expected, and felt under-prepared for this.
		22% of parents felt that the number of therapy sessions was insufficient
		Parents in the untreated group reported more anxiety, and a number (18 of 88, 20%) dropped out of the control group and sought services.
Researchers' conclusions		Findings suggest the need for further research on the amount of therapy, and the need to investigate the role of parent-provided practice in the efficacy of therapy
Critical appraisal		The contribution of these findings to interpret the 2000 results raises the suggestion that this kind of mixed methodology would be useful in similarly focussed research using an Action Research approach.

of therapy. The role of mixed methodologies such as those involved in this research is clearly useful, and in addressing such clinical questions as these, we suggest that the incorporation of such methodologies within an Action Research approach would serve to provide more rapid adjustment of efficacious approaches to therapy for clients. Ideas for further research using questionnaires and surveys are presented in Table 8.19.

Table 8.19 Summary of potential project 12

Aim		What are parents' expectations of their role and ability to provide practice support for speech-language therapy? How do these expectations differ from those of speech-language pathologists? (An alternative would be to investigate teachers' expectations)
Method	Participants	50 parents of children receiving speech and language therapy (in a particular educational or health service) for questionnaire
		10 parents for in-depth interview
		50 speech-language pathologists
		10 speech-language pathologists for in-depth interview
	Data collection	Questionnaire (note that the development and piloting of such a questionnaire would in itself constitute a specific research study)
		In-depth interview (these interviews could inform the development of the questionnaire)
	Data analysis	Quantitative and qualitative analyses
Results		Comparison of parents' and speech-language pathologists' expectations
Possible implications		Findings would assist in identifying where speech-language pathologists need to adjust their expectations as well as to identify ways that speech-language pathologists might increase the skills and willingness of parents to assist with practice tasks.
Critical appraisal		This comparative study might serve to inform the development of a more wide-ranging research project within an Action Research approach with the aim of developing a more collaborative partnership between parents and therapists.

8.7   Concluding comments

As mentioned at the opening of this chapter in relation to Figure 8.1, there is a range of research questions that can be formulated to investigate any particular area. It can be seen from the examples presented throughout this chapter, that different ways of formulating the research

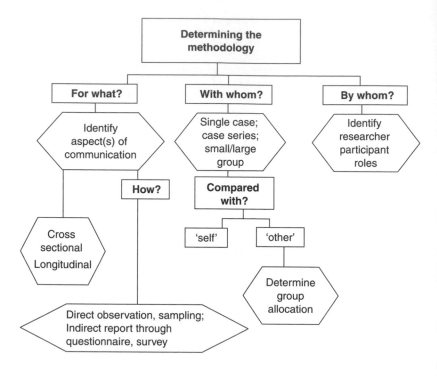

Figure 8.2   Determining the methodology

question tend to require a different methodology or combination of methodologies – and we have summarized this notion in Figure 8.2.

To summarize, if, for example, a researcher is seeking a description of the nature of an aspect of communication, that is, asking a 'What is the ...?' sort of question, then the researcher might look to either a descriptive single case study, or if practicable, a larger cohort study. Research questions that ask 'how' or 'why' tend to be seeking an understanding of relationships, and such questions might be usefully addressed using small group studies, particularly making use of the manipulations of variables possible through case-control designs. Research into the presence and extent of differences associated with particular contexts or interventions can be conducted equally well through well-controlled experimental single case studies and well-matched small group case-control studies. The use of questionnaires and other methods of obtaining participants' perspectives such as in-depth interviewing provide the opportunity to explore subjective data in either quantitative or qualitative ways. While most applied research is designed to translate readily into practice, action research provides a particular dynamic and immediate methodology for developing and evaluating changes in practice.

Further reading

Denzin, N. K., & Lincoln, Y.S. (eds), *The Sage handbook of qualitative research* (3rd edn). London: Sage Publications.
This book provides a comprehensive coverage of qualitative research methodology. It is divided into sections, with Section IV probably the most useful in terms of concrete guidance regarding methodology.
Minichiello, V., Sullivan, G., Greenwood, K., & Axford, R. (eds). (2004). *Handbook of research methods for nursing and health sciences* (2nd edn). Frenchs Forest, NSW: Prentice-Hall Health.
This book consists of numerous short chapters, each of which provides an introduction to the main methodologies used within the health sciences. It is useful for speech-language pathologists and psychologists to explore alternative methods, as well as providing applied linguists with sufficient information to assist with decision-making regarding appropriate methodologies for applied projects in the area of communication disorders within healthcare contexts.

9
Programme Development

This chapter maps out pathways to develop research from pilot stages and smaller scale projects such as those initiated by single practitioners or small teams through to longer term research programme development. An example of the development of a particular research programme in the area of stuttering is provided by way of illustration of the ways in which research can develop from small beginnings to a long-term programme which can contribute to the field of communication disorders. While small-scale projects may be conducted with only limited resources, longer term and large-scale programmes of research need substantial and continuing support, and so this chapter introduces some of the steps in obtaining funding to support such developments.

9.1 Development of a clinical research programme

Case study

As an example of programme development, it is interesting to look at the development of stuttering treatment research which has been conducted over the last 20 years through collaboration between academic researchers at University of Sydney and speech-language pathologists (now under the umbrella of the Australian Stuttering Research Centre, http://www3.fhs.usyd.edu.au/asrcwww). The three main arms of this research programme includes early stuttering treatment studies, advanced stuttering treatment studies and methodological studies which describe the work underpinning both treatment arms, and in this chapter, the focus will be on the early stuttering treatment studies as these provide a good example of how a research programme developed out of a practitioner-driven single case study project (see Figure 9.1).

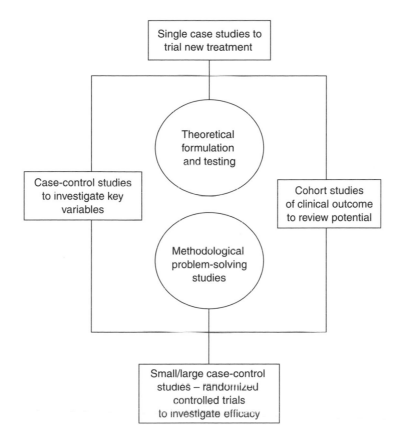

Figure 9.1 Aspects of a programme of clinical research development

In the field of stuttering there is a disjuncture between the theoretical formulations as to the nature of stuttering and the development of practice to provide successful interventions (Packman & Onslow, 2002). Theories abound as to the nature of stuttering, both in terms of its fundamental causes and in terms of describing what constitutes a 'stutter'. Only some of these theories lead direct to the formulation of treatment strategies, and one of the most successful treatment approaches as applied in both children and adults, that of behavioural modification, is explicitly neutral as to the nature of stuttering. Thus, while the researchers involved in developing a clinical interventions have explored particular aspects of the linguistic nature of stuttering, these studies are separate from the theoretical underpinnings as to why particular treatments work (e.g. of research into the linguistic aspects of stuttering, see Onslow & Packman, 2002; Packman & Onslow, 2002; Spencer *et al.*, 2005)

The initial research undertaken by this research team involved the trial of a new operant treatment for early stuttering which has come to be known as the 'Lidcombe Program' (since the research was conducted at the university and hospital campuses in the suburb of Lidcombe in Sydney) – (Onslow, 2001; Onslow *et al.*, 1997). At the time of its initial development in the early 1990s, there was a generally held view that direct treatment with a young child who was stuttering might, at best, be unnecessary since periods of disfluency were often seen to resolve, and at worst, be harmful, in drawing attention to the problem to both parents and the child with possible resultant increases in anxiety and potential increases in likelihood of stuttering. However, previous experimental laboratory research by Martin *et al.* (1972) had shown that frequency of stuttering in two very young children (2–3 years old) was rapidly reduced under a behavioural modification 'time-out' condition (involving a puppet who disappeared from view when the child stuttered and returned to interact when the child's speech was fluent), with no apparent ill-effects on the child or their speech. Onslow and colleagues set out to research (a) whether stuttering in young children could be reduced, and (b) whether there was any indication that treatment was harmful.

(a) Can stuttering in young children be reduced? Four single case studies were used to trial the effects of the behavioural treatment, with all four pre-school aged children achieving fluency within two months and maintaining fluency at the follow up nine months later (Onslow *et al.*, 1990). With these positive results, the team moved on to conduct a case-control study involving 12 more pre-school aged children, which was similarly successful (Onslow *et al.*, 1994).

(b) Is treatment for stuttering in young children harmful? Over the next few years, a number of studies were conducted which sought to establish if treatment was harmful. No harmful psychosocial effects were found in a small group cohort study of eight children (Woods *et al.*, 2002), and no harmful effects on children's language development and communicative interaction were found in other small group cohort studies.

Having established that the treatment protocol was efficacious, the research team wanted to know which particular aspects of the protocol were essential in contributing to the outcome. This is an important question, since potentially not all parts of the protocol might be required, in which case perhaps treatment could be conducted more effectively. On the other hand, perhaps there might be particular aspects of the protocol that, if left out, might mean that the treatment could not work. This is very important to know, since speech-language pathologists using the treatment protocol need to know the extent to which they can adapt the protocol for individual clinical settings and individual client.

(c) Which parts of the protocol are essential? This question was explored using both small group designs as well as large group randomized controlled studies to explore the following aspects of the protocol:

- Duration of treatment (Kingston *et al.*, 2003)
- Role of contingent reinforcement (Harrison *et al.*, 2004)
- Alternative modes of service delivery (Wilson *et al.*, 2004)
- Older age group (school-age) (Lincoln *et al.*, 1996)

Research into clinical treatments is conducted with tight control over the selection of participants and the clinical setting, and the treatments are provided by highly trained specialists. One of the questions that arises for all clinical intervention research is whether the same results will be found in the real-world, where clients are highly diverse, the settings vary and the treatments are provided by clinicians who are less specialized (e.g. provide services to a wider caseload). The research team wanted to know whether this treatment could achieve similar positive outcomes in the real world.

(d) What are the outcomes of treatment protocol in the clinical setting? A large cohort study was conducted looking at the outcomes for 261 pre-school children which confirmed the attainment of zero- to near-zero dysfluency within a median of 11 sessions (Jones *et al.*, 2000).

As this research progressed, the team faced many challenges in developing the methods they needed to conduct the research. Such methodological challenges themselves became the focus of research studies for the team, which are as follows:

(e) Is the methodology sound?

- Can listeners reliably identify stuttering in children? (Onslow *et al.*, 1992)
- How many participants does this type of research need to ensure that there is sufficient power in the statistical analysis of change? (Jones *et al.*, 2002)

- What terminology can we use that will assist us in making sure that we are all identifying and referring to the same stuttering behaviours? (Teesson *et al.*, 2003).

These research foundations allowed the programme to develop a randomized controlled trial comparing the effects of the Lidcombe Program for 29 children with a control group of 25 children (Jones *et al.*, 2005). Results of the study were that there was a significant difference in stuttering between the groups immediately post-treatment and this was maintained at three, six and nine months, and that this difference was also clinically significant.

In considering how this research programme has been able to sustain this productive extended period of development, it can be suggested that the following ingredients may be important.

- *Leadership*: The research programme has had consistent leadership through Professor Mark Onslow.
- *A team of experts*: This research has been supported by the consistent presence of qualified and experienced practitioners undertaking doctoral research studies under the supervision of both Professor Onslow and Associate Professor Ann Packman.
- *National and international dissemination*: The research programme has built a wide national and international network of both academic researchers and practitioners through dissemination of the research findings across a wide range of forums, including workshops, professional development activities, e-newsletters, web-based resources, conferences, journals and reference books.
- *Interdisciplinary collaboration*: The research programme has been interdisciplinary, in drawing upon the fields of psychology and linguistics, as well as in its use of diverse research methodologies from both quantitative and qualitative paradigms.
- *Incremental development*: By conducting small-scale research involving single case studies, the programme was able to obtain initial funding for small group research, and the published outcomes of this research enhanced the ability of the programme to attract successively larger funding support for each subsequent development.

For a researcher embarking on a particular line of investigation, it is unlikely that all the stages and steps can be foreseen in developing towards a larger scale research programme. However, the key ingredients of leadership, disciplinary and interdisciplinary networks, staged and sequential development, ongoing publication, and funding support are suggested to promote a successful programme.

9.2 Finding resources to support project development

Probably the single most important factor in determining whether research proceeds to completion is success in obtaining the funding to support the many costs involved (Ries & Leukefeld, 1995). One of the biggest challenges faced by beginning researchers is that the criteria for allocation of funding is generally based more on what is described as the 'track record' of the researchers at least to an equal extent to the significance of the research. The funding body is, in essence, an investor in the research, but rather than necessarily seeking monetary returns, the investor in this case seeks returns of successfully completed research, as evidenced by changes brought about by the project, and dissemination of outcomes via publications, presentations of the work indicating acceptance by professional peers and the community at large. So, the funding body is seeking evidence from the track record of the team that funds are likely to bring the planned outcomes.

For the beginning researcher, it can be advantageous to collaborate with an established research team so that an individual track record can start to be built. For this reason, speech-language pathologists in the field are often looking for academic research partners, and vice versa, in order to build collaborative teams with track records showing evidence of expertise and experience across the particular domains of theory and practice required for a particular project. It is also useful for beginning researchers to seek smaller amounts of funding to 'seed' their research, and the successful outcomes of these smaller projects begin to develop track records which provide evidence of the researchers' knowledge and expertise in the area, and their ability to implement research and complete projects to the stage of dissemination of findings. University academics may have access to seed funding for the early stages of research development, while speech-language pathologists sometimes have access to hospital-based funding for service innovation and evaluation which may provide a base for future research development.

Another funding source to explore is through local charitable institutions, for example it is not uncommon for organizations such as Rotary International to support small-scale research, and independent advocacy groups may have foundations set up with the purpose of advancing research in particular areas (e.g. Multiple Sclerosis). One of the advantages for linguistic researchers in building partnerships with speech-language pathologists is the access to these funding sources which are closely allied to particular types of communication disorders. In line with the theory-practice continuum (as discussed in Chapter 1), research with practical outcomes for people with a communication disorder frequently provides an important opportunity for theory building and testing.

Government grants may be available for research, and it is useful to take the time to review the nature of different funding options and the different criteria which apply. One feature of all grant applications is the need to provide a detailed budget of the costs (personnel, equipment, consumables, travel and other miscellaneous costs). Budgets need to be realistic, as to over-inflate the potential costs may damage the credibility of the application, but to under-estimate the potential costs may leave the project unable to achieve its planned outcomes. Applications for funding require careful writing (see Chapter 7), and will generally undergo a critical or peer review process (for further guidance, see Locke *et al.*, 2007).

9.3   Finding resources to support the researcher

So far this chapter has discussed funding that would be paid directly to the institution in which the researcher works or with which the researcher is affiliated in some way. In such cases, if any monies were to come to the researcher then they would do so via a salary payment through the institution. However, individual researchers can obtain funding support for themselves to assist in their research through applying for scholarships and fellowships.

Generally speaking scholarships provide funds which support the living and education expenses of a researcher undertaking a formal study programme at an education institution (e.g. Masters by research, or doctoral research programme), while fellowships provide funds which support the living and travel costs of a researcher undertaking a self-initiated programme of learning and professional development in relation to their research area (e.g. a study tour of overseas institutions working in a similar area).

The sources of funding for scholarships and fellowships include government and private charitable institutions, with the bulk of these being made available through universities. Scholarships that are specifically focused on studies in areas relevant to communication disorders are very rare, but the competitive field for these is relatively smaller than the more generic scholarships and grants. An important requirement generally required for applications for scholarships and fellowships is the requirement for a number of referees to be listed, and the choice of these can be crucial. Referees need to be experts in the area(s) of the research, and need to know the applicant's work and proposed project well. With cross-disciplinary research in linguistics and speech pathology, it is a good idea to draw referees from across the disciplinary areas. It is important to request permission to provide someone's name as a referee, and time spent in discussion with the main referee will be worthwhile, as will sending referees either a copy or summary of the application and the award guidelines.

As discussed previously in relation to submissions for presentation and publication, seeking funding support requires considerable persistence. Unlike submission for publication however, it is appropriate to submit applications simultaneously to multiple sources of funding (assuming there are no specific guidelines for a particular funding body that preclude this). Generally, the application will provide the opportunity for such simultaneous requests to be reported, and guidelines as to whether or not multiple sources can be held concurrently if successful.

Whether or not researchers are working in institutional contexts outside the demands of particular formal programmes of study, there is always the need to juggle the competing needs of the 'day job' and the development and implementation of research. There needs to be recognition of when the particular research will have substantial benefits to developments in theory or practice in order to allow windows of opportunity to be prioritized to work on obtaining research support. This is an ongoing challenge, and creating workplace environments which value the contribution of research is a necessary pre-requisite to the formation and maintenance of long-term research programmes. One of the most important keys to facilitating the creation of this type of environment is for the researcher to maintain a continued line of communication with co workers and employers about the significance and progress of the work in development or underway.

9.4 Concluding comments

Individually, developing a coherent research programme requires stamina, and the ability to respond positively to fair criticism. Teams of researchers benefit from both continuity in leadership and membership, as well as the flexibility to widen or shift the team depending on expertise. Nurturing early career researchers makes good sense for established teams, in order to allow for the research scope to be widened and continued beyond the productive span of individuals. All of this visionary work in establishing a long-term research programme provides an exciting pathway, underpinned by extensive information seeking, planning and preparation.

Throughout this book, we have sought to emphasize the diversity of issues that await further research, and the multiplicity of ways in which significant contributions can be made to the field of communication disorders. It is clear that such contributions are made by individuals, and by teams of individuals. It is also clear that these contributions grow cumulatively through the life of individuals as their expertise grows with experience and the life of teams as they tackle particular problems or sets of problems. It is also evident that research is a powerful means by which the lives of individuals with communication disorders are improved, and so we conclude this book with an invitation to readers to continue their progress along this worthwhile pathway.

Further reading

Ries, J. B., & Leukefeld, C. G. (1995). *Applying for research funding: Getting started and getting funded*. Thousand Oaks, CA: Sage Publications.
    This book provides a more in-depth coverage of some of the issues discussed in this chapter.
Rothwell, N. (2002). *Who wants to be a scientist?: Choosing science as a career*. Cambridge, UK: Cambridge University Press.
    Although this book is designed more for the 'hard science' reader, the central principles discussed regarding career decision-making are highly relevant to the applied researcher in the field of communication disorders. Chapters include coverage of funding support and intellectual property.

Part IV
Further Resources

10
Resources for Researching Communication Disorders

10.1 Examples of standardized tests

10.1.1 Child language

Bishop, D. V. M. (2003). *Test for reception of grammar,* (2nd edn). San Antonio, TX: Harcourt Assessment Inc.

Dodd, B., Hua, Z., Crosbie, S., Holm, A., & Ozanne, A. (2006). *Diagnostic Evaluation of Articulation and Phonology (DEAP).* San Antonio, TX: Pearson.

Dunn, L. M., & Dunn, D. M. (2007). *Peabody Picture Vocabulary Test (PPVT-4)* (4th edn). Bloomington, MN: Pearson Assessment Group.

Fisher, H. B., & Logemann, J. A. (1971). *Fisher-Logemann Test of Articulation Competence (F-LTOAC).* Austin, TX: Pro-Ed.

Goldman, R., & Fristoe, M. (2000). *Goldman-Fristoe Test of Articulation (G-FTA-2)* (2nd edn). Austin, TX: Pro-Ed.

Hodson, B. W. (2004). *Hodson Assessment of Phonological Patterns (HAPP-3).* Austin, TX: Pro-Ed.

Renfrew, C. (1997). *Action picture test.* Bicester, UK: Speechmark.

Semel, E., Wiig, E. H., & Secord, W. A. (2003). *Clinical Evaluation of Language Fundamentals (CELF-4)* (4th edn). San Antonio: Harcourt Brace & Co, The Psychological Corporation.

Semel, E., Wiig, E. H., & Secord, W. A. (2006). *Clinical Evaluation of Language Fundamentals (CELF-4)* (4th - Australian standardised ed.). Marrickville, NSW: Harcourt Assessment.

Wagner, R., Torgesen, J. K., & Rashotte, C. A. (1999). Comprehensive test of phonological processing. CTOPP. Austin TX: Pro-Ed.

Zimmerman, I. L., Steiner, V. G., & Evatt Pond, R. (2002). *Pre-school language scales,* (4th edn) (PLS-4). San Antonio, TX: Harcourt Assessment Inc.

10.1.2 Adolescent language

Bowers, L., Huisingh, R., & LoGuidice, C. (2007). *Test of Problem Solving 2 - Adolescent (TOPS 2)* (2nd edn). East Moine, IL: LinguiSystems.

10.1.3 Adult language: aphasia

Bastiaanse, R., Edwards, S., & Rispens, J. (2002). *Verb & sentence test.* Oxford, UK: Pearson Assessment.

Dabul, B. L. (2000). *Apraxia Battery for Adults* (ABA-2) (2nd edn). Austin, TX: Pro-Ed.

Goodglass, H., Kaplan, E., & Barresi, B. (2000). *Boston diagnostic aphasia examination*, (3rd edn). San Antonio, TX; Harcourt Assessment Inc.

Holland, A., Frattali, C., & Fromm, D. (1999). *Communication Activities of Daily Living (CADL-2)* (2nd edn). Austin, TX: Pro-Ed.

Howard, D., & Patterson, K. (1992). *Pyramids and palm trees*. Oxford, UK: Pearson Assessment.

Kay, J., Lesser, R., & Coltheart, M. (1992). *Psycholinguistic Assessments of Language Processing in Aphasia (PALPA)*. Hove, East Sussex, England: Psychology Press.

Kertesz, A. (2006). *Western Aphasia Battery – Revised*. San Antonio, TX; Harcourt Assessment Inc.

Paradis, M., & Libben, G. (1987). *The assessment of bilingual aphasia – the bilingual aphasia test*. Hove, UK: Psychology Press.

10.1.4   Cognitive communication disorders

Adamovich, B., & Henderson, J. (1992). *Scales of cognitive ability for traumatic brain injury (SCATBI)*. Austin, TX: Pro-Ed Pub.

Bayles, K., & Tomoeda, C. (1993). *Arizona battery for communication disorders of dementia (ABCD)*. Arizona, TX: Pro-Ed.

Bryan, K. (1994). *The right hemisphere language battery* (2nd edn). Chichester, West Sussex, England: John Wiley & Sons.

10.2   Examples of behavioural checklists

10.2.1   Child language

Bishop, D. (2006). *Children's Communication Checklist-2 (CCC-2)* (2nd edn). San Antonio, TX: Pearson.

Prutting, C. A. & Kirchner, D. M. (1987). A clinical appraisal of the pragmatic aspects of language. *Journal of Speech and Hearing Disorders, 52*(2), 105–19.

10.3   Quality of life scales

Code, C., & Muller, D. J. (1992) *Code-Muller Protocols: Assessing Perceptions of Psychosocial Adjustment in Aphasia and Related Disorders*. Chichester, West Sussex: John Wiley & Sons.

Hilari, K., Byng, S., Lamping, D. L., & Smith, S. C. (2003). Stroke and Aphasia Quality of Life Scale – 39 (SAQOL-39): Evaluation of acceptability, reliability and validity. *Stroke, 34*(8), 1944–50.

van Weel, C., Konig-Zahn, C., Touw-Otten, F. W. M. M., van Duijn, N. P., & Meyboom-de Jong, B. (1995). *Measuring functional health status with the COOP/ WONCA Charts: A manual (PDF version, available from www.globalfamilydoctor. com/publications)*. The Netherlands: World Organization of Family Doctors (WONCA), European Research Group on Health Outcomes (ERGHO), Northern Centre for Health Care Research (NC), University of Gronigen.

Ware, J., & Sherbourne, C. D. (1992). The MOS 36-item short-form survey (SF-36): I Conceptual framework and item selection. *Medical Care, 30*, 473–83.

10.4 Examples of professional associations

(Examples only – more comprehensive list available on the American Speech Hearing Language Association website)

American Speech Hearing Language Association
www.asha.org

Canadian Association of Speech Language Pathologists and Audiologists
www.caslpa.ca

Speech Pathology Association of Australia
www.speechpathologyaustralia.org.au

International Association of Logopaedics and Phoniatrics
www.ialp.info/joomla

Royal College of Speech and Language Therapists
www.rcslt.org

South African Speech-Language-Hearing Association
www.saslha.co.za

Speech Language Hearing Association Singapore
www.shas.org.sg

New Zealand Speech-Language Therapists Association
www.nzsta-speech.org.nz

Irish Association of Speech and Language Therapists
www.iaslt.com

Malaysian Association of Speech-Language and Hearing
www.mash.org.my

Association of Speech Language Pathologists Malta
www.aslpmalta.org

Japanese Association of Speech-Language-Hearing Therapists
www.jaslht.gr.jp (Japanese)
www.jaslht.gr.jp/e_top.html (English)

Asia Pacific Society for the Study of Speech, Language and Hearing
www.shrs.uq.edu.au/asiapacific

10.5 Examples of support group websites

10.5.1 Disorder: aphasia

Adler Aphasia Center, New Jersey, USA
www.adleraphasiacenter.org

Aphasia Institute, Toronto, Canada
www.aphasia.ca

Aphasia Center of California
www.aphasiacenter.org

Australian Aphasia Association
www.aphasia.org.au

UK Connect, London
www.ukconnect.org

Stroke Recovery Association of NSW, Australia
www.strokensw.org.au

National Aphasia Association, USA
www.aphasia.org

Speakability, UK
www.speakability.org.uk

10.5.2   Disorder: Parkinson's disease

Parkinson's Australia
www.parkinsons.org.au

Parkinson's Disease Society, UK
www.parkinsons.org.uk

Parkinson Society Canada
www.parkinson.ca

Parkinson's Disease Society of Singapore

10.5.3   Disorder: stuttering/dysfluency

National Stuttering Association (USA)
www.nsastutter.org

Australian Speakeasy Association
www.speakeasy.org.au

Canadian Stuttering Association
www.stutter.ca

10.6   Examples of journals in the field of communication disorders

Journal	Description
American Journal of Speech-Language Pathology	Speech pathology audience
Aphasiology	Focus on aphasia
Augmentative & Alternative Communication	Focus on assistive technology
Brain & Language	Interdisciplinary
Clinical Linguistics & Phonetics	Interdisciplinary
Clinical Neuropsychologist	Neuropsychology audience
Cognitive Neuropsychology	Neuropsychology audience
Disability & Rehabilitation	Interdisciplinary
International Journal of Language & Communication Disorders	Speech pathology audience
International Journal of Speech Language Pathology (formerly, *Advances in Speech Language Pathology*)	Speech pathology audience

Continued

Continued

Journal	Description
Journal of Applied Linguistics	Disciplinary
Journal of Communication Disorders	Speech pathology audience
Journal of Intellectual & Developmental Disability	Multidisciplinary audience
Journal of Speech, Hearing & Language Research	Disciplinary
Journal of Voice	Focus on voice
Journal of Fluency Disorders	Focus on stuttering
Journal of Psycholinguistic Research	Interdisciplinary
Journal of Psychology	Disciplinary
Language & Cognitive Processes	Multidisciplinary audience
Learning Disabilities Research & Practice	Multidisciplinary audience

10. 7 Examples of publishers in the field of communication disorders (Comprehensive list available from ASHA website)

Publisher	Description
Cengage (including former Thomson Learning)	Psychology, education
Elsevier	Linguistic, psychology, education
Lippincott, Williams & Wilkins	Psychology, medical
Plural	Allied health, including speech-language pathology
Pro-Ed	Clinical resources
Sage	Applied linguistic
Thieme	Medical

10.8 Examples of conferences in the field of communication disorders

Conference	Description
Academy of Aphasia conference	International, focus on aphasia
Association Internationale de Linguistique Appliquee World Congress (International Association of Applied Linguistics)	International, interdisciplinary, linguistic
American Speech Hearing and Language Association Convention	National, speech-language pathology
Asia-Pacific Conference on Speech, Language & Hearing	International, interdisciplinary, speech-language pathology
British Aphasiology Society's conference	National, focus on aphasia

Continued

Conference	Description
Clinical Linguistics & Phonetics	International, interdisciplinary, linguistic
CUNY Conference on Human Sentence Processing	Cognitive neuropsychology
International Dysarthria Conference	International, speech pathology, medical
International Systemic Functional congress	International, linguistic
International Voice Symposium	International, voice disorders
World Congress of the International Association of Logopedics and Phoniatics (IALP)	International, speech-language pathology

10.9   Resources for transcription

The methods used for transcription of spoken interaction vary greatly across different research projects.

Paradis *et al.* (2003) used the transcription method and conventions from the CHAT system (Codes for the Human Analysis of Transcripts), and the analysis system provided through CLAN (Computerized Language Analysis), which are the most widely accepted computer-assisted methods in the field of child language disorders, and are part of Child Language Data Exchange System (CHILDES – MacWhinney 1996, 2000). For further information, see http://childes.psy.cmu.edu.

The CHAT system is able to convert transcripts using the transcription conventions set out for use with the Systematic Analysis of Language Transcripts software ('SALT' – Miller (1984–2004)). Such software provides for consistent and reliability count measures from transcribed data. For further information see http://www.saltsoftware.com.

References

Adamovich, B., & Hendershon, J. (1992). *Scales of cognitive ability for traumatic brain injury (SCATBI)*. Austin, TX: Pro-Ed.

Ambrose, N. G., & Yairi, E. (2002). The Tudor study: Data and ethics. *American Journal of Speech-Language Pathology, 11*, 190–203.

Anson, K., & Ponsford, J. (2006). Coping and emotional adjustment following traumatic brain injury. *Journal of Head Trauma Rehabilitation, 21*(3), 248–59.

APA. (1994). *Diagnostic and statistical manual of mental disorders: DSM-IV*. Washington, DC: American Psychiatric Association.

Armstrong, E. (2001). Connecting lexical patterns of verb usage with discourse meanings in aphasia. *Aphasiology, 15*, 1029–46.

Armstrong, E. (2005). Language disorder: A functional linguistic perspective. *Clinical Linguistics & Phonetics, 19*(3), 137–53.

Armstrong, E., Ferguson, A., Mortensen, L., & Togher, L. (2005). Acquired language disorders: Some functional insights (ch.14). In R. Hasan, C. Matthiessen & J. Webster (eds), *Continuing discourse on language: A functional perspective (vol. 1)* (pp. 383–412). London: Equinox.

Armstrong, E., Ferguson, A., Mortensen, L., & Togher, L. (2007). Acquired language disorders perspective. In J. Webster, R. Hasan & C. Matthiessen (eds), *Continuing discourse on language: A functional perspective (ch.14)*. London: Equinox.

Avent, J. R., & Austermann, S. (2003). Reciprocal scaffolding: A context for communication treatment in aphasia. *Aphasiology, 17*(4), 397–404.

BAAL. (1994). *Recommendations on good practice in applied linguistics*: British Association for Applied Linguistics.

Balandin, S., Hemsley, G., Sigafoos, J., Green, V., Forbes, R., Taylor, C., et al. (2001). Communicating with nurses: The experiences of 10 individuals with an acquired severe communication impairment. *Brain Impairment, 2*(2), 109–18.

Ball, M., & Duckworth, M. (eds). (1996). *Advances in clinical phonetics*. Amsterdam: John Benjamins.

Ball, M. J., & Muller, N. (2002). The use of the terms phonetics and phonology in the description of disordered speech. *Advances in Speech-Language Pathology, 4*(2), 95–108.

Bamberg, M. (ed.). (1997). *Narrative development: Six approaches*. Mahwah, NJ: Lawrence Erlbaum.

Barlow, D. H., & Hersen, M. (1984). *Single case experimental designs: Strategies for studying behaviour change* (2nd edn). New York: Pergamon Press.

Baron-Cohen, S. (1995). *Mindblindness: An essay on autism and Theory of Mind*. Cambridge, MA: MIT Press.

Bastiaanse, R., Edwards, S., & Rispens, J. (2002). *Verb and Sentence Test (VAST)*. Oxford, UK: Pearson Assessment.

Bates, E., Thal, D., & MacWhinney, B. (1991). A functionalist approach to language and its implications for assessment and intervention. In T. M. Gallagher & N. Rees (eds), *Pragmatics of language: Clinical practice issues*. San Diego, CA: Singular Group.

Bayles, K., & Tomoeda, C. (1993). *Arizona Battery for Communication Disorders of Dementia (ABCD)*. Arizona, TX: Pro-Ed.

Beeke, S., Wilkinson, R., & Maxim, J. (2003a). Exploring aphasic grammar 1: A single case analysis of conversation. *Clinical Linguistics & Phonetics, 17*(2), 81–107.

Beeke, S., Wilkinson, R., & Maxim, J. (2003b). Exploring aphasic grammar 2: Do language testing and conversation tell a similar story? *Clinical Linguistics & Phonetics, 17*(2), 109–34.

Beeke, S., Maxim, J., & Wilkinson, R. (2007). Using conversation analysis to assess and treat people with aphasia. *Seminars in Speech & Language, 28*(2), 136–47.

Beins, B. C., & Beins, A. M. (2008). *Effective writing in psychology: Papers, posters, and presentations*. Malden, MA: Blackwell.

Bishop, D. V. (2003). *Test for Reception of Grammar – version 2*. Oxford: Psychological Corporation.

Bishop, D. (2006). *Children's Communication Checklist-2 (CCC-2)* (2nd edn). San Antonio, TX: Pearson.

Blum-Harasty, J. A., & Rosenthal, J. B. M. (1992). The prevalence of communication disorders in children: A summary and critical review. *Australian Journal of Human Communication Disorders, 20*(1), 63–80.

Booth, S., & Perkins, L. (1999). The use of conversation analysis to guide individualized advice to carers and evaluate change in aphasia: A case study. *Aphasiology, 13*(4/5), 283–303.

Booth, S., & Swabey, D. (1999). Group training in communication skills for carers of adults with aphasia. *International Journal of Language & Communication Disorders, 34*(3), 291–309.

Bower, A. R. (1997). The role of narrative in the study of language and aging. *Journal of Narrative and Life History, 7*, 265–74.

Bowers, L., Huisingh, R., & LoGuidice, C. (2007). *Test of Problem Solving 2 - Adolescent (TOPS 2)* (2nd edn). East Moine, IL: LinguiSystems.

Boyd, K., & Davies, A. (2002). Doctors' orders for language testers: The origin and purpose of ethical codes. *Language Testing, 19*(3), 296–322.

Brazil, D. C. (1981). Intonation. In R. M. Coulthard & M. M. Montgomery (eds), *Studies in discourse analysis*. Routledge and Kegan Paul.

Broca, P. (1861). Remarque sur le siege de la faculte du language articule suivies d'une observation d'aphemie (perte de la parole). *Bulletin de la Societe d'Anatomie de Paris, 6*, 330–57.

Brookshire, R. H., & Nicholas, L. E. (1994). Speech sample size and test-retest stability of connected speech. *Journal of Speech & Hearing Research, 37*(2), 399–407.

Brown, R. (1973). *A first language: The early stages*. London: Allen and Unwin.

Brundage, S. B., Bothe, A. K., Lengeling, A. N., & Evans, J. J. (2006). Comparing judgements of stuttering made by students, clinicians, and highly experienced judges. *Journal of Fluency Disorders, 31*, 271–83.

Bryan, K. (1994). *The Right Hemisphere Language Battery* (2nd edn). Chichester, West Sussex, England: John Wiley & Sons.

Candlin, S. (2003). Issues arising when the professional workplace is the site of applied linguistic research. *Applied Linguistics, 23*(4), 386–94.

Candlin, C. N., & Sarangi, S. (2004). Editorial: Making applied linguistics matter. *Journal of Applied Linguistics, 1*(1), 1–8.

Caramazza, A., & Badecker, W. (1991). Patient classification in neuropsychological research. *Brain & Cognition, 16*(2), 198–210.

Chan, J., Carter, S., & McAllister, L. (1994). Contributions to anxiety in clinical education in undergraduate speech-language pathology students. *Australian Journal of Human Communication Disorders, 22*(1), 57–73.

Chapey, R., Duchan, J. F., Elman, R. J., Garcia, L. J., Kagan, A., Lyon, J. G., et al. (2001). Life participation approach to aphasia: A statement of values for the future. In R. Chapey (ed.), *Language intervention strategies in aphasia and related neurogenic communication disorders (ch.10, pp.235–245)* (4th edn). Baltimore, MD: Lippincott Williams & Wilkins.

Christie, J., Roskos, K., Vukelich, C., & Han, M. (2003). The effects of a well-designed literacy program on young children's language and literacy development. In *The first eight years – Pathways to the future: Implications for research, policy, and practice* (pp. 447–8). New York: Head Start Bureau, Mailman School of Public Health, Columbia University.

Clarke, A. (2003). On being an object of research: Reflections from a professional perspective. *Applied Linguistics, 24*(3), 374–85.

Clegg, J., Hollis, C., Mawhood, L., & Rutter, M. (2005). Developmental language disorders – a follow-up in later adult life. Cognitive, language and psychosocial outcomes. *Journal of Child Psychology & Psychiatry, 46*(2), 128–49.

Code, C., & Muller, D. J. (1992). *The Code-Muller Protocols: Assessing perceptions of psychosocial adjustment to aphasia and related disorders.* Chichester, West Sussex, England: John Wiley and Sons.

Code, C., Muller, D. J., Hogan, A., & Herrmann, M. (1999). Perceptions of psychosocial adjustment to acquired communication disorders: Applications of the Code-Muller Protocols. *International Journal of Language & Communication Disorders, 34*(2), 193–207.

Cohen, D. J., & Volkmar, F. R. (eds). (1997). *Autism and pervasive developmental disorders* (2nd edn). New York: John Wiley & Sons.

Cohen, J. (1969). *Statistical power analysis for the behavioral sciences.* New York: Academic Press.

Cole-Virtue, J., Nickels, L., & Coltheart, M. (2000). Spoken word-picture matching: What affects performance? *Asia Pacific Journal of Speech, Language and Hearing, 5*(3), 149–55.

Coltheart, M. (2005). Analysing developmental disorders of reading. *Advances in Speech Language Pathology, 7*(2), 49–57.

Cook, V. J. (1996). *Chomsky's universal grammar: An introduction.* Oxford, OX: Blackwell Publishers.

Copland, D., McMahon, K., de Zubicaray, G., Nickels, L., & Smith, E. (2006). *Brain mechanisms underlying phonological treatment effects in aphasia.* Paper presented at the 12th Aphasiology Symposium of Australia, Macquarie University, November 30–December 1 (retrieved 10 June 2008 from http://www.maccs. mq.edu.au/news/conferences/2006/ASA2006/schedule.htm).

Coupland, N., & Coupland, J. (1998). Reshaping lives: Constitutive identity work in geriatric medical consultations. *Text, 18*(2), 159–89.

Creswell, J. W. (2003). *Research design: Qualitative, quantitative and mixed method approaches.* Thousand Oaks: Sage Publications.

Cruice, M., Worrall, L., Hickson, L., & Murison, R. (2003). Finding a focus for quality of life with aphasia: Social and emotional health, and psychological well-being. *Aphasiology, 17*(4), 333–54.

Crystal, D. (1992). *Profiling linguistic disability*. London: Whurr.

Crystal, D., Fletcher, P., & Garman, M. (1976). *Grammatical analysis of language disability*. London: Whurr.

Dabul, B. L. (2000). *Apraxia Battery for Adults* (ABA-2) (2nd edn). Austin, TX: ProEd.

Damico, J. S., & Augustine, L. E. (1995). Social considerations in the labeling of students as attention deficit hyperactivity disordered. *Seminars in Speech & Language, 16*(4), 259–74, 317–18.

Damico, J. S., & Simmons-Mackie, N. (2003). Qualitative research and speech-language pathology: A tutorial for the clinical realm. *American Journal of Speech-Language Pathology, 12*(2), 131–43.

Damico, J. S., Oller, J. W., & Tetnowski, J. A. (1999). Investigating the interobserver reliability of a direct observational language assessment technique. *Advances in Speech Language Pathology, 1*(2), 77–94.

De Vaus, D. (1995). *Surveys in social research* (4th edn). Sydney: Allen & Unwin.

Deane, K. H. O., Whurr, R., Playford, E. D., Ben-Shlomo, Y., & Clarke, C. E. (2005). Speech and language therapy for dysarthria in Parkinsons disease: A comparison of techniques. *The Cochrane Library, 4*.

Dell, G. S., Juliano, C., & Govindjee, A. (1993). Structure and content in language production: A theory of frame constraints in phonological speech errors. *Cognitive Science, 17*, 149–95.

Desai, R., Conant, L. L., Waldron, E., & Binder, J. R. (2006). fMRI of past tense processing: The effects of phonological complexity and task difficulty. *Journal of Cognitive Neuroscience, 18*(2), 278–97.

Devitt, R., Colantonio, A., Dawson, D., Teare, G., Ratcliff, G., & Chase, S. (2006). Prediction of long-term occupational performance outcomes for adults after moderate to severe traumatic brain injury. *Disability & Rehabilitation, 28*(9), 547–59.

Dodd, B., Hua, Z., Crosbie, S., Holm, A., & Ozanne, A. (2006). *Diagnostic Evaluation of Articulation and Phonology (DEAP)*. San Antonio, TX: Pearson.

Duffy, J. R. (2005). *Motor speech disorders: Substrates, differential diagnosis, and management*. St Louis, Missouri: Elsevier Mosby.

Dunn, L. M., & Dunn, D. M. (2007). *Peabody Picture Vocabulary Test (PPVT-4)* (4th edn). Bloomington, MN: Pearson Assessment Group.

Dunn, L. M., Dunn, L. M., Whetton, C., & Burley, J. (1999). *The British Picture Vocabulary Scale (BPVS)*. Windsor: NFER-Nelson.

Dworzynski, K., Remingston, A., Rijskijk, F., Howell, P., & Plomin, R. (2007). Genetic etiology in cases of recovered and persistent stuttering in an unselected, longitudinal sample of young twins. *American Journal of Speech-Language Pathology, 16*(2), 169–78.

Eggins, S., & Slade, D. (1997/2004). *Analysing casual conversation*. London: Cassell(1997)/Equinox Publishing.

Ellis, A. W., & Young, A. W. (1988). *Human cognitive neuropsychology*. London: Lawrence Erlbaum.

Elman, R. J., & Bernstein-Ellis, E. (1999). Psychosocial aspects of group communication treatment: Preliminary findings. *Seminars in Speech and Language, 20*(1), 65–72.

Engell, B., Hutter, B. O., Willmes, K., & Huber, W. (2003). Quality of life in aphasia: Validation of a pictorial self-rating procedure. *Aphasiology, 17*(4), 383–96.

Fabbro, F. (2001). The bilingual brain: Cerebral representation of language. *Brain and Language, 79*, 211–22.

Faircloth, C. A., Boylstein, C., Rittman, M., Young, M. E., & Gubrium, J. (2004). Sudden illness and biographical flow in narratives of stroke recovery. *Sociology of Health & Illness, 26*(2), 242–61.

Ferguson, A. (1994). The influence of aphasia, familiarity and activity on conversational repair. *Aphasiology, 8*(2), 143–57.

Ferguson, A. (1998). Conversational turn-taking and repair in fluent aphasia. *Aphasiology, 12*(1), 1007–31.

Ferguson, A. (2002). The place of peer review in research. *ACQuiring knowledge in speech, language and hearing, 4*(1), 61.

Ferguson, A., & Elliot, N. (2001). Analysing aphasia treatment sessions. *Clinical Linguistics & Phonetics, 15*(3), 229–43.

Ferguson, A., & Peterson, P. (2002). Intonation in partner accommodation for aphasia: A descriptive single case study. *Journal of Communication Disorders, 35*, 11–30.

First, M. B., & Tasman, A. (2004). *DSM-IV-TR mental disorders: Diagnosis, etiology, and treatment.* Chichester, West Sussex: J. Wiley.

Fisher, H. B., & Logemann, J. A. (1971). *Fisher-Logemann Test of Articulation Competence (F-LTOAC).* Austin, TX: Pro-Ed.

Fisher, N., Happe, F., & Dunn, J. (2005). The relationship between vocabulary, grammar, and false belief task performance in children with autistic spectrum disorders and children with moderate learning difficulties. *Journal of Child Psychology & Psychiatry, 46*(4), 409–19.

Fodor, J. (1983). *The modularity of mind: An essay on faculty psychology.* Cambridge, MASS: MIT Press.

Frank, A. W. (1995). *The wounded storyteller: Body, illness, and ethics.* Chicago: The University of Chicago Press.

Fredericksen, C. H. (1986). Cognitive models and discourse analysis. In C. R. Cooper & S. Greenbaum (eds), *Written communication annual, vol. I: Studying writing: Linguistic approaches* (pp. 227–67). Beverley Hills: Sage.

Friedland, D., & Penn, C. (2003). Conversation analysis as a technique for exploring the dynamics of a mediated interview. *International Journal of Language & Communication Disorders, 38*(1), 95–111.

Fries, P. H. (1983). On the status of theme in English: Arguments from discourse. In J. S. Petofi & E. Sozer (eds), *Micro and macro connexity of discourse* (pp. 116–52). Hamburg: Buske.

Gallois, C., Giles, H., Jones, E., Cargile, A. C., & Ota, H. (1995). Accommodating intercultural encounters: Elaborations and extensions. In R. L. Wiseman (ed), *Intercultural accommodation theory* (pp. 115–147). Thousand Oaks, CA: Sage.

Garrett, M. (1988). Processes in language production. In F. J. Newmeyer (ed.), *The Cambridge survey of linguistics: Language: Psychological and biological aspects* (Vol. 3, pp. 69–96). Cambridge: Harvard University Press.

Ghadessy, M. (ed.). (1995). *Thematic development in English texts*. London: Pinter.

Giles, H., Taylor, D. M., & Bourhis, R. (1973). Towards a theory of interpersonal accommodation through language: Some Canadian data. *Language in Society, 2,* 177–192.

Glogowska, M., & Campbell, R. (2000). Investigating parental views of involvement in pre-school speech and language therapy. *International Journal of Language & Communication Disorders, 35*(3), 391–405.

Glosowska, M., Roulstone, S., Enderby, P., & Peters, T. J. (2000). Randomised controlled trial of community based speech and language therapy in preschool children. *British Medical Journal, 321,* 923–926.

Glosowska, M., Campbell, R., Peters, T. J., Roulstone, S., & Enderby, P. (2002). A multimethod approach to the evaluation of community preschool speech and language therapy provision. *Child: Care, Health & Development, 28*(6), 513–21.

Goldman, R., & Fristoe, M. (2000). *Goldman-Fristoe Test of Articulation (G-FTA-2)* (2nd edn). Austin, TX: Pro-Ed.

Goodglass, H., Kaplan, E., & Barresi, B. (2001). *Boston diagnostic aphasia examination* (3rd edn). Philadelphia: Lea & Febiger.

Goodwin, C. (1995). Co-constructing meaning in conversations with an aphasic man. *Research on Language and Social Interactions, 28*(3), 233–260.

Goodwin, C. (ed.). (2003). *Conversation and brain damage*. Oxford: Oxford University Press.

Greenbaum, S., & Quirk, R. (1990). *A student's grammar of the English language*. Harlow: Longman.

Grodzinsky, Y. (1990). *Theoretical perspectives on language deficits*. Cambridge: MIT Press.

Grodzinsky, Y. (2006). The language faculty, Broca's region, and the mirror system. *Cortex, 42*(4), 464–68.

Gumperz, J. J. (1982). *Discourse strategies*. New York: Cambridge University Press.

Haddon, M. (2003). *The curious incident of the dog in the night-time*. London: Random House.

Hagstrom, F. (2004). Including identity in clinical practices. *Topics in Language Disorders, 24*(3), 225–38.

Halliday, M. A. K. (1975). *Learning how to mean: Explorations in the development of language*. London: Edward Arnold.

Halliday, M. A. K. (1985). *An introduction to functional grammar*. London: Edward Arnold.

Halliday, M. A. K. (1994). *An introduction to functional grammar* (2nd edn). London: Arnold.

Halliday, M. A. K., & Hasan, R. (1976). *Cohesion in English*. London: Longman.

Halliday, M. A. K., & Matthiessen, C. M. I. M. (2004). *An introduction to functional grammar* (3rd edn). London: Arnold.

Hammersley, M., & Atkinson, P. (1983). *Ethnography: Principles in practice*. London: Tavistock.

Han, M., Roskos, K., Christie, J., Mandzuk, S., & Vukelich, C. (2005). Learning words: Large group time as a vocabulary development opportunity. *Journal of Research in Childhood Education, 19*(4), 333–45.

Harrison, E., Onslow, M., & Menzies, R. (2004). Dismantling the Lidcombe Program of early stuttering intervention: verbal contingencies for stuttering and clinical measurement. *International Journal of Language & Communication Disorders, 39*(2), 257–67.

Hasan, R., & Perrett, G. (1994). Learning to function with the other tongue: A systemic functional perspective on second language learning. In T. Olin (ed.), *Perspectives on pedagogical grammar*. New York: Cambridge University Press.

Higgs, J., McAllister, L., & Rosenthal, J. (2005). Learning academic writing. In J. Higgs, A. Sefton, A. Street, L. McAllister & I. Hay (eds), *Communicating in the health and social sciences (ch.4)* (pp. 29–41). Oxford: Oxford University Press.

Hilari, K., Byng, S., Lamping, D. L., & Smith, S. C. (2003). Stroke and Aphasia Quality of Life Scale-39 (SAQOL-39): Evaluation of acceptability, reliability, and validity. *Stroke, 34*(8), 1944–1950.

Hilari, K., Byng, S., & Pring, T. (2001). Measuring well-being in aphasia: The GHQ-28 versus the NHP. *Advances in Speech Language Pathology, 3*(2), 129–37.

Hinckley, J. J. (2007). *Narrative-based practice in speech-language pathology.* San Diego, CA: Plural Publishing.

Hodson, B. W. (2004). *Hodson Assessment of Phonological Patterns (HAPP-3).* Austin, TX: Pro-Ed.

Holland, A. L., Frattali, C., & Fromm, D. (1999). *Communication Activities of Daily Living (CADL-2)* (2nd edn). Austin, TX: Pro-Ed.

Holm, A., & Dodd, B. (1999). A longitudinal study of the phonological development of two Cantonese-English bilingual children. *Applied Psycholinguistics, 20*, 349–76.

Horton, S. (2006). A framework for description and analysis of therapy for language impairment in aphasia. *Aphasiology, 20*(6), 528–64.

Horton, S., Byng, S., Bunning, K., & Pring, T. (2004). Teaching and learning speech and language therapy skills: The effectiveness of classroom as clinic in speech and language therapy student education. *International Journal of Language & Communication Disorders, 39*(3), 365–90.

Howard, D., & Gatehouse, C. (2006). Distinguishing semantic and lexical word-retrieval deficits in people with aphasia. *Aphasiology, 20*(9–11), 921–50.

Howard, D., & Patterson, K. (1992). *Pyramids and Palm Trees.* Oxford, UK: Pearson Assessment.

Hua, Z., & Dodd, B. (eds). (2006). *Phonological development and disorders in children: A multilingual perspective.* Clevedon: Multilingual Matters.

Hyland, K. (2004). *Disciplinary discourses: Social interactions in academic writing.* Ann Arbor: University of Michigan Press.

Hymes, D. (1974). *Foundations in sociolinguistics: An ethnographic approach.* Philadelphia: University of Pennsylvania Press.

Ingham, R. J. (2001). Brain imaging studies of developmental stuttering. *Journal of Communication Disorders, 34*(6), 493–516.

Ingham, R. J., & Cordes, A. K. (1997). Identifying the authoritative judgments of stuttering: Comparisons of self-judgments and observer judgments. *Journal of Speech, Language, and Hearing Research, 40*(3), 581–94.

Ingham, R. J., Ingham, J. C., Onslow, M., & Finn, P. (1989). Stutterers' self-ratings of speech naturalness: assessing effects and reliability. *Journal of Speech & Hearing Research, 32*(2), 419–31.

Irwin, D. L., Pannbacker, M., & Lass, N. J. (2008). *Clinical research methods in speech-language pathology and audiology.* San Diego, CA: Plural.

Isaac, K. M. (2002). *Speech pathology in cultural and linguistic diversity.* London: Whurr.

Joanette, Y., & Ansoldo, A. I. (1999). Clinical note: Acquired pragmatic impairments and aphasia. *Brain and Language, 68*(3), 529–34.

Jones, M., Gebski, V., Onslow, M., & Packman, A. (2002). Statistical power in stuttering research: a tutorial. *Journal of Speech, Language, and Hearing Research, 45*(2), 243–55.

Jones, M., Onslow, M., Harrison, E., & Packman, A. (2000). Treating stuttering in young children: Predicting treatment time in the Lidcombe Program. *Journal of Speech, Language, and Hearing Research, 43*(6), 1440–50.

Jones, M., Onslow, M., Packman, A., Williams, S., Ormond, T., Schwarz, I., & Gebski, V. (2005). Randomised controlled trial of the Lidcombe programme of early stuttering intervention. *British Medical Journal, 331*(7518), 659–61.

Kambanaros, M., & van Steenbrugge, W. (2004). Interpreters and language assessment: Confrontation naming and interpreting. *Advances in Speech Language Pathology, 6*(4), 247–52.

Kay, J., Lesser, R., & Coltheart, M. (1992). *Psycholinguistic Assessment of Language Processing in Aphasia (PALPA).* Hove, East Sussex, England: Psychology Press.

Kazdin, A. E. (1982). *Single-case research designs: Methods for clinical and applied settings.* New York: Oxford University Press.

Kazdin, A. E. (2003). *Research design in clinical psychology.* Boston: Allyn & Bacon.

Kemmis, S., & McTaggart, R. (2005). Participatory action research. In N. K. Denzin & Y. S. Lincoln (eds), *The Sage handbook of qualitative research (ch.23, pp.559–603)* (3rd edn). London: Sage Publications.

Kemper, S., Ferrell, P., Harden, T., Finter-Urczyk, A., & Billington, C. (1998). Use of elderspeak by young and older adults to impaired and unimpaired listeners. *Aging, Neuropsychology, and Cognition, 5*(1), 43–55.

Kertesz, A. (2006). *Western Aphasia Battery – Revised.* San Antonio, TX: Harcourt Assessment.

Kingston, M., Huber, A., Onslow, M., Jones, M., & Packman, A. (2003). Predicting treatment time with the Lidcombe Program: Replication and meta-analysis. *International Journal of Language & Communication Disorders, 38*(2), 165–77.

Kintsch, W., & Van Dijk, T. (1978). Toward a model of text comprehension and production. *Psychological Review, 85*(5), 363–94.

Klein, J. F., & Hood, S. B. (2004). The impact of stuttering on employment opportunities and job performance. *Journal of Fluency Disorders, 29*, 255–73.

Klippi, A. (2003). Collaborating in aphasic group conversation: Striving for mutual understanding. In C. Goodwin (ed.), *Conversation and brain damage (ch.5)* (pp. 117–43). Oxford: Oxford University Press.

Laakso, M., & Klippi, A. (1999). A closer look at the 'hint and guess' sequences in aphasic conversation. *Aphasiology, 13*, 345–63.

Labov, W., & Fanshel, D. (1977). *Therapeutic discourse: Psychotherapy as conversation.* New York, NY: Academic Press.

Lesser, R. (2003). When conversation is not normal: The role of conversation analysis in language pathology. In C. L. Prevignano & P. J. Thibault (eds), *Discussing conversation analysis* (pp. 141–56). Amsterdam: John Benjamins.

Levelt, W. J. M. (1989). *Speaking: From intention to articulation*. Cambridge, MA: MIT Press.

Liamputtong, P., & Ezzy, D. (2005a). Making sense of qualitative data (ch.12). In *Qualitative research methods* (2nd edn, pp. 257–85). Oxford: Oxford University Press.

Liamputtong, P., & Ezzy, D. (2005b). *Qualitative research methods* (2nd edn). Oxford: Oxford University Press.

Lincoln, M., Adamson, B., & Covic, T. (2004). Perceptions of stress, time management and coping strategies of speech pathology students on clinical placement. *Advances in Speech-Language Pathology, 6*(2), 91–9.

Lincoln, M., Onslow, M., Lewis, C., & Wilson, L. (1996). A clinical trial of an operant treatment for stuttering school-age children. *American Journal of Speech-Language Pathology, 5*, 73–85.

Lindsay, J., & Wilkinson, R. (1999). Repair sequences in aphasic talk: A comparison of aphasic-speech and language therapist and aphasic-spouse conversations. *Aphasiology, 13*, 305–25.

Locke, L. F., Spirduso, W. W., & Silverman, S. J. (2007). *Proposals that work: A guide for planning dissertations and grant proposals* (5th edn). Thousand Oaks, CA: Sage.

Locke, S., Wilkinson, R., & Bryant, K. (2001). *Supporting partners of people with aphasia in relationships and conversation*. Oxon, UK: Speechmark.

Lomas, J., Pickard, L., Bester, S., Elbard, H., Finlayson, A., & Zoghaib, C. (1989). The communicative effectiveness index: Development and psychometric evaluation of a functional communication measure for adult aphasia. *Journal of Speech & Hearing Disorders, 54*, 113–24.

MacWhinney, B. (1996). The CHILDES system. *American Journal of Speech-Language Pathology, 5*, 5–14.

MacWhinney, B. (2000). *The CHILDES project: Tools for analyzing talk*. Mahwah, NJ: Lawrence Erlbaum.

Magill-Evans, J., Hodge, M., & Darrah, J. (2002). Establishing a transdisciplinary research team in academia. *Journal of Allied Health, 31*(4), 222–6.

Martin, J. R. (2000). Beyond exchange: Appraisal systems in English. In S. Hunston & G. Thompson (eds), *Evaluation in text* (pp. 143–75). Oxford: Oxford University Press.

Martin, J. R., & Rose, D. (2003). *Working with discourse: Meaning beyond the clause*. London: Continuum.

Martin, R., Kuhl, P., & Haroldson, S. (1972). An experimental treatment with two preschool stuttering children. *Journal of Speech and Hearing Research, 15*, 743–52.

Matthiessen, C. (1995). Theme as an enabling resource in ideational 'knowledge' construction. In M. Ghadessy (ed.), *Thematic development in English texts* (pp. 20–54). London: Pinter.

Matyas, T. A., & Greenwood, K. M. (1996). Serial dependency in single-case time series (ch.7). In R. D. Franklin, D. B. Allison & B. S. Gorman (eds), *Design and analysis of single-case research* (pp. 215–43). Mahway, NJ: Lawrence Erlbaum.

Maxwell, D. L., & Sataki, E. (1997). *Research and statistical methods in communication disorders*. Baltimore: Williams and Wilkins.

McCready, V., Roberts, J. E., Bengala, D., Harris, H., Kingsley, G., & Krikorian, C. (1996). A comparison of conflict tactics in the supervisory process. *Journal of Speech and Hearing Research, 39*, 191–9.

McDonald, J., Brown, L., & Murphy, A. (2002). Strengthening primary health care: Building the capacity of rural communities to access health funding. *Australian Journal of Rural Health, 10*, 173–7.

McNamara, T. F. (2000). *Language testing.* Oxford: Oxford University Press.

McNeil, M. R., & Pratt, S. R. (2001). Defining aphasia: Some theoretical and clinical implications of operating from a formal definition. *Aphasiology, 15*(10/11), 901–91.

McReynolds, L. V., & Kearns, K. P. (1983). *Single-subject experimental designs in communicative disorders.* Baltimore: University Park Press.

Meline, T., & Schmitt, J. F. (1997). Case studies for evaluating statistical significance in group designs. *American Journal of Speech-Language Pathology, 6*(1), 33–41.

Minichiello, V., Sullivan, G., Greenwood, K., & Axford, R. (eds). (2004). *Handbook of research methods for nursing and health sciences* (2nd edn). Frenchs Forest, NSW: Prentice-Hall Health.

Morse, J. M., & Field, P. A. (1995). *Qualitative research methods for health professionals* (2nd edn). London: Sage.

Munoz, K., & Jeris, L. (2005). Learning to be interdisciplinary: An action research approach to boundary spanning. *Health Education Journal, 64*(1), 5–12.

Nash, H., & Snowling, M. (2006). Teaching new words to children with poor existing vocabulary knowledge: A controlled evaluation of the definition and context methods. *International Journal of Language & Communication Disorders, 41*(3), 335–54.

Nelson, R., & Ball, M. J. (2003). Models of phonology in the education of speech-language pathologists. *Clinical Linguistics & Phonetics, 17*(4–5), 403–9.

NHMRC. (1999). *National statement on ethical conduct in research involving humans*: National Health & Medical Research Council, Australia.

NHMRC. (2002). *Human research ethics handbook: Commentary on the national statement on ethical conduct in research involving humans*: National Health & Medical Research Council, Australia.

NHMRC. (2003). *Values and ethics: Guidelines for ethical conduct in Aboriginal and Torres Strait Islander health research*: National Health & Medical Research Council, Australia.

Nickels, L. A. (ed.). (2002). *Cognitive neuropsychological approaches to spoken word production in aphasia.* Hove, UK: Psychology Press.

Noble, K., Glosser, G., & Grossman, M. (2000). Oral reading in dementia. *Brain and Language, 74*(1), 48–69.

O'Brian, S., Cream, A., Onslow, M., & Packman, A. (2001). A replicable nonprogrammed, instrument free method for control of stuttering with prolonged speech. *Asia Pacific Journal of Speech, Language and Hearing, 6*, 91–6.

Oliver, O. (1983). *Social work with disabled people.* Tavistock: MacMillan.

Onslow, M. (2001). Re: Frequency altered feedback as an alternative to 'prolonged speech' techniques for the control of stuttered speech. *International Journal of Language & Communication Disorders, 36*(3), 409–11.

Onslow, M., Andrews, C., & Lincoln, M. (1994). A control/experimental trial of an operant treatment for early stuttering. *Journal of Speech & Hearing Research, 37*(6), 1244–59.

Onslow, M., Costa, L., & Rue, S. (1990). Direct early intervention with stuttering: some preliminary data. *Journal of Speech & Hearing Disorders, 55*(3), 405–16.

Onslow, M., Gardner, K., Bryant, K. M., Stuckings, C. L., & Knight, T. (1992). Stuttered and normal speech events in early childhood: the validity of a behavioral data language. *Journal of Speech & Hearing Research, 35*(1), 79–87.

Onslow, M., O'Brian, S., & Harrison, E. (1997). The Lidcombe Programme of early stuttering intervention: Methods and issues. *European Journal of Disorders of Communication, 32*(2), 231–50.

Onslow, M., & Packman, A. (2002). Stuttering and lexical retrieval: inconsistencies between theory and data. *Clinical Linguistics & Phonetics, 16*(4), 295–8.

Owens, R. E. (2007). *Introduction to communication disorders: A lifespan perspective* (3rd edn). Boston: Pearson/Allyn&Bacon.

Owens, R. E. (2008). *Language development: An introduction* (7th edn). Boston: Pearson Education.

Packman, A., & Onslow, M. (2002). Searching for the cause of stuttering. *Lancet, 360*(9334), 655–6.

Paradis, J., & Libben, G. (1987). *The assessment of bilingual aphasia: the Bilingual Aphasia Test.* Hove, UK: Psychology Press.

Paradis, J., Crago, M., Genesee, F., & Rice, M. (2003). French-English bilingual children with SLI: How do they compare with their monolingual peers? *Journal of Speech, Language, and Hearing Research, 46*(1), 113–27.

Paradis, M. (ed.). (1995). *Aspects of bilingual aphasia.* Oxford, UK: Pergamon.

Parr, S., Byng, S., Gilpin, S., & Ireland, C. (1997). *Talking about aphasia.* Buckingham: Open University Press.

Paul, R. (2007). *Language disorders from infancy through adolescence: Assessment and intervention.* St Louis, Missouri: Mosby Elsevier.

Peck, K. K., Moore, A. B., Crosson, B. A., Gaiefsky, M., Gopinath, K. S., White, K., et al. (2004). Functional magnetic resonance imaging before and after aphasia therapy: Shifts in hemodynamic time to peak during an overt language task. *Stroke, 35*(2), 554–9.

Penfield, W., & Roberts, L. (1959). *Speech and brain mechanisms*: Princeton University Press.

Perkins, L. (1995). Applying conversation analysis to aphasia: Clinical implications and analytic issues. *European Journal of Disorders of Communication, 30*, 372–83.

Perkins, L., Crisp, J., & Walshaw, D. (1999). Exploring conversation analysis as an assessment tool for aphasia: The issue of reliability. *Aphasiology, 13*(4–5), 259–82.

Perrin, R. (2007). *Pocket guide to APA style* (2nd edn). Boston: Houghton Mifflin.

Phillips, B., Ball, C., Sackett, D., Badenoch, D., Strause, S., & Dawes, M. (2001). *Oxford Centre for Evidence-based Medicine levels of evidence.* Retrieved 17 June, 2008, from http://www.cebm.net/index.aspx?o=1025

Plante, E. (1998). Criteria for SLI: The Stark and Tallal legacy and beyond. *Journal of Speech, Language, and Hearing Research, 41*, 951–957.

Poeppel, D., & Hickok, G. (2004). Towards a new functional anatomy of language. *Cognition, 92*, 1–12.

Pring, T. (2005). *Research methods in communication disorders*. London: Whurr.
Prutting, C. A., & Kirchner, D. M. (1987). A clinical appraisal of the pragmatic aspects of language. *Journal of Speech and Hearing Disorders, 52*(2), 105–19.
Psathas, G., & Anderson, T. (1990). The 'practices' of transcription in conversation analysis. *Semiotica, 78*(1–2), 75–99.
Ramig, L. O., Countryman, S., Thompson, L. L., & Horii, Y. (1995). Comparison of two forms of intensive speech treatment for Parkinson Disease. *Journal of Speech and Hearing Research, 38*, 1232–51.
Rao, R. R. (1994). The aphasia syndromes: Localization and classification. *Topics in Stroke Rehabilitation, 1*(2), 1–13.
Reason, P., & Bradbury, H. (eds). (2001). *Handbook of action research: Participative inquiry and practice*. London: Sage Publications.
Reilly, S., Douglas, J., & Oates, J. (eds). (2004). *Evidence based practice in speech pathology*. London: Whurr.
Renfrew, C. (1997). *Action Picture Test*. Bicester, UK: Speechmark.
Rescorla, L., Alley, A., & Book Christine, J. (2001). Word frequencies in toddlers' lexicons. *Journal of Speech, Language, and Hearing Research, 44*(3), 598–609.
Ries, J. B., & Leukefeld, C. G. (1995). *Applying for research funding: Getting started and getting funded*. Thousand Oaks, CA: Sage Publications.
Ripich, D., & Spinelli, F. M. (1985). An ethnographic approach to assessment and intervention. In D. N. Ripich & F. M. Spinelli (eds), *School discourse problems*. San Diego, CA: College-Hill Press.
Roberts, C., & Sarangi, S. (2003). Uptake of discourse research in interprofessional settings: Reporting from medical consultancy. *Applied Linguistics, 24*(3), 338–59.
Rodriquez, A. D., Raymer, A. M., & Rothi, L. J. G. (2006). Effects of gesture+verbal and semantic-phonologic treatments for verb retrieval in aphasia. *Aphasiology, 20*(2–4), 286–97.
Rogers, T. T., Ivanoiu, A., Patterson, K., & Hodges, J. R. (2006). Semantic memory in Alzheimer's disease and the frontotemporal dementias: A longitudinal study of 236 patients. *Neuropsychology, 20*(3), 319–35.
Rose, M. L. (2006). The utility of arm and hand gestures in the treatment of aphasia. *Advances in Speech Language Pathology, 8*(2), 92–109.
Rose, T. A., Worrall, L. E., & McKenna, K. T. (2003). The effectiveness of aphasia-friendly principles for printed health education materials for people with aphasia following stroke. *Aphasiology, 17*(10), 947–64.
Ross, K. B., & Wertz, R. T. (2003). Quality of life with and without aphasia. *Aphasiology, 17*(4), 355–64.
Sacks, H., Schegloff, E. A., & Jefferson, G. (1974). A simplist systematics for the organization of turn taking for conversation. *Language, 50*, 696–735.
Saffran, E. M., Sloan-Berndt, R., & Schwartz, M. (1989). The quantitative analysis of agrammatic production: Procedure and data. *Brain and Language, 37*, 440–79.
Saur, D., Lange, R., Baumgaertner, A., Schraknepper, V., Willmes, K., Rijntjes, M., *et al.* (2006). Dynamics of language reorganization after stroke. *Brain, 129*(6), 1351–6.
Seliger, H. W., & Vago, R. M. (eds). (1991). *First language attrition*. Cambridge: Cambridge University Press.

Semel, E., Wiig, E. H., & Secord, W. A. (2003). *Clinical Evaluation of Language Fundamentals (CELF-4)* (4th edn). San Antonio: Harcourt Brace & Co, The Psychological Corporation.

Semel, E., Wiig, E. H., & Secord, W. A. (2006). *Clinical Evaluation of Language Fundamentals (CELF-4)* (4th - Australian standardised edn). Marrickville, NSW: Harcourt Assessment.

Shadden, B. B., & Agan, J. P. (2004). Renegotiation of identity: The social context of aphasia support groups. *Topics in Language Disorders, 24*(3), 174–86.

Shapiro, D. A. (1994). Interaction analysis and self-study: A single-case comparison of four methods of analyzing supervisory conferences. *Language, Speech, and Hearing Services in Schools, 25*, 67–75.

Shapiro, K. A., Mottaghy, F. M., Schiller, N. O., Poeppel, T. D., Fluss, M. O., Muller, H. W., *et al.* (2005). Dissociating neural correlates for nouns and verbs. *Neuroimage, 24*(4), 1058–67.

Shohamy, E. (2004). Reflections on research guidelines, categories, and responsibility. *TESOL Quarterly, 38*(4), 728–31.

Silveri, M. C., Perri, R., & Cappa, A. (2003). Grammatical class effects in brain-damaged patients: Functional locus of noun and verb deficit. *Brain and Language, 85*(1), 49–66.

Silvia, P. (2007). *How to write a lot: A practical guide to productive academic writing.* Washington, DC: American Psychological Association.

Simmons-Mackie, N., Code, C., Armstrong, E., Stiegler, L., & Elman, R. J. (2002). What is aphasia? Results of an international survey. *Aphasiology, 16*(8), 837–48.

Simmons-Mackie, N., & Damico, J. S. (1999). Qualitative methods in aphasia research: Ethnography. *Aphasiology, 13*(9–11), 681–7.

Simmons-Mackie, N., Damico, J. S., & Damico, H. L. (1999). A qualitative study of feedback in aphasia treatment. *American Journal of Speech-Language Pathology, 8*(3), 218–30.

Sowman, R., Robinson, D., O'Riordan, R., Connolly, S., & O'Neill, D. (2006). Rapidly deteriorating speech and language in a case of probably sporadic Creutzfeldt-Jakob disease. *Aphasiology, 20*(6), 579–92.

SPAA. (2000). *Code of ethics.* Melbourne, VIC: The Speech Pathology Association of Australia.

Spencer, E., Packman, A., Onslow, M., & Ferguson, A. (2005). A preliminary investigation of the impact of stuttering on language use. *Clinical Linguistics & Phonetics, 19*(3), 191–201.

Stemler, S. E. (2004). A comparison of consensus, consistency, and measurement approaches to estimating interrater reliability. *Practical Assessment, Research & Evaluation, 9*(1), Retrieved 19 July 2006 from http://PAREonline.net/getvn. asp?v=2009&n=2004.

Taylor, R., & Iacono, T. (2003). AAC and scripting activities to facilitate communication and play. *Advances in Speech-Language Pathology, 5*(2), 79–93.

Teesson, K., Packman, A., & Onslow, M. (2003). The Lidcombe behavioral data language of stuttering. *Journal of Speech, Language, and Hearing Research, 46*(4), 1009–15.

Tesak, J., & Code, C. (2008). *Milestones in the history of aphasia: Theories and protagonists.* Hove: Psychology Press.

Thody, A. (2006). *Writing and presenting research.* London: Sage.

Thomson, J. (2003). Clinical discourse analysis: One theory or many? *Advances in Speech-Language Pathology, 5*, 41–9.

Thomson, J. (2005). Theme analysis of narratives produced by children with and without Specific Language Impairment. *Clinical Linguistics & Phonetics, 19*(3), 175–90.

Thompson, C. K., Shapiro, L. P., Kiran, S., & Sobecks, J. (2003). The role of syntactic complexity in treatment of sentence deficits in agrammatic aphasia: The Complexity Account of Treatment Efficacy (CATE). *Journal of Speech, Language, and Hearing Research, 46*(3), 591–607.

Threats, T. T. (2006). Towards an international framework for communication disorders: Use of the ICF. *Journal of Communication Disorders, 39*(4), 251–65.

Togher, L., Hand, L., & Code, C. (1997). Measuring service encounters in the traumatic brain injury population. *Aphasiology, 11*, 491–504.

Togher, L., McDonald, S., Code, C., & Grant, S. (2004). Training communication partners of people with traumatic brain injury: A randomised controlled trial. *Aphasiology, 18*(4), 313–35.

Trinder, L., & Reynolds, S. (eds). (2000). *Evidence-based practice: A critical appraisal.* Oxford: Blackwell Science.

Ulatowska, H. K., Allard, L., & Bond Chapman, S. (1990). Narrative and procedural discourse in aphasia. In Y. Joanette & H. H. Brownell (eds), *Discourse ability and brain damage: Theoretical and empirical perspectives* (pp. 180–98). New York: Springer-Verlag.

Ulatowska, H. K., Olness, G. S., & Williams, L. J. (2004). Coherence of narratives in aphasia. *Brain and Language, 91*, 42–3.

van Weel, C., Konig-Zahn, C., Touw-Otten, F. W. M. M., van Duijn, N. P., & Meyboom-de Jong, B. (1995). *Measuring functional health status with the COOP/ WONCA Charts: A manual (PDF version, available from www.globalfamilydoctor. com/publications).* The Netherlands: World Organization of Family Doctors (WONCA), European Research Group on Health Outcomes (ERGHO), Northern Centre for Health Care Research (NC), University of Gronigen.

Vinten-Johansen, P., Brody, H., Rachman, S., Rip, M., & Zuck, D. (2003). *Cholera, chloroform, and the science of medicine: A life of John Snow*: Oxford University Press.

Voets, N. L., Adcock, J. E., Flitney, D. E., Behrens, T. E., Hart, J., Stacey, R., *et al.* (2006). Distinct right frontal lobe activation in language processing following left hemisphere injury. *Brain, 129*(3), 754–66.

Wagner, R., Torgesen, J. K., & Rashotte, C. A. (1999). *Comprehensive Test of Phonological Processing (CTOPP).* Austin, TX: Pro-Ed.

Ware, J., & Sherbourne, C. D. (1992). The MOS 36-item short-form survey (SF-36): I Conceptual framework and item selection. *Medical Care, 30*, 473–483.

Weir, C. (2005). *Language testing and validation: An evidence-based approach.* Basingstoke, Hampshire: Palgrave Macmillan.

Weismer, S. E., Plante, E., Jones, M., & Tomblin, J. B. (2005). A functional magnetic resonance imaging investigation of verbal working memory in adolescents with specific language impairment. *Journal of Speech, Language, and Hearing Research, 48*(2), 405–25.

Wernicke, C. (1893). Der aphasische symptomenkomplex: Eine psychologische studie auf anatomischer basis. In C. Wernicke (ed.), *Gesamelte aufsatze und kritische referat zur pathologie des nervensystems* (pp. 1–170). Berlin, Germany: Fischer. [Original work published 1874].

Whitworth, A., Perkins, L., & Lesser, R. (1997). *Conversation Analysis Profile for People with Aphasia (CAPPA)*. London: Whurr.

Whitworth, A., Webster, J., & Howard, D. (2005). *A cognitive neuropsychological approach to assessment and intervention in aphasia: A clinician's guide*. New York: Psychology Press.

WHO. (2000). ICIDH-2 International classification of impairments, activities, and participation: World Health Organisation (http://www.who.int/icidh).

WHO. (2001). *ICF: International classification of functioning, disability and health*. Geneva: World Health Organisation.

WHO. (2002). *Towards a common language for functioning, disability and health*. Geneva: World Health Organization.

Wilkinson, R. (1999). Sequentiality as a problem and resource for intersubjectivity in aphasic conversation: Analysis and implications for therapy. *Aphasiology, 13*, 327–43.

Wilson, L., Onslow, M., & Lincoln, M. (2004). Telehealth adaptation of the Lidcombe Program of Early Stuttering Intervention: five case studies. *American Journal of Speech-Language Pathology, 13*(1), 81–93.

Wingate, M. E. (1988). *The structure of stuttering: A psycholinguistic analysis*. New York: Springer-Verlag.

WMA. (1964–2004). *World Medical Association Declaration of Helsinki: Ethical principles for medical research involving human subjects*: World Medical Association.

Woods, S., Shearsby, J., Onslow, M., & Burnham, D. (2002). Psychological impact of the Lidcombe Program of early stuttering intervention. *International Journal of Language & Communication Disorders, 37*(1), 31–40.

Worrall, L., & Hickson, L. (eds). (2003). *Communication disability in aging*. West Brunswick, VIC: Coordinates Occupational Therapy Services.

Worrall, L., Rose, T., Howe, T., Brennan, A., Egan, J., Oxenham, D., *et al.* (2005). Access to written information for people with aphasia. *Aphasiology, 19*(10/11), 923–9.

Yaruss, J. S. (1998). Describing the consequences of disorders: Stuttering and the international classification of impairments, disabilities, and handicaps. *Journal of Speech, Language, and Hearing Research, 41*, 249–57.

Zimmerman, I. L., Steiner, V. G., & Pond, R. E. (2002). *Pre-school Language Scales (PLS-4)* (4th edn). San Antonio, TX: Harcourt Assessment.

Index